China Dreams

China Dreams

20 Visions of the Future

WILLIAM A. CALLAHAN

OXFORD
UNIVERSITY PRESS

OXFORD

UNIVERSITY PRESS

Oxford University Press is a department of the University of Oxford.
It furthers the University's objective of excellence in research, scholarship,
and education by publishing worldwide.

Oxford   New York
Auckland   Cape Town   Dares Salaam   Hong Kong   Karachi
Kuala Lumpur   Madrid   Melbourne   Mexico City   Nairobi
New Delhi   Shanghai   Taipei   Toronto

With offices in
Argentina   Austria   Brazil   Chile   Czech Republic   France   Greece
Guatemala   Hungary   Italy   Japan   Poland   Portugal   Singapore
South Korea   Switzerland   Thailand   Turkey   Ukraine   Vietnam

Oxford is a registered trademark of Oxford University Press
in the UK and certain other countries.

Published in the United States of America by
Oxford University Press
198 Madison Avenue, New York, NY 10016

Library of Congress Cataloging-in-Publication Data
Callahan, William A.
China dreams : 20 visions of the future / William A. Callahan.
pages cm
Includes bibliographical references and index.
ISBN 978-0-19-989640-0 (hardback); 978-0-19-023523-9 (paperback)
1. China—Foreign relations—2002   2. China—Forecasting.   3. China—Foreign relations—
United States.   4. United States—Foreign relations—China.   5. Social change—China.
6. Politics and culture—China.   7. China—Intellectual life.   8. Intellectuals—China—Biography.
I. Title.
DS779.47.C25 2013
327.51073—dc23
2012047002

To the memory of Anne Bruls (1960–2011)
Classmate, scholar, diplomat, friend

There's something happening here,
What it is ain't exactly clear.

—Buffalo Springfield

Contents

List of Figures

Preface

JUST AS I was finishing up the copyedits for the first edition of *China Dreams: 20 Visions of the Future* in November 2012, newly anointed Chinese Communist Party General Secretary Xi Jinping announced to the world that his "China dream" is for the "great rejuvenation of the Chinese nation," which, as he later explained, means "achieving a rich and powerful country, the revitalization of the nation, and the people's happiness." Over the past two years, "The China Dream" has become Xi's key concept, and it now dominates discussion of China's future and the world's future in the PRC. It has inspired a major propaganda campaign that includes popular TV shows like "The Voice of the China Dream" singing contest, and book titles like *The China Dream: A Reader for Party Members and Cadres*; *The China Dream Is Our Dream*; and *Uphold the China Dream*. It has also provoked spirited debate among China's citizen intellectuals over whether China's dream is individual, collective, or national, whether it is about constitutional rights or Confucian order, and whether it grows out of civilizational values or China's martial spirit.

Although most now assume that the China Dream is a top-down state-centric project, Xi Jinping himself recognizes that the ideal grows out of discussions among Chinese people. In November 2012 he said that "everyone has their own ideals and aspirations, and all have their own dream. Now, everyone is talking about the China Dream."

This book is valuable because it places the China Dream phenomenon in the context of debates that have been raging in Chinese civil society over the past few years. The contours of this discussion—over the meaning of "civilization," the importance of the martial values, the proper relation of state and society, the question of Chinese exceptionalism, and the PRC's new role as a superpower—that are explored in these pages are defining features of the debate in China over Xi Jinping's official China Dream. Indeed, Chinese elites are interested in *China Dreams: 20 Visions of the Future* as well. It is my first book to make it past the censors in the PRC intact, and it is being published by the Central Compilation and Translation Bureau, which is the think tank of the Central Committee of the Chinese Communist Party.

London, October 2014

Acknowledgments

THIS RESEARCH WAS supported by a Leverhulme Trust Fellowship (2010–2011), and the British Inter-university China Centre's grant from the Economic and Social Research Council and the Arts and Humanities Research Council (RES-580-28-0008).

For their helpful comments and advice, I thank Elena Barabantseva, Geremie R. Barmé, Roland Bleiker, Shaun Breslin, Chris Buckley, Sumalee Bumroongsook, Kelvin Chi-kin Cheung, Patrick Chovanec, David Kelly, Prasenjit Duara, Michael Dutton, Rosemary Foot, John Garnaut, Han Lijing, Robert Hathaway, Yinan He, Wei Hsueh, Christopher R. Hughes, Malgorzata Jakimow, David Kerr, Richard Curt Kraus, James Leibold, Lin Xiaofang, Rana Mitter, Astrid Nordin, Evan Osnos, Michael Pettis, Frank N. Pieke, William Schroeder III, Shi Yinhong, Suwanna Satha-Anand, James T.H. Tang, Jeffrey N. Wasserstrom, Thongchai Winichakul, David Tobin, Jianying Zha, Zheng Yongnian, Zhu Jie, Zhu Wei, and the participants at the British Inter-university China Centre's "China's Futures and the World's Future" workshop held in Manchester (2011). The book also benefited from students' comments at my Identity and Security in China and East Asia class at the University of Manchester (2012).

I especially thank Elena Barabantseva, Mary Erbaugh, and Richard Curt Kraus for commenting on the full manuscript: many of the book's best arguments and clever formulations come from their comments. At Oxford Univerity Press, I thank David McBride and Alexandra Dauler, who helped me focus and clarify my ideas.

Finally, I thank Sumalee for all her help and support.

Chapters 2 and 5 are refined versions of:

"China's Strategic Futures: Debating the Post-American World Order?" *Asian Survey* 52:4 (2012): 617–642.

"Shanghai's Alternative Futures: The World Expo, Citizen Intellectuals and China's New Civil Society," *China Information* 16:2 (2012): 251–273.

I thank the publishers for their permission to use this material.

China Dreams

Introduction

CHINA IS THE FUTURE

IT'S AN EXCITING time to be Chinese. While in the West the first decade of the 21st century was defined by pessimism due to 9/11, the Iraq War, and the Great Recession, Chinese people are very optimistic that the 21st century will be the "Chinese century." The fruits of China's three decades of rapid economic growth are there for all to see: by 2010, the People's Republic of China (PRC) had the fastest computer in the world and the smartest students in the world, and it was enthusiastically entering the space age—just as the United States was retiring its fleet of Space Shuttles.[1]

These headline achievements are the tangible result of Deng Xiaoping's reform and opening policy, which, starting in 1978, shifted China's focus away from Maoist class struggle to concentrate on economic development. After lifting more than 300 million people out of poverty, the PRC passed Japan in 2010 to become the second-largest economy in the world. Reflecting on their country's recent economic success, China's policymakers and opinion-makers are now asking "what comes next?" How can the PRC convert its growing economic power into enduring political and cultural influence in Asia and around the globe?

We can see China's official dream of a strong and prosperous future in the party-state's three centrally orchestrated mega-events: the 2008 Beijing Olympics presented China as a soft superpower, the National Day military parade in 2009 reminded everyone that China also has hard power, and the Shanghai World Expo in 2010 was billed as the "Olympics for Culture, Economy and Technology." On the other hand, "Charter 08," co-authored by future Nobel laureate Liu Xiaobo, was a powerful critique of the party-state's rule of the PRC. It argues that China needs to match its market-based economic reforms with democratic political reforms. On Christmas day in 2009, "Charter 08" earned this dissident eleven years in jail for "inciting subversion of state power." These two views of China's future—either as a powerful authoritarian state or as the world's next liberal democratic country—dominate discussions in the West.

Yet what do they leave out? What is going on in between the officials who parrot state policy and the dissidents who directly challenge the party-state?

Once you get below the surface of the baroquely choreographed debate between officials and dissidents that reduces complex situations to pro- and anti-communist party polemics, you can see how these two groups are involved in a dance for power and influence with a third group: citizen intellectuals. This new group, which I will describe in more detail in chapter 1, is an unintended consequence of Deng's reform and opening policy. While Deng's goal was economic reform, the "opening policy" has gone far beyond liberalizing markets to create much more space for discussion in China. The past two decades have witnessed an explosion of new social and cultural activities as the party-state loosened its control over daily life. The economic reforms, thus, have opened up a wide variety of cultural opportunities, ranging from elite literature to the popular culture of China's *American Idol*-like show *Go! Oriental Angel*.

If we widen our view of activism beyond dissidents to include citizen intellectuals—the bloggers, novelists, filmmakers, scholars, and artists who are thinking up new ways of being Chinese—then we can see the enormous energy and optimism of people who are busy building the future in China. While not political in the sense of directly criticizing the party-state, citizen intellectuals are certainly political in the broader sense of probing the boundaries of what is allowed (and not allowed) in Chinese society.

For many in China, we are entering the "Era of Peace and Prosperity" (*Taiping Shengshi*), a period when China will reclaim not just national strength, but also global power. Until recently, the term was primarily used to describe the apex of China's imperial civilization in the Tang dynasty (618–907); but according to cultural critic Chan Koonchung, the idea reappeared 2008 to signal that China's time had come—again.[2] Along with limitless possibilities, China faces many problems: enduring rural and urban poverty, runaway inflation, environmental degradation, a graying population, a housing bubble, and official corruption.

While Beijing is in many ways converging with the West in terms of technical and social norms, there is a hunger in the PRC for indigenous Chinese political and cultural models that are different from those that originate in Europe and America. The popularity of such nativist urges has been growing since the fantastic success of Beijing's 2008 Olympics, which showcased China as the top gold medal winner and the city of Beijing as a new center of global prosperity and order. The Olympics motto, after all, was "One World,

同一个世界 同一个梦想
One World One Dream

FIGURE 0.1 Olympic slogan sign at Beijing airport
Source: William A. Callahan

One Dream." (see Fig. 0.1) That the Great Recession started in New York less than one month after the Beijing Olympics confirmed for many that China could be successful on its own terms, especially in comparison with America. Thus, the China dream is starting to replace the American dream in the global imagination.

New voices are also emerging in China as a result of the long transition to China's new generation of leaders, who took control after President Hu Jintao and Premier Wen Jiaobao retired at the 18th Party Congress in 2012. This informal transition period, which spans from 2009 to 2014, has opened up new intellectual space as China's new leaders, Xi Jinping and Li Keqiang, try to differentiate themselves from their predecessors. Hu Jintao, for example, didn't start to consolidate his official policy narrative—"scientific development concept" (2004), "harmonious society" (2004), and "harmonious world" (2005)—until two years after he took power in 2002. As we will see in chapter 1, before he took office in 2012–2013 President Xi Jinping offered few clues about his policy priorities. Similar to Hu's regime, Xi and others will spend the next few years coming up with new ideas to guide China's long-term national strategy.

The ambiguous situation created by this long informal leadership transition has opened up opportunities to discuss China's future direction, in part, as a way of influencing the PRC's new rulers. Here citizen intellectuals have been quite successful: In his first public speech as leader of the CCP, Xi

Jinping declared, "Now, we are all discussing the China Dream. In my view, to achieve the great rejuvenation of the Chinese nation is the greatest dream of the Chinese nation in modern times."[3]

While previously the debate among citizen intellectuals was marked by a clear division between China's New Left, who celebrated state power, and the Liberals, who criticized it, current debates show no clear direction. In other words, even China's elite is unsure about the country's future—which makes it an even more fascinating topic.

In the face of these uncertainties, citizen intellectuals express an abundance of hope that China can find its own way to become prosperous and powerful. Artist-activist Ai Weiwei's reaction in October 2008 to the spreading global economic crisis is typical: "I am very optimistic.... I think that it's very important for everyone to see that we're entering a new world, a new condition, and a new structure, and to see the possible potential damage. It's a very, very exciting time and I think that everybody will learn something from it."[4]

Although the American dream might be in trouble, philosopher Richard Rorty's way of thinking about political possibilities can help us understand how new visions of the future are emerging in China: "You have to describe the country in terms of what you passionately want it to become, as well as what you know it to be now. You have to be loyal to a dream country rather than to the one to which you wake up every morning. Unless such loyalty exists, the ideal has no chance of becoming actual."[5] Although a pragmatic nonideological approach to economic development has defined the PRC's reform era, the Chinese are incurably idealistic about their "dream country." We should not be surprised that many Chinese—from Xi Jinping to people on the street—express their aspirations and anxieties in terms of "The China Dream" itself.

To get a sense of the various dream countries—and dream worlds—that are proposed by officials, dissidents, and citizen intellectuals, I think we need to take a new approach. The standard operating procedure for political scientists who study Chinese government policy is to gather facts through elite interviews and to survey China's "restricted" (neibu) publications. Yet, over the last decade, I have found that trying to acquire "secret knowledge" from well-connected sources has often led me away from important new developments in China. Most interlocutors, for understandable reasons, either tell me what they think foreigners want to hear or tell me what the party-state wants outsiders to hear.

Rather than try to eavesdrop on the Politburo's secret discussions, in this book we will listen in on what Chinese people are saying to each other in public space; indeed, often what they are yelling and screaming at each other in the mass media and popular culture. Although there is harsh censorship of direct criticism of the party and the leadership, there is also a very broad space for people to think about different ways of being Chinese.

Often this is not just an intellectual exercise; for many citizen intellectuals, their work reflects their life choices and even life styles. Han Han, who as China's top blogger is one of the party-state's most eloquent critics, is not a member of China's literati elite; rather, he is a high school dropout who pursued his personal ambition to become a professional race car driver. Han thus is seen by many as the voice of the first generation of one-child policy children who were born in the 1980s (known as the "post-1980 generation") and who grew up in the reform era's environment of increasing prosperity and freedom. Han's sense of China's future possibilities echoes Rorty's "dream country" hopes: "my country right now is not good enough. So, even though I am a weak individual, the only thing I can do is to try to help make the country that I dream of."[6]

Justin Yifu Lin, who as the vice president and chief economist of the World Bank from 2008 to 2012 became the top formulator of the emerging "China model" of economic development that combines authoritarian state governance and free market capitalism, also has a fascinating life story that shapes his views. When Lin abandoned his Taiwanese army post and swam to the mainland in 1979, he became one of the few people to actually defect *into* the PRC. Leaving his pregnant wife behind, Lin left Taiwan because he felt that Beijing had a better chance of building a strong and prosperous "China."

While Han dropped out of China's elite society to pursue his China dream, Lin swam in to pursue his. By seeing how social, historical, and political contexts inform the work of citizen intellectuals such as Han and Lin, we can join China's lively conversations about where the PRC should go in the 21st century.

This broad view of Chinese politics enables us to better explore the grand aspirations and deep anxieties of a wide variety of officials, dissidents, and citizen intellectuals. Rather than try to discover the one true Future China, it is important to appreciate the plurality of many possible Chinas and the tension between these competing China dreams; indeed, ideas and influence grow out of the discussions among officials, dissidents, and citizen intellectuals. Although they may not talk directly to each other, these people are involved in a raucous debate over the direction of China's future. Analyzing the party-state's official documents is still important; but the goal also is to consider what the films, novels, art, and blogs of China's unofficial futurologists can tell us about what it means to be Chinese in the 21st century.

While analyses of the "Chinese Century" focus largely on economic growth, I think that it's necessary to see how China's rise presents a challenge of ideas and norms, in the drive to build a new world order. While officials in Beijing often talk about the "win-win opportunities" of China's "peaceful development," many others see close links between the rise of China and the fall of America. Books such as *When China Rules the World: The Rise of the Middle Kingdom and the End of the Western World* (2009) graphically describe how Beijing is constructing an alternative modernity for a post-American world order.[7]

This is more than an academic issue. Henry Kissinger's *On China* (2011) and Chinese strategist Yan Xuetong's *Ancient Chinese Thought, Modern Chinese Power* (2011)[8] show how discussions of China's destiny are informing how elites in China and the West conceptualize the future world order in terms of Confucian China versus the democratic West.

This book's goal is to challenge popular English-language books that assert stereotypes of China's civilizational challenge to the West because, as Howard W. French notes, they seldom get beyond Beijing's "official cant" and often "read like a compilation of ideas gleaned by the water cooler at the Chinese Academy of Social Sciences, the state's official think tank."[9]

The new trend of Chinese-language books about China's future shows that we need to look beyond such official plans for the future to see what Chinese people are telling each other—rather than see what they like to tell foreigners. Once you enter the Chinese discourse, you can see that simplistic formulations of the China model versus the American model actually obscure the fascinating debate about China's future. Although exotic Chinese ideas are part of this discussion, so are the more familiar discourses of socialism, statism, nationalism, and even liberal democracy. Rather than assuming that Confucianism has replaced communism, we need to appreciate the dynamic tensions among socialism, democracy, and indigenous ideals in the PRC. Indeed, one of the debates is over how to understand the Chinese term *wenming*: does it refer to the conservative values of China's ancient "civilization" or does it mean "civility" in the sense of people caring about each other in a democratic civil society?

The spirited discussion about the PRC's future direction highlights how the problem of "how to understand China" challenges not only outsiders, but Chinese people as well. Since even officials can't agree about the meaning of the China dream, the future is up for grabs.

The Future Returns to China

Why should we study China's futures? Or the China dream? Predictions of China's economic growth, for example, have consistently been wrong, grossly underestimating the rate of change. Perhaps the only accurate prediction we can make is that futurologists' forecasts will be wrong. But as futures studies pioneer Jim Dator tells us, "any useful statement about the future should appear to be ridiculous."[10]

In spite of the problems inherent in forecasting, many Chinese intellectuals have caught the futurology bug. The past five years have seen an explosion of futures studies activity among officials, scholars, and citizen intellectuals. In 2010–2011 much discussion took place in public space about the party-state's 12th Five-Year Plan (2011–2015). In addition, scholars and citizen intellectuals have published dozens of consciously futuristic studies: *China's Future*; *China: Moving Towards 2015*; *China in 2020*; *2025: The China Dream*; *2030 China: Towards Common Prosperity*; *China: 30 Years in the Future*; *2049: Believe in China*; and *China Shock*.[11]

It is important to study the future not because the various forecasts are necessarily "true." Chinese futurology is important for political rather than epistemological reasons: The emergence in the PRC of new ways of thinking about the future is part of the shift in normative power from the West to the East. Futures studies thus is important not because it is true, but because it is new in China. As in American and European futures studies, knowledge and power are interlinked in Chinese futurology, where the objective is not just to know the future, but also to control it.[12] These futuristic plans and dreams are important because they can tell us how Chinese people relate to their past, present, and future as well as how they interact with people in other countries in the present.

You can get a sense of the energy of Chinese futurology by reading books by outsiders; John and Doris Naisbitt's *China's Megatrends: The 8 Pillars of a New Society* (2010) is part of this optimistic trend when the authors proclaim that "China in 2009 was creating an entirely new social and economic system—and a political model, which may well prove that 'the end of history' was just another pause along history's path."[13] The Naisbitts came to these conclusions in a novel way: in 2007, they founded the Naisbitt China Institute in Tianjin as an independent think tank to conduct their research. While Martin Jacques's *When China Rules the World* was translated from English into Chinese, in 2009 the Naisbitts published *China's Megatrends* in Chinese—and only later in English.

Although the content of *China's Megatrends* is of minimal value—it does little more than reproduce Beijing's official propaganda slogans—the process of its research and publication shows two significant trends in Chinese futurology: (1) a shift from locating the future outside China (by figuring China as backward and the West as advanced) to see China itself as the future, and (2) a shift from officials centrally planning the future (through the party-state's Five-Year economic development plans) to having many different people dreaming about many different futures. Thus, the battle for the future is not necessarily waged only between China and the West (as we are incessantly told), but also takes place within the PRC itself among different groups of Chinese intellectuals.

In the 20th century, the future was located outside of China. The country was weak after suffering imperial encroachments from the West and Japan as the Qing dynasty slowly died out at the turn of the 20th century, in what Chinese call their "Century of National Humiliation."[14] Many intellectuals lost faith in China's traditional way of organizing economics, politics, and society. After China's republican revolution unseated two millennia of imperial rule in 1911, activists and intellectuals looked abroad for modernity. The "New Culture Movement" (1915–1922) consciously imported the exotic Western entities "Science" and "Democracy" to cure the ills of China's "backward" traditional culture. After the communist revolution in 1949, New China was more advanced than imperial or republican China; but Mao Zedong still famously predicted that "the Soviet Union's today will be China's tomorrow." During the Great Leap Forward (1958–1961) and the Cultural Revolution (1966–1976), China presented itself to the globe as a revolutionary model of the future—but the tragic results of these mass movements underlined the PRC's failure to embody the future for itself, let alone for the rest of the world. With Deng Xiaoping's reform and opening policy (1978), the West— and especially the American dream of consumer prosperity—became China's model for the future. For the children of China's "post-1980 generation," who were born under the one-child policy, the China dream is not only to pursue the American dream in China. As a Chinese teenager in the northeastern city of Dalian declared, "it's my dream to live in a nice suburb in America!"[15]

Many Chinese analysts likewise take America as the standard of modernity, development, and the future; as historian Arthur Waldron writes: "If one were to name a single metric by which the Chinese government judges itself, it would be the United States."[16] As we will see, the main goal of many Chinese futurologists is less to achieve a utopian society than it is simply to surpass the United States economically, militarily, and politically. Futurology in China is seen as a Western practice: a survey of Chinese newspaper and academic articles shows that the term "futurologist" (*weilai xuezhe*) is characteristically modified as "American futurologist" or "Western futurologist." Joe Studwell's book *The China Dream* and James Mann's book *The China Fantasy* are not about Chinese people's dreams, but about Western dreams of China as a vast untapped economic market or as the next liberal democracy.[17] Discussing the Asia-Pacific Century in the 1990s, historian Alexander Woodside noted how Chinese intellectuals treated American futurologists Alvin Toffler (author of *The Third Wave* [1980]) and John Naisbitt (whose *Megatrends* was published in 1982) as "oracles." Yet, Woodside wondered at the lack of native Chinese futurologists.[18] Naisbitt's recent experience confirms this: in 1996, he told President Jiang Zemin that "Taiwan has a small story to tell, and tells it very well. China has a big story to tell, and does a terrible job in telling it." To which Jiang replied: "Why don't you tell it? We will give you all the support you need."[19] The result, of course, was *China's Megatrends*.

Toffler, Naisbitt, and a host of other Western futurologists continue to shape Chinese ideas about the future. According to this dominant view of modernization and progress, both the future and futurology are located outside China.

But things are changing. At the end of his glowing assessment of *China's Megatrends*, a Chinese reviewer suggests that it is time for China to tell its own story: "Chinese have the ability to create a great story, Chinese also definitely are able to learn how to tell our own story, allowing China's story to spread to the world, to emotionally move the world."[20]

To many in the PRC, the West is no longer the future: as we saw with the dozens of books with titles such as *China: 30 Years in the Future*, China itself is now the future. This shift is confirmed by the appearance over the past few years of arguments for the "China Dream," the "China Model," and the various "Chinese Schools" of social science (e.g., the Chinese school of international relations theory).[21] Most of these new futurologists see China as an alternative to the universals of Western modernity. Rather than taking "the outside" as the measure of China's development status, such books directly criticize what they call the Soviet model and the American model to avoid either repeating the shocking collapse of the Soviet Union or falling into the "booby-trap" of Westernization. They argue that because of China's unique history and civilization, it needs to tread its own developmental road; otherwise, it is on the "road to suicide," just like the former Soviet Union.[22]

Curiously, many of these Chinese futurologists look to the past to explain their objectives. "Confucian futures studies" should be an oxymoron since the classics gaze back to an ancient golden age rather than to a future utopia. Yet, noted scholars are now looking to the past to plan China's future and the world's future, combing ancient texts for ideas to guide the Chinese century: Under-Heaven (*tianxia*), Great Harmony (*datong*), and the Kingly Way (*wangdao*). China's current rise to global power, they tell us, is not without precedent; it is actually the rejuvenation of the Chinese nation to its "natural place" at the center of the world.[23]

Beijing is also starting to export futures. Either because China is big (with one-fifth of the world's population) or because it is good (China can make great contributions to human civilization), many Chinese authors assert that their country's future is the world's future: "China and other countries all need to focus on this question: what does China's future development mean for world order?"[24] In its conclusion, *2049: Believe in China* confidently answers this question: "not far in the future the world will accept China's model ... a model that surpasses its potential" to make China a country "as rich as America, but one that loves peace and social harmony more, and is capable of lasting a long time."[25]

While it is common for pundits in China and the West to proclaim that the American dream has been replaced by the Chinese dream, we will see how even China's nativists are still fascinated by America. U.S.-China relations now constitutes the most important bilateral relationship in global politics and economics. This dynamic, which British historian Niall Ferguson and German economist Moritz Schularik call "Chimerica," is more than an economic relationship that binds together the PRC as producer and the United States as consumer;[26] it also points to the transnational connections between American people and Chinese people, if not the governments in Beijing and Washington.

Actually, most of the citizen intellectuals considered in this book have had an international experience that includes studying, living, and working in the United States. For some, it led them to formulate more complex views of China's relation to the world; for others, it hardened their belief in a zero-sum notion of "China versus the West." For both groups, living abroad was an important experience that shaped their views. Thus, this book will consider U.S.-China relations in a different way by exploring how the China dream is interwoven with the American dream.

The absence of Japan in China's discussions of its future direction is both odd and understandable. Over the past century China has sent many students to study in the West; but it has sent many more to study in Japan. Japan served as an attractive model in the early 20th century because it was the first Asian country to master modernity through economic and social reforms. Japan became a model again in the 1980s when its developmental state model of economic organization challenged America's laissez-faire capitalism. The current hype about China as the next superpower also resembles the combination of fascination and fear that characterized Western reactions to Japan's rise as an economic superpower in the 1980s. Ezra Vogel's *Japan as Number One: Lessons for America* could equally have been subtitled "lessons for China" since the PRC used a similar state-capitalist model for its own economic miracle.

But as we will see in chapters 2 and 3, China's citizen intellectuals go out of their way to stress the irrelevance of Japan's political and economic experience. There are three reasons for this. First, since memories of Japan's wartime atrocities continue to shape both official policy and popular perceptions toward Japan, it is culturally and politically difficult for Chinese elites to take Japan as a model. Second, Chinese economists now see Japan as a negative example; they are actually trying to avoid the economic slow-down that characterized Japan's two lost decades since 1990. The last reason is ideological: as Japan's experience in the 1980s shows, promoting your country's unique values is an important part of being the new superpower, and China is no exception to this trend.

Japan thus is rarely mentioned in Chinese futurology; when it is discussed, it is primarily to celebrate how China passed Japan in 2010 to become the world's second-largest economy. (The European model is largely absent as well, especially since China's GDP passed Germany's in 2007.) In this global marathon, Beijing's objective now is to pass the United States in terms of economic, political, and cultural power. Although the bulk of the book explores what citizen intellectuals have to say about the China dream, we will also consider the important role that "America" plays in Chinese people's plans for the future.

Chapter 6 will directly compare the meaning of the China dream and the American dream, relating both to American exceptionalism and to Chinese exceptionalism. We can easily summarize the American dream by looking to the Declaration of Independence's promise of the rights of life, liberty, and the pursuit of happiness. Yet, as we will see in chapter 6, the American dream is surprisingly complex, and it has grown out of the tension between freedom for individuals and equality for social groups. While the American dream primarily focuses on the individual advancement of "self-made men," we will see how the China dream is still taking shape in debates between different citizen intellectuals.

Exceptionalism, for both American and Chinese thinkers, means that their country is not only unique, but also uniquely superior. Each country's uniquely superior values, then, are so great that they need to be exported to other countries—whether those other countries like it or not. American exceptionalism grows out of the idea that the United States is the world's first new nation, while Chinese exceptionalism looks to the country's 5,000 years of continuous history to see China as the world's first ancient civilization.[27] American exceptionalism informs a foreign policy of spreading freedom and democracy around the world—often through military intervention. Chinese exceptionalism looks to China's uniquely peaceful civilization to unite the globe in a World of Great Harmony that promises order and prosperity, usually as an alternative to liberal democracy.

Although some Chinese people dream of individual freedom, and some Americans dream of collective equality, the trend is clear: The American dream is for individual freedom and the China dream is for national rejuvenation. The book's concluding scenario, however, seeks to complicate this view of American individuals versus the Chinese nation by charting the partial overlaps and strange crossovers of a particular Chimerican dream.

Different Roads to the Future

Alongside the shift in the future's location from outside China to inside the PRC, the method of forecasting the future is moving from centralized state planning to more decentralized activity among a multitude of citizen intellectuals.

Although it is reasonable to assume that futures studies emerged from post–World War II movements in Europe and America—such as RAND Corporation in the United States or Bertrand de Jouvenel's *Comité International Futuribles* in France—we should remember that Marxism is also a futuristic ideology that charts its own path from the problematic present to the communist future. Science is a key element in Marxism; indeed, to separate himself from the dreamy ideas of utopian socialists such as Pierre-Joseph Proudhon, Marx promoted his new ideology as "scientific socialism." In the PRC, science is an important site where socialist ideology and futurology overlap: Hu Jintao's "scientific development concept" slogan was added to the constitution of the Chinese Communist Party in 2007. Modernization, progress, and development thus are presented as scientific facts rather than ideological positions.

However, as with the Soviet Union, the PRC's futurism is better described as Leninist due to its top-down notion of development that relies on the centralized planning of the command economy, which also regulates social and cultural life. China's first Five Year Plan began in 1953, and the current 12th Five-Year Plan (2011–2015) was approved in 2011. Hence, even though Deng Xiaoping's economic reforms introduced markets to China, official futures studies still employs state-led centralized notions of modernization, progress, and development. To introduce China's 12th Five-Year Plan to a general audience, top economist Hu Angang outlined his methodology and goals: "Comprehensively know China, deeply analyze China, meticulously plan China, scientifically develop China." The title of the *Beijing Review*'s interview with Hu about the 12th Five-Year Plan—"A Plan Is Born"—says it all.[28] Here China's future is centralized in terms of both the "knowability" of hard science and the "governability" of state planning,[29] both of which seek to discover a future that is singular, inevitable, and undeniable.

Yet, alongside this centralized view of the future, new voices are emerging to propose a multitude of different dreams, possibilities, and futures for China. The PRC's recent success, especially when contrasted with continuing crisis in the West, is leading many Chinese to think in new ways about China's future—and the world's future. Rather than promoting the singular future of "The Real China," they are dreaming of plural futures for many Chinas.

One of the most interesting developments has been the appearance of the citizen intellectuals mentioned above, who consciously work in public space to imagine China's preferred futures. Citizen intellectuals are "independent voices" not because they stand in opposition to state power, but because they take advantage of China's new social and economic opportunities to choose when to work with the state and when to work outside state institutions. Hu Angang, for example, works within the system on the committee that draws up China's Five-Year Plans; but he also uses his status as a citizen intellectual to push a "green development model" that is often at odds with the political leadership in Beijing.[30] While many experts once criticized people who worked so closely with the party-state as "sell-outs," China's new social and economic freedoms mean that we need to take citizen intellectuals—and their new ideas—more seriously.

Like Hu Angang, many citizen intellectuals appeal to science to ground their forecasts. But a host of others are dreaming of alternative futures that are more critical and open-ended. The liberal newspaper *Southern Weekend*, for example, engages in unofficial futurology when it gives out "China Dreamer" awards each year to diplomats, journalists, artists, and writers in

a grand ceremony at Peking University.[31] Most notably, Hong Kong writer
Chan Koonchung's critique of the China model in his science-fiction novel
The Golden Age: China, 2013 (published in English as *The Fat Years*), provoked a firestorm of commentary among Chinese intellectuals about what
China should be.[32] But not all citizen intellectuals are liberal critics; this new
trend also includes conservative voices: Senior Colonel Liu Mingfu's *China
Dream* (2010) of building up the PRC's military power to challenge America
is a personal commentary rather than an official statement from the Ministry
of Defense.[33]

This move from planning a singular future through computer modeling to
imagining alternative futures matches the shift from outside to inside China
discussed above; recall that the Naisbitts' book reviewer reframed China's
futurology from scientific discovery to "creating a great story" that would
"emotionally move the world."

Great changes are certainly taking place in China. But they are complex
and multilayered. Hence, I am not arguing that there has been a grand one-way
shift from the state to civil society, from central planning to decentered dreaming, or from the future as outside China to China as the future. Rather, I want
to highlight how understanding the productive tension between the state and
civil society, planning and dreaming, and outside and inside China is what is
most important—and most interesting.

The book addresses this complex situation by examining twenty China
dreams, which were selected because they are part of key discussions of
China's domestic politics (chapter 1), grand strategy (chapter 2), economic
development model (chapter 3), social dynamic (chapter 4), and cultural
activities (chapter 5). Chapter 6 summarizes these China dreams and explores
the tension between them and the American dream, and between American
exceptionalism and Chinese exceptionalism.

The objective is not to provide a singular prediction of when China will be
the world's number one power; rather, each chapter offers a range of scenarios
that show us where Chinese people think they are going. The book concludes
with a "Scenario" that explores the complexities of China's rise and how it
interrelates with the West. In this way, I hope to illuminate a specific range of
possibilities for China's future role in the world, which entails a specific set of
outcomes for the West.

Certainly, we could argue over whose dream should be included and
whose shouldn't; in fact, these dreams were chosen after heated discussions with friends and colleagues in China and around the world. I decided
that the ideas of these twenty-some people—who are typically ethnic Han

men—were noteworthy because they are important in the PRC. Others, like ethnic Uighur businesswoman Rabeeya Kadeer and Tibetan poet Woeser, are doing fascinating things; but since they are not provoking key debates in China I will save discussion of their work for another day.

Patriotically Worrying about the Future

While most English-language books, e.g. Jacques's *When China Rules the World* and the Naisbitts' *China's Megatrends,* contrast Chinese success with Western failure, the Chinese-language literature is often more complex. Beijing's *zeitgeist* includes a complicated mix of hopes and fears about the opportunities offered by the "Chinese Century." Chinese writers certainly are triumphalist, typically defining China's current and future success as a return to the country's "natural status" at the center of the world. But many also engage in what Chinese call "patriotic worrying" (*youhuan*), where China itself is seen as "the problem" that intellectuals are morally obligated to solve—otherwise they fear that the Chinese race-nation risks being wiped off the face of the earth.[34]

Although Liu Mingfu's plan to overtake the United States to become the world's number one power is often criticized as "extremist," at times his analysis is nuanced. His last chapter, "We Need a 'China Collapse Theory.'" is consciously anti-triumphalist. It starts with praise for America's self-critical practice of patriotic worrying, which he calls "American declinism." Liu is fascinated with this self-criticism because he is surprised that people could so harshly judge their own country. While many in China celebrate the end of the American century since the financial crisis began in 2008, Liu is more circumspect. He notices that this is not the first time that Americans have self-critically discussed their country's current problems as a sign of national demise; Liu finds that, since World War II, each "crisis in domestic policy or foreign affairs" has provoked a debate in the United States about whether or not it is a turning point that signals the start of a serious national decline. Liu concludes that this thorough self-criticism is not a weakness but rather a strength: "Americans often cry out to themselves 'American decline,' to protect against the decline."

Liu laments that such a self-critical "worrying mentality" is scarce in China, especially in discussions of security and foreign affairs: only foreigners talk about China's collapse. The greatest threat, however, is not Westerners' demonization of China through China Collapse Theory,[35] but a lack of Chinese voices singing the song of China collapse. Thus, the China dream, according to Liu, needs to include both good dreams and nightmares because "while we Chinese are in the midst of our rise, we must listen for the sound of 'China collapse' because this will protect us against the collapse, and help us make the rise a reality."[36]

In addition to celebrating China's global ambitions, many citizen intellectuals are worrying about China's national anxieties: the risk of being a loser (again) in what I call China's pessoptimism (a mixture of optimism and pessimism).[37] China's dreams of global greatness here are interwoven with its nationalist nightmares. China's rise thus is best described as *uneasy*; as it fulfills its grand aspirations, China simultaneously encounters nagging political, social, and economic uncertainties. According to both Five-Year Planners and military strategists, China is in an "era of strategic opportunity," where the "strategic window" for China's success may soon close. The stakes are high—if Beijing misses this great opportunity for grand success many feel that it risks total failure: "If China in the 21st century cannot become world number one, cannot become the top power, then inevitably it will become a straggler that is cast aside."[38]

I
_____

Officials, Dissidents, and Citizen Intellectuals

TO UNDERSTAND CHINESE politics, it used to be enough to read leaders' speeches and interview a few well-connected officials and scholars. But since Deng Xiaoping's economic reforms opened up society, China's politics have become much more complex. In this chapter, I will show how ideas and policy interact in a more open China by exploring the interplay of the China dreams of officials, dissidents, and citizens through real life examples: Xi Jinping, Bo Xilai, Liu Xiaobo, Ai Weiwei, Pan Wei, and Zhang Wei-wei. These six prominent people ask and answer some of the main questions facing China today: Is China being westernized as it modernizes? Can Chinese values combine with Western values in a new cosmopolitan civilization? Or should Chinese values replace Western values in a new post-American world order?

Officials: The Rise of the Princelings

The PRC is in the midst of a long transition from the fourth generation leaders—President Hu Jintao and Premier Wen Jiabao—to the fifth generation leadership of Xi Jinping and Li Keqiang, who served out their apprenticeships under Hu and Wen. The official transition takes place in three steps: in November 2012 Xi Jinping took over as general secretary of the Chinese Communist Party (CCP) at the 18th Party Congress and was appointed chair of the Central Military Commission, and in March 2013 he was elected president of the PRC at the National People's Congress. The informal transition is much longer, roughly between 2009, as the fourth generation's power began to wane, and 2014, when the fifth generation will have consolidated its control.

Although this sounds routine, the CCP is actually still in the process of formalizing the succession process: the transition to the fourth generation leadership in 2002 was the PRC's first constitutional transfer of power. The previous handovers were actually coups d'état: Jiang Zemin became secretary general after the June 4th massacre ousted Zhao Ziyang in 1989 and Deng Xiaoping illegally unseated Mao's chosen successor, Hua Guofeng. In many ways, the systematization of leadership politics is a response to the Cultural Revolution (1966–1976), when Mao's personality-based strong-man politics severely damaged the CCP. Hence, the reform era is as much known for party-building as it is for economic reform.

Since 2007, a mandatory retirement age of sixty-eight has been instituted for the Politburo Standing Committee (PBSC), China's top decision-making body. Presidents and vice presidents are limited to two five-year terms in office. Soon after they took office in 2012–2013, Xi and Li put in motion the whole transition process again when they started grooming the sixth generation leadership that will take over in 2022. Although the process is getting more predictable, right up until the 18th Party Conference huge uncertainties remained about the make-up of the seven places in China's top decision-making body, the PBSC. Everyone but Xi Jinping and Li Keqiang retired in 2012; as we will see below, intense competition erupted for the five empty seats.

Even so, official politics in China is secretive. While voters in the West are barraged with campaign messages from aspiring politicians for months—or years in the case of American presidential elections—China's leaders are chosen in a way that more closely resembles a papal conclave. The electorate is neither the PRC's 1.3 billion citizens, nor the CCP's 80 million party members, but rather the 300-odd members of the CCP's Central Committee—if not the nine men (and they were all men) on the previous PBSC. The workings of power are cloaked: Decisions are made through the collective responsibility of consensus-building in the PBSC. Although the members certainly debate behind the scenes, one of the hallmarks of communist party leadership is a highly disciplined public façade of unity.

Thus, the political audience is internal. Former president Hu Jintao was known primarily for his stiff personal style and for a pronounced *lack* of enthusiasm for press conferences. Although former premier Wen Jiabao was popularly known as "Grandpa Wen" for his common touch, some criticized this kindly image as empty and insincere: the author of a recent book satirically dubbed him "China's Best Actor."[1] Hence, even after Hu's ten years as president and Wen's decade as premier, we still know very little about their

FIGURE 1.1 Xi Jinping
Source: Hong Kong Culture and Arts Press

political views. Their hopes and dreams for China's future can be summarized in the laudable—but rather anodyne—policy statements of "building a harmonious society" at home and "building a harmonious world" abroad.

Who is Xi Jinping, and what does he believe? These are difficult questions to answer. Because of the party's secrecy, reliable sources are scarce. The Chinese people learned about Xi's military service, for example, only in his official biography, which was published when he was appointed vice chair of the Central Military Commission in 2010. Otherwise, the main sources are leaked American diplomatic cables and a biography by a Hong Kong journalist.[2] Hence, beyond the potted official career history, most of what we know about Xi's personal life and his beliefs comes from rumor and gossip. Even with all these problems, outsiders often know more than the Chinese people.

With these caveats in mind, a few things are clear. Like many of the fifth generation leaders, Xi is a "princeling" (*taizi*): a member of an informal group of around 300 children of veteran communist revolutionaries. Xi's father, Xi Zhongxun, joined the CCP in 1928, and he was a revolutionary hero who founded a key communist guerrilla base area in northern China. After falling out with Mao, he was imprisoned in 1962 and spent the Cultural Revolution in jail. In 1978, the elder Xi was rehabilitated by Deng Xiaoping. He become the party head of Guangdong Province, where he launched the Shenzhen economic reform experiment that initiated China's economic opening to the world in the 1980s.

Xi Jinping was born in Beijing in 1953. His father was head of the CCP's Central Propaganda Department and deputy minister of culture and education, so Xi grew up in the gated communities and elite schools of China's red aristocracy. Like many of the princelings, Xi has used family connections to grease the wheels of his career. But while other princelings have gone into business to make vast fortunes, Xi primarily used his network for political advancement.

According to a childhood friend cited in a U.S. diplomatic cable, Xi has been "single-minded" and "exceptionally ambitious" in his pursuit of high office. Even though his father was denounced and tortured during the Cultural Revolution, Xi decided to join the CCP during this turbulent period. To avoid Beijing's hypercompetitive political climate, Xi decided to start his career outside the capital, so, in 1983, he requested a position in the provinces. Over the next twenty-five years, Xi rose through the ranks of the party leadership, starting in the poor northern province of Hebei (1983–1985), before being transferred to the wealthy southeastern provinces of Fujian (1985–2002) and Zhejiang (2002–2007). Due to successful anti-corruption drives, he has the reputation of being Mr. Clean. Hence, in 2007 Xi was parachuted in to lead Shanghai, which was in the midst of a corruption scandal. Xi dealt with the scandal so effectively that within seven months he was summoned to Beijing to join the PBSC in October 2007, and he became vice president of the PRC in March 2008. In this sense, Xi has followed the career trajectory of Hu Jintao; the only thing missing is experience managing social unrest and ethnic minority issues.

As this impressive professional biography shows, Xi is Mr. Resume. Rather than pursuing a specific political program—either as an economic reformer or as a political conservative—Xi's career shows that he's a careerist. Instead of being ideological, he is most well known for being pragmatic and loyal. While his father was in jail during the Cultural Revolution, Xi survived this tumultuous period by becoming "redder than red." Later, when he worked in the prosperous Southeast, Xi promoted economic reform. Speaking as the president of the CCP's Central Party School in 2010, Xi enjoined people to study the Marxist classics. In other words, Xi is loyal to the party, whatever the particular party line is at the time. Like most of China's leaders, Xi has no experience outside the system; he reportedly divorced his first wife because she wanted to live abroad.

When meeting with American politicians and officials he is engaging and even friendly: according to the leaked diplomatic cables, Xi told an

American ambassador that he liked Hollywood movies because they show that "Americans have a clear outlook on values and clearly demarcate between good and evil." But for other audiences, he lashes out at the West: "Some foreigners with full bellies and nothing better to do engage in finger-pointing at us," he told overseas Chinese in Mexico in 2009. "First, China does not export revolution; second, it does not export famine and poverty; and third, it does not mess around with you. So what else is there to say?" On the other hand, Xi sent his daughter to study at Harvard University and two of his siblings live abroad. Like many Chinese, he has mixed views about the United States; his foreign policy ideas, like his policy preferences in other areas, are more flexible than ideological.

Flexibility certainly can be a strength; however, it doesn't tell us much about what Xi will do now that he is China's leader. According to the diplomatic cables, Xi believes that the princelings are China's "legitimate heirs" who are entitled to lead because "rule by a dedicated and committed communist party leadership is the key to enduring social stability and national strength." Thus, Xi's beliefs about his natural leadership role in China have much in common with popular feelings about China's natural leadership role on the world stage: both Xi and the PRC are pragmatic, ambitious, and successful, and they see themselves as destined to rule. While the rise of the princelings in 2012 heralds the return to power of the red aristocracy, the rise of the PRC in the 21st century marks the return of China as the center of the world.

From these sketchy sources, we can't be sure what Xi's hopes and dreams for China are. Since the main task of an heir apparent in China is to *not* stand out, leadership style and policy preferences come out only after they gain the top job. Still, soon after Xi was summoned to the capital in 2007, he was put at the helm of China's mega-events: the 2008 Olympics and the celebrations of the sixtieth anniversary of the PRC in 2009. During his short tenure as Shanghai's party secretary in 2007, he was an ardent supporter of Shanghai's World Expo 2010. This shows how he was involved in shaping Beijing's official view of China as an authoritarian capitalist civilization-state.

This was confirmed in Xi's first public speech as China's new helmsman, when he declared that his "China dream" is to "achieve the great rejuvenation of the Chinese nation," in which "each person's future and destiny is closely linked with the future and destiny of the country and the nation."[3] Although "rejuvenation" (*fuxing*) is a very broad and ambiguous term, here Xi is declaring that he is more nationalistic than Hu or Wen. His nationalism could be

FIGURE 1.2 Major General Peng Liyuan
Source: Global Times

more militaristic too: even before the transfer of power in 2012–2013, Xi was leading the policymaking behind China's territorial disputes in the South China Sea and the East China Sea.[4]

While Hu Jintao turned out to be a weak leader who generally lacked confidence, Xi's self-confident charm could make him a strong leader who makes bold choices. Unlike his predecessors, Xi was able to hit the ground running because he became head of the communist party and commander-in-chief of the armed forces in a complete transfer of power in November 2012. Expectations are high in China for Xi to act quickly on a range of issues; there is a sense of urgency in Beijing because people feel that China's "window of opportunity" for global greatness is closing. But as only the first among equals in the PBSC's collective decision making, it is unlikely that Xi will be a trans-formational leader like Mao or Deng.

Perhaps the most intriguing thing about Xi is his second wife, Peng Liyuan. Peng is one of China's most famous folk singers. As the long-time host of CCTV's Chinese New Year Gala—the most important event in Chinese television—Peng was probably more famous than her husband, at least until recently. Peng's patriotic crooning as a major-general in the PLA's premier singing troupe makes her popular with rank-and-file soldiers, which adds a populist element to Xi's military connections. In 2011, Peng's fame went global: She was appointed goodwill ambassador by World Health

Organization director-general Margaret Chan, who is from Hong Kong. Many expect Xi's glamorous wife to give a Kennedyesque feel to his tenure.

Most analysts compare Xi and China's new premier Li Keqiang, pointing out that they come from rival factions in the CCP. Xi is a princeling who is part of former president Jiang Zemin's Shanghai gang. Li has risen through the ranks under the patronage of former president Hu Jintao and the Communist Youth League faction of the CCP, which is seen as more populist than the elitist princeling group. But rather than probe the dance of these two factions, it is more important to compare two "princelings": Xi Jinping and Bo Xilai, who until recently was party secretary of the southwestern city of Chongqing (2007–2012).

Xi and Bo make an interesting comparison because their experience illustrates not only how to succeed in China's elite politics, but also how to fail: in 2012, Xi became the leader of the CCP, while Bo was expelled from the party. Bo's fall triggered the party's most serious crisis since 1989. It exposed factionalism, corruption, and abuses of power at the very heart of the CCP leadership, which damaged the party's legitimacy in the eyes of both the elite and ordinary people.

This scandal was shocking because it was so unexpected; everyone was predicting a smooth transition to the fifth generation leadership. Before his fall, Bo Xilai used the mass media to capture the national imagination by courting populist audiences as well as elite patronage. He was handsome, articulate, and media-savvy; if Peng Liyuan is Jackie O, then Bo was China's JFK (see Fig. 1.3). He was the "crown prince" among princelings: His father Bo Yibo was a top revolutionary veteran who held key posts under both Mao and Deng; he was one of the powerful Communist Party veterans who backed Deng's crackdown after the June 4th massacre in 1989.

In 2007, Bo Xilai was in the running to become China's vice president, and, thus, its president in 2012; but after much politicking, Xi Jinping beat him out to be the princeling candidate for the vice presidency and the PBSC. Bo was named to the Politburo in 2007, but he was sent to the provinces. Rather than take this demotion as the end of his career, Bo decided to use his time in Chongqing to openly campaign for a seat on the PBSC.

But Bo campaigned for the PBSC in an atypical way. Rather than just rely on personal networks to broker a back-room deal in the Politburo, he started a number of high-profile political campaigns. Soon after arriving in Chongqing, Bo launched a crackdown on the city's notorious criminal syndicates that controlled prostitution, drugs, and other illegal businesses. Bo's "Strike Black" anti-crime drive led to nearly 3,500 arrests and thirteen

FIGURE 1.3 Bo Xilai and Gu Kailai
Source: http://uscpf.org/v3/?p=4249

executions as well as sixty-four criminal syndicates that were closed down and some 2.1 billion yuan ($330 million) in assets seized.[5] The anti-mafia campaign made Bo enormously popular in Chongqing and throughout China. Liberal critics, however, said that the Strike Black crackdown was overzealous: Its use of torture to extract confessions and a heavy-handed approach to the law were seen as undermining the growing independence of China's judicial system.

However, Bo is most famous for his Mao-style mass campaigns: the "Red Culture" movement included singing revolutionary songs, reading communist classics, broadcasting red television programs, and texting Mao quotes. This rather traditional propaganda campaign culminated in 2011 with Chongqing's official celebration of the ninetieth anniversary of the Chinese Communist Party (CCP): 70,000 people filled a soccer stadium to sing revolutionary songs such as "The East Is Red" and "Without the Communist Party, There Would Be No New China." Bo even recruited arch-geostrategist Henry Kissinger, who was in town promoting his book *On China*, to join in the communist sing-along.

Alongside the Strike Black and Sing Red campaigns, Bo pursued other populist policies, including subsidized housing for the poor, free tuition below the ninth grade, and more police in crime-ridden neighborhoods. Bo even revived the Cultural Revolutionary practice of sending bureaucrats to the countryside to work alongside peasants for one month each year.[6] Bo's egalitarian policies, thus, were very popular among the anti-reform groups and China's New Left intellectuals.

The success of Bo's mass campaign might have something to do with Chongqing's particular demographics. Chongqing, which is the size of Austria and has a population of 33 million people, is technically the largest city in the world. Yet, in fact, this huge territory includes large tracts of land beyond the urban core, so Chonqqing's population is 70 percent rural. Bo's populist campaigns that used traditional communist propaganda techniques had greater appeal to less-educated people in the countryside. And much like with conservative politicians in the United States, complaints by "liberal critics" only made Bo Xilai more popular.

Leaders in Beijing were initially wary of Bo's populist style. Since they prefer a behind-the-scenes collective responsibility approach to politics, Bo's populism with an iron fist was a little too close for comfort to Mao's strong-man tactics, which decimated the CCP in the Cultural Revolution.

Bo is a strange sort of Maoist considering that, during the Cultural Revolution, his father was tortured and his mother was beaten to death. Bo's actions came less from deep-seated beliefs than from his quest for power. Like Xi Jinping, Bo was a political chameleon who seized opportunities: when Bo was minister of commerce, he was very cosmopolitan; as general secretary of Chongqing, he was a populist. Bo also hedged his bets through his children: His son went to Oxford and then to Harvard. For the princelings, the main ideology is not communism, nationalism, or reform; rather, everything is about power.

While Bo's supporters said that he was media-savvy, he was also criticized for his "flashy" style; even before his fall in 2012, the Hoover Institution's Alice Miller concluded that "Bo is seen by other high-ranking party leaders as something of a showboater playing to the foreign press and grandstanding to local audiences."[7] In 2011, the leadership started to show some interest: after months of silence, Xi praised Bo's policies and most of the other PBSC members went to visit Bo to commend his "Chongqing model."

But Bo's quest for power ran aground in February 2012, when Wang Lijun, his right-hand man and the city-state's super-cop and vice major, fled Chongqing to request asylum at the U.S. consulate in Chengdu. When Bo Xilai found out, he sent seventy police cars over 200 miles to surround the consulate, which actually is outside Chongqing's jurisdiction. During his thirty-six-hour stay at the American consulate, Wang told a story of elite corruption and the abuse of power in Chongqing, including details of how

Bo's wife, Gu Kailai, poisoned British businessman Neil Heywood after he threatened to expose the family's shady foreign business deals.[8] (see Fig. 1.3) When Wang finally left the consulate, he was taken—together with his evidence of Bo's misdeeds—to Beijing by the central government's State Security Bureau. Wang was later convicted for, among other things, trying to defect to a foreign power. Why did this well-connected police chief willingly risk such a serious outcome? Wang was convinced that the alternative would have been worse: He figured that Bo would have had him assassinated if he stayed in Chongqing.

This event precipitated Bo's downfall because foreign factors—killing a Briton and involving the U.S. consulate—exposed the party to international embarrassment. As the exposés of the fabulous wealth of the families of former premier Wen Jiabao and current president Xi Jinping show, corruption is common among China's political and military elites. But the way Bo ran Chongqing as a personal fiefdom for personal economic and political gain went too far. The outrageous wealth of Bo and his family—and the violence used to obtain it—shocked many people in China. In a way, Bo had to go because he was too popular and his Chongqing model was too successful. Bo's ideological campaigns, which challenged the authority of the central government, threatened to split the party leadership. Bo was subsequently expelled from the party, and the political aspects of his Chongqing model were quickly dismantled. (Some of the economic policies of the Chongqing model have survived his fall, as we will see in chapter 3).

The Brookings Institution's Cheng Li concludes that China will benefit from this political crisis; he sees the opportunity for the Chinese leadership to develop a new consensus to promote meaningful political reform; otherwise, he states that "the party will continue to lose its credibility."[9] However, the calls for party unity and the crackdown on "rumors"—meaning news from outside the propaganda system—after Bo's fall suggest that the party learned a different lesson from its most serious crisis since Tiananmen. The CCP used traditional propaganda strategies to reestablish political control; hence, rather than being a part of the solution, transparency is seen as a problem. In other words, just because the CCP successfully stopped the rise of an ultra-nationalist strongman does not mean that it will pursue liberal political reforms.

The main conclusion that we can draw from the Bo Xilai crisis is that the party is more fragile than most experts thought. We were expecting to witness a well-scripted—and, frankly, boring—transition from the fourth to the fifth generation leadership. This crisis—and the elite infighting that it exposed—shows the fragility of China's leadership and the uncertainties of a power transition that was anything but smooth. Struggles emerged not just between the CCP's two main factions—the princelings and the China Youth League—but, as Bo's challenge shows, also within the princeling faction.

More broadly, the power transition changed the character of the PBSC. While most of the members of the fourth generation leadership were trained as engineers, the fifth generation leadership studied the humanities and social sciences, including law, economics, history, and journalism. The fourth generation technocrats worked to modernize China according to the universal logic of science: Their achievements are evident in China's rapid economic growth and in huge projects such as the Three Gorges Dam, the high-speed rail network, and the 2008 Olympic Games.

The fifth generation social scientists, however, are more interested in China as an exceptional civilization that needs to pursue its own culturally determined China model of economic, political, and social development. The fifth generation may be more open in terms of presenting themselves to China and the world; but they are more elitist in their politics. Hence, this transition will not provide a democratic or a liberal opening. Even before he was arrested in 2011, artist-activist Ai Weiwei was pessimistic about the prospects for political change: "we are not expecting much from this generation of leaders. Maybe the generation after. After a decade, they will be more open in their ideas."[10]

Dissidents: Challenging the System

On December 10, 2008—Human Rights Day—a group of dissidents published "Charter 08" on the Internet. Like everyone else in Beijing, its authors are concerned about China's future direction. Thus, "Charter 08" asks: "Where is China headed in the 21st century? Will it continue with 'modernization' under authoritarian rule, or will it embrace universal human values, join the mainstream of civilized nations, and build a democratic system?"[11]

This manifesto, which recalls Czechoslovakia's famous "Charter 77" declaration, was co-authored by future Nobel laureate Liu Xiaobo, and signed by hundreds of—and eventually more than 10,000—Chinese intellectuals and activists. After explaining the recurring problem of authoritarian rule, "Charter 08" sets down the principles that are necessary to achieve the dream of a liberal democratic China where people have political, civil, and economic rights and are entrusted with the responsibility to govern themselves.

For drafting this manifesto, Liu was sentenced in December 2009 to eleven years in jail for "inciting subversion of state power." The Nobel Committee cited Liu's "long and non-violent struggle for fundamental human rights in China," in its announcement awarding him the Nobel Peace Prize in 2010.

According to literary scholar Julia Lovell, Beijing has a "Nobel complex," namely that officials and public intellectuals alike see winning the prize as a sign that the world has accepted China.[12] Yet, for many, this was the *wrong* Nobel prize. There was little sympathy among intellectuals in China; I was in China when the award was announced in October 2010, and I found that many of my social science colleagues were hostile to Liu and to the Nobel Prize itself, which they criticized as part of a "foreign plot" to "westernize and split up" China. The most sympathetic response I received was from a long-time liberal friend who conceded that perhaps Liu's jail sentence was a bit too long: "maybe seven years is enough," he told me. Two years later, Chinese novelist Mo Yan, who had just won the Nobel Prize for Literature, caused a stir when he declared that he hoped that Liu could "achieve his freedom as soon as possible."[13]

Although Liu Xiaobo and Xi Jinping are contemporaries—Liu was born in 1955 and Xi in 1953—they have had very different life experiences in following different career trajectories. While Xi made the best of being sent down to the countryside during the Cultural Revolution to become his new village's local party leader, Liu celebrated the closure of schools as "a temporary emancipation from the educational process" that he saw as authoritarian.[14] Once universities opened again, Liu passed the entrance exam to become part of China's celebrated "Class of '77," the best and the brightest of the era. At Beijing Normal University, Liu studied to earn a BA and an MA, and he received his PhD in Chinese literature in 1988. Liu was already on course to have a successful career as a teacher and a literary critic. But the 1989 student movement gave him an opportunity to apply the political theory he had been thinking about since 1988.

Before 1989, Liu was famous for being iconoclastic. His speeches and essays ruthlessly criticized China's literati and establishment intellectuals, often in a harsh mocking tone. He reveled in being an outsider, a loner who was unpopular with his peers; but this "angry young man" was very popular with students, who were impatient with China's slow pace of political reform. For Liu, 1988–1989 was a turning point: after graduating in 1988, he went abroad for fellowships in Oslo, the East-West Center in Honolulu, and Columbia University in New York. During this time he wrote a series of political essays that discussed the prospects for democracy and civil society in China. When in the spring of 1989 student demonstrations erupted in Beijing, Liu felt compelled to return. As he told his friend, the poet Bei Ling: "Haven't we been preparing for this moment all our lives?" He left Columbia early and arrived back in Beijing on April 27th.

While Liu was known previously for his take-no-prisoners approach to debate—and to life—in Tiananmen Square he became a moderating force for students who ran the democratic demonstrations in an authoritarian way. In both his discussions with students and his various writings during the Tiananmen movement, Liu criticized the emotional sloganeering of the student leaders, and he demanded a rational egalitarian approach to building a democratic society. This marked a huge shift for someone whose career was built on being a "renegade critic and cultural nihilist." As Australian Sinologist Geremie R. Barmé writes, "Liu Xiaobo, a figure labeled in China as the evil champion of nihilism and the irrational was, ironically, now the chief advocate of positive and rational civil action."[15]

In the "June 2nd Hunger Strike Declaration," Liu called on everyone to be democratic in both goals and methods, that is to promote equality, respect, and responsibility in China's new civil society by adopting "legal, nonviolent, rational and peaceful methods in its pursuit of freedom, democracy, and human rights." Liu thus used his experience at Tiananmen Square to formulate a more nuanced understanding of democracy that goes beyond elections to foster robust civil society.

Most interestingly, while many of the other intellectuals and student leaders were denouncing Deng Xiaoping and Li Peng as enemies, Liu and his fellow hunger strikers called on their comrades to "abandon the enemy mentality and hate psychology" because "hatred leads only to violence and dictatorship. We must begin to build democracy in China in a spirit of tolerance and with conscious cooperation."[16] This call marked a novel move in modern Chinese politics, and it constituted a part of Liu's new interest in civic consciousness and civil society. According to Barmé, this was indicative of an important shift in political vocabulary: previously students and intellectuals were elitist, seeing themselves as the "soul of the nation" and referring to others in patronizing terms as "the masses." Liu now argued that everyone was an equal citizen, each one of whom was equally responsible for China's future.

Liu is more than a thinker; he is a man of action who, on the night of June 3–4, negotiated with the troops and persuaded the students to leave Tiananmen Square, saving hundreds of lives. This commitment to nonviolent action and peaceful change is the main reason that he was awarded the Nobel Peace Prize in 2010.

Liu's interest in building civil society as a positive tolerant space developed in the 1990s and 2000s. "Charter 08" presents an alternative history of modern China in viewing democracy and human rights as the solution to China's problems of official corruption, income inequality, forced evictions, and environmental degradation, among others. Liu and his co-authors make a compelling argument that China needs to follow its economic modernization with political modernization. Although "Charter 08" is radical because it demands an end to one-party rule, it is moderate in the sense that it calls on the government to live up to its own laws: Beijing signed the UN's human rights covenants in 1998, and human rights guarantees were added to the PRC constitution in 2004.

In his thoughts and actions, Liu has probed the ideas of community, civility, and civil society. Although he was a lone critic before 1988, since then he worked closely with others to write the "June 2nd (1989) Hunger Strike Declaration" and "Charter 08," both of which explore how citizens acting together in civil society form the foundation of democracy. While writing "Charter 08" he worked with many Chinese intellectuals and activists to shape the document and build up the list of signatories. According to Chinese writer Jianying Zha, "Even as he solicited signatures for Charter 08, he was gracious toward those who declined to sign."[17] In this way, Liu and the other "Charter 08" writers were doing what they describe in the manifesto: employing a generous and tolerant civic spirit to address the "sharpening animosity between officials and ordinary people."

In "I Have No Enemies," Liu's "Final Statement" to the court in 2009, he pursues the themes of tolerance and civility even further, declaring that "none of the police who have watched, arrested, or interrogated me, none of the prosecutors who have indicted me, and none of the judges who will judge me are my enemies." This is because "hatred only eats away at a person's intelligence and conscience, and an enemy mentality can poison the spirit of an entire people, lead to cruel and lethal internecine combat, destroy a society's tolerance and humanity, and block a nation's progress toward freedom and democracy."

Rather than expressing total opposition to the party-state, Liu recognizes how Deng Xiaoping's reform and opening policy has "gradually weakened the enemy mentality and the psychology of hatred," thus providing "gentle and humane grounds for restoring mutual affection among the people." Liu declares that he is an "optimist" who "looks forward to the advent of a future free China."[18]

In light of Beijing's response to Liu's Nobel Peace Prize, this is sadly ironic. While the prisoner is magnanimous toward his captors, it would not be an exaggeration to say that the official response was hateful. It treated Liu as a traitor and saw the prize itself as "blasphemous" and "disgraceful," an "obscenity" that is part of a Western plot to destroy China.

When we compare Xi Jinping and Liu, the ironies proliferate. As we saw above, before he became president, Xi kept mum: not rocking the boat with personal opinions is part of being an heir apparent in China. Since 1989, on the other hand, Liu has been forbidden from teaching, publishing, and publicly speaking in China. When he did speak out, Liu was imprisoned for "speech crimes." Indeed, as he told the court in 2009, the only time since 1989 that he has been allowed to make a public statement has been at "trial sessions at the Beijing Municipal Intermediate People's Court."

There is one more comparison provoked by Xi and Liu, namely their personal relationships with their wives. Xi and Peng got married in 1987; but until Xi moved to Beijing in 2007, they chose to live separate lives. Liu and his wife, Liu Xia, however, have been forcibly separated by Liu's multiple incarcerations. After Liu won the Peace Prize, Liu Xia herself was kept under illegal house arrest. This makes the last part of Liu's "Final Statement" even more poignant—it is a love letter to his wife:

> I am serving my sentence in a tangible prison, while you wait for me in the intangible prison of the heart. Your love is the sunlight that leaps over high walls and shines through the iron bars of my prison window, that caresses every inch of my skin and warms every cell of my body, allowing me to always keep peace, openness, and brightness in my heart, and filling every minute of my time in prison with meaning.[19]

Xi Jinping's chameleon-like changes raise a number of uncertainties about where he will lead China. Liu Xiaobo, however, is interesting and important because he has changed in a principled way, shifting from the bad boy of Chinese literature in the 1980s to a level-headed demonstration organizer in 1989 to one of China's top democracy thinkers and activists in the 2000s.

Ai Weiwei's journey into politics—and eventually to jail in 2011—is similar to Liu Xiaobo's trajectory of dissidence. Initially, Ai wasn't overly political. He participated in the Democracy Wall movement in the 1970s, but he spent most of China's early reform era abroad in New York (1981–1993). His East Village apartment became a hub of activity for visiting Chinese artists and poets, including Liu Xiaobo during his Columbia sojourn in 1989. Bei Ling, who is friends with both Liu and Ai, describes how Ai always carried around a camera and usually persuaded his friends and guests to pose nude with him:

Ai and Bei are smilingly nude in an iconic photo at the World Trade Center's plaza (1985), which is now Ground Zero.

While Liu was drawn home to Beijing in 1989, Ai chose to stay in New York, where he organized various protest activities. He returned to Beijing in 1993 because his father, the famous communist poet Ai Qing, was ill. Ai Weiwei's home/studio in Beijing served a similar purpose to his apartment in New York: due to his fluency in English, he became an intermediary between Western artists and China's newly vibrant cultural scene. He is most famous for being the artistic consultant for the Beijing's "Bird's Nest" Olympic stadium, which was designed by Swiss firm Herzog & de Meuron; just before the Olympics, Ai became *infamous* when he denounced it as China's "fake smile" to the world.

Ai's art has been political for some time. His "Study in Perspective" (1995) shows him giving the finger to Tiananmen—the Gate of Heavenly Peace—the traditional site of political authority that is now adorned with Mao's portrait. (see Fig. 1.4) This provocative photograph, which is part of series where Ai flips off the White House, the Eiffel Tower, and other seats of power, was exhibited at Shanghai's "Fuck Off" exhibition in 2000.

While Liu expanded from literary criticism to political organization in 1989, Ai's turning point came in 2008. Along with denouncing the Bird's Nest stadium, Ai was very critical of the official response to the earthquake

FIGURE 1.4 "Study in Perspective" (1995)
Source: Courtesy of Ai Weiwei Studio

in Sichuan. Noticing that public schools were destroyed more often than surrounding buildings, many people felt that the schools collapsed due to substandard construction stemming from official corruption. After the party-state refused to investigate, Ai enlisted volunteers in what he called a "Citizens' Investigation" to compile and publish a list of the names of the 5,212 children who were killed in the earthquake. Ai and his team eventually shamed the government into releasing its own list of 5,335 names. Blurring the lines between art and politics, Ai turned this tragedy into the massive mosaic "Remembering" (2009) at Munich's Haus der Kunst in which he lined up 9,000 school bags to spell out one mother's reaction to her daughter's death: "She lived happily on this earth for seven years."

According to Bei Ling, this social activism constitutes a natural extension of Ai's provocative photographs: "Ai does not just like to get naked by himself or with friends, he has also helped to lay bare 'China,' from the Central Committee to regional administrations. He has his own brand of indignation, mixed with an easy humor, to face the violence of state power."[20]

Ai's style and tactics are, thus, quite different from Liu's. Liu Xiaobo is a quintessentially 20th-century activist: he drafts manifestos demanding radical change, thinks in terms of grand visionary goals, and acts in ways that are earnest, thoughtful, and rational. "Charter 08" is like a Five-Year Plan for the fifth modernization: democracy. As we saw, it is easy for the party-state to clamp down on such dissidents, turning them into martyrs and feeding what critics call their "hero mentality." Ultimately, however, Liu is still an optimist.

Although only two years younger, Ai Weiwei takes a distinctively 21st-century approach that blurs art, life, politics, and activism. Liu is an essayist who published primarily in overseas journals and only later online. Ai, however, feels most comfortable on the Internet; as one of his Tweets explains: "My motherland, if I have to have one, would be the Internet because it can fulfill the space and boundaries of my imagination. As for other so-called countries, you can have them" (December 29, 2009). Ai's blog started in 2005, and, over the next few years, it grew into a popular site of outrage at China's social injustices.[21] Along with those of other bloggers, his critical posts were periodically scrubbed.

When Ai's blog site was shut down permanently in May 2009, he shifted to Twitter (@aiww), which concentrated his critique and anger even more. While Liu rationally declares that he has no enemies, Ai ruthlessly criticizes the Chinese system as evil: "Evil exists to test our courage" (August 3, 2009). Rather than seeing emotions as a weakness, Ai uses them as a political strategy to build community through "shared feelings of love and anger"[22] on the Web and with colleagues and volunteers.

Ai's tactics thus are similar to those of Bo Xilai, who, likewise, made a name for himself through family connections and audacious media campaigns. Certainly, some people—including Ai's artistic peers—think that Ai is a clown; his mocking and irreverent style makes him look like a smart ass. The scene described by *New Yorker* correspondent Evan Osnos, in which Ai's visit to a police station in Chengdu is filmed by four of Ai's own videographers and two more from the police, certainly sounds like a circus. Yet Osnos concludes that Ai's use of new media has "subverted the usual Chinese method of dissent: favoring bluntness and spectacle over metaphor and anonymity. He shamed the system with his own transparency."[23]

Perhaps the Manichean nature of Twitter, which encourages a sloganeering of good versus evil at the expense of nuanced argument, pushed Ai too far. On April 3, 2011, he was arrested at Beijing's airport and was held incommunicado until his release eighty-one days later. It isn't clear what triggered the arrest. Ai's celebrity as a top artist and his "princeling" family background—his father Ai Qing was a famous communist poet—protected him for a while. But according to Beijing's hypernationalist newspaper, the *Global Times*, this "maverick" had finally crossed the party-state's "red line," the characteristically vague quasi-legal boundary of what is allowed in Chinese society.[24] Ai's detention was not unique: in 2011, the party-state engaged in its most intense crackdown since 1989 to make sure that an "Arab Spring" didn't happen in China. Many lawyers, activists, and NGO leaders were also harassed and imprisoned.

Ai was released on bail but with a host of conditions: He was barred from making political statements, talking to foreigners, and using Twitter, among other restrictions. Less than a month after his conditional release, Ai broke his silence to describe his ordeal. His first major political critique described Beijing as a "city of violence" with "no hope"—a Kafkaesque city that drives you mad. Rather than seeing Beijing as the center of the China dream, Ai concludes that "Beijing is a nightmare. A constant nightmare."[25]

This essay was published in English in *Newsweek* magazine; thus, within China, both Liu and Ai have "been harmonized" (*bei hexie le*): slang for being censored on the web in China. The party-state has turned these dissidents into "criminals" who have a limited—if any—chance to express their views to Chinese compatriots. In the spring of 2011, Ai Weiwei himself was "harmonized": The characters for his name were blocked online, and so people came up with homophones such as "Ai Weilai-love the future," which in turn were blocked. Hence, "the future" (*weilai*) was harmonized by China's party-state.

Citizen Intellectuals: Debating the China Model

Because the state is so strong in China, it is easy to frame politics in terms of officials versus dissidents. However, in "The Power of the Powerless" (1978) Czech dissident and later president Vaclav Havel explains a different way of being political that avoids the limitations of being pro- or anti-communist party and pro- or anti-nationalist. Havel, who is very popular among China's liberals, suggests that being a dissident can be counterproductive because it isolates intellectuals as an exclusive group from the rest of society. Rather than arguing that an elite movement should lead a grand revolution, Havel thinks that everyone can make their own revolution by "living in truth." Living in truth starts with rejecting the lies that the regime produces to buttress its legitimacy. But it is also positive in the sense of engaging in "small-scale work" to build parallel cultures and parallel markets, and thus a parallel society that exists side-by-side with the party-state's official culture, economy, and society. Havel argues that when these various small-scale work activities are gathered together they can constitute a parallel *polis*. Ultimately official structures "simply begin to wither away ... to be replaced by new structures that have evolved from 'below' and are put together in a fundamentally different way."[26]

Beijing takes this possibility very seriously. Even as it feels obliged to open up social space to encourage technical innovation and economic growth, the Chinese leadership is very wary of civil society movements. According to the civil administration law, all NGOs have to be sponsored by party-state organizations. Thus, NGOs in China are, by definition, GONGOs (government-organized NGOs) or even PONGOs (party-organized NGOs). Hence, civil society in China is characteristically unorganized; it is built largely through the small-scale work of individuals and informal groups.

To live and work in this ambiguous social space, China's citizen intellectuals have developed a few strategies. One is to consciously avoid being pigeonholed as a dissident. This marks a switch from the 1990s when a tried-and-true strategy for success for many Chinese artists, writers, and filmmakers actually was to seek out censorship by the Chinese government. Censorship created a ready market for this "packaged dissident" in greater China and the West, leading to fame and fortune as a dissident intellectual.[27] Ai Weiwei thus is criticized for catering to a foreign audience: He has never had a major exhibition in China, and Twitter, which is blocked by the Great Firewall, caters to foreigners and China's elite. More to the point, Ai's anti-party and anti-government tactics played into the battle of officials versus dissidents, which is characteristically won by the party-state.

In the 2000s, things changed, opening up opportunities for a more nuanced way of being political. More space opened in China to allow formerly dissident artists to become legal—and popular—within the PRC. Filmmaker Jia Zhangke's experience is a good example of a citizen intellectual's work. In the 1990s, he was internationally known for his underground films; but, starting with "The World" (*Shijie*, 2004) his films have been legal—and popular—in China. Although many people criticize Jia for selling out, we should take him seriously when he says that the reason that his films now pass the censors is not because he has changed; rather, it is because China's propaganda system itself has loosened up. Unlike dissident directors who work with an elite and often foreign audience in mind, Jia's target audience is the Chinese public because he "believes his social critique is strongest not as a protestor on the sidelines but as a legal—and marketable—filmmaker."[28]

China thus is interesting because it presents a paradoxical situation. While political space is quite narrow in the PRC (especially since 1989), Beijing's reform and opening policy has also created a wide variety of social and economic opportunities for citizen intellectuals in China's expanding arena of civil society. Thus, instead of looking for alternative organizations (such as NGOs), we need to see how civil society emerges through the "alternative civilities"[29] of the many China dreams of the country's citizen intellectuals.

China's citizen intellectuals are, thus, slightly different from the public intellectuals found in more liberal societies. Citizen intellectuals have emerged in the shadow of state censorship, which continues to shape modern Chinese thought. "Citizen" here is not a legal term (i.e. passport holder); rather, it describes the social responsibility that such intellectuals feel when they think about China's preferred future. As novelist Chan Koonchung puts it in *The Golden Age*, Chinese intellectuals are 90 percent free. While he and others lament the 10 percent who are lost to (self)censorship, in this book we will explore what citizen intellectuals are doing with their newly expanded freedom.

The "China model" is one of the hottest topics in the PRC, provoking debate among top scholars and opinion-makers in the popular press. In its most basic sense, the China model is about economic development. It challenges the market fundamentalism of the Washington Consensus by combining a strong authoritarian state with free market capitalism. But as we will see in this chapter and in chapter 3, the China model is more than state capitalism. Although Chinese economic success spawned this idea, with the rise of confidence in 2008–2009 due to the successful Olympics and the celebration of the PRC's sixtieth birthday, the China model took on new life to describe a whole "Chinese system" of politics, economics, and society that is seen as *unique*.

Yet, it is not part of official discourse: neither Hu Jintao nor Wen Jiaobao ever mentioned the China model in their official statements—except to deny its existence.[30] Other party leaders have actually warned their compatriots about the dangers of discussing this topic since foreigners might see it as a threat. This mix of vociferous debate in the public domain and deafening silence from official quarters makes the China model a great example of citizen intellectual work.

Just as we saw with "Charter 08," the China model discourse is part of a broader discussion about China's future direction. Indeed, many of the reactions to Liu Xiaobo's Nobel Peace Prize—both positive and negative—invoke the China model.[31] The China model's triumphalism shows Beijing's supreme confidence, but its combative style also suggests that serious doubts are harbored about China's future. Citizen intellectual discourse typically intertwines aspirations and anxieties, and discussions about the China model are no exception. According to Zhang Wei-wei, one of the concept's key advocates, the debate reveals the "enormous challenges and endless opportunities that China now faces."[32]

As we will see, these citizen intellectuals are trying to influence China's path. In one sense, many are like old-fashioned establishment intellectuals because they are trying to directly influence China's new leaders and official state policy. But new voices are emerging that are interested in shaping public opinion as well.

Two citizen intellectuals—Pan Wei, a political scientist at Peking University, and Zhang Wei-wei, who specializes in international politics at the Geneva School of Diplomacy and International Relations—are actively promoting this new China model through their books, *The China Model* (2009) and *China Shock* (2011), respectively.[33] Pan sees the China model less in terms of a set of policy prescriptions than as the sign of China's "cultural renaissance." Zhang credits the PRC's recent achievements to China's unique status as the world's only "civilization-state," one that benefits from 5,000 years of continuous history. Although the China model appears to be concerned only with the PRC's domestic issues, it is actually discussed in terms of what citizen intellectuals see as a grand Cold War–type battle between rival social systems: the China model versus the Western model.

The curious thing about this nativist view of China's dream is that both Pan and Zhang have had extensive international experience. Pan received his PhD from the University of California at Berkeley on a scholarship provided by an American foundation; Zhang received his PhD from the University of Geneva, and he has worked in Switzerland for decades. As Deng Xiaoping's official English-language interpreter in the mid-1980s, Zhang traveled to more than one hundred countries. Yet, in the 2000s both began to change. Initially, Pan, in his PhD dissertation and, then, in his first book, analyzed "the politics of marketization in rural China," explaining the problems that peasants faced in the new system.[34] He then became well known for his advocacy of political reform in terms of promoting the rule of law and a neutral judiciary, although as an alternative to liberal democracy. Zhang's first two books analyzed the relationship between economic and political reform in China.[35] Thus, both of these citizen intellectuals looked primarily to (Western) social science to understand economic and political reform in the PRC.

However, in the mid-2000s, as part of a broader trend among Chinese intellectuals, Pan and Zhang started to draw on cultural arguments to explain Beijing's new power. Like many of China's other New Left intellectuals who now argue for neoconservative values, Pan comes from an elite academic family and spent his youth in the countryside during the Cultural Revolution. Rather than pursuing transnationally shared social goals—like equality—Pan and Zhang both now proclaim that, to achieve its full potential, China needs to jettison the "Western model" and find its own way. In recent years, they have gone one step further to preach the China model in Europe's halls of power: Zhang lectured before the Dutch Senate and Pan the British Parliament. Although Deng Xiaoping condemned Chinese culture as "feudal superstition," Zhang and Pan criticize liberal democracy as a "superstition," and they look to China's traditional values to chart the world's future. More importantly, while dissidents Liu Xiaobo and Ai Weiwei expanded their views from culture to politics, Pan and Zhang are narrowing their views from universal social science to the peculiarities of China's unique civilization.

Pan and Zhang, like many other citizen intellectuals, look to China's indigenous ideas to describe their China model. For both, the PRC's strength is built on China's historical and cultural continuity: Pan rehabilitates the Maoist period (1949–1978) in praising the PRC's sixty years of success, and Zhang points to China's unbroken history of 5,000 years of civilization. The present version of the China model stresses three intertwined factors: stability, legitimacy, and statism. One of its the main goals is to affirm and support Beijing's current system of governance, which is dominated by the CCP.

While Pan and Zhang discuss grand Cold War–style ideological battles of the Chinese system versus the Western system, their China model is actually part of a broader debate among China's citizen intellectuals. The stress on the indigenous ideas of Chinese civilization constitutes a reaction to liberal arguments that China should be open to global civilization's universal values of democracy, constitutionalism, free markets, human rights, and the rule of law. Certainly, some liberals participate in the apocalyptic hyperbole by advocating "total Westernization" or denouncing official scholars who "sing the praises of the Chinese model" that is actually "filthy, anti-human rights, immoral, unconstitutional, and secretive."[36] But it would be a mistake to think that this is a free debate; while liberal websites are harassed and liberal activists are arrested, websites that promote ultranationalist and anti-Western ideas are rarely disciplined. The Maoist website "Utopia" was shut down by the government in April 2012 due to its vocal support for Bo Xilai, rather than because it threatened violence towards liberal activists.

This debate sometimes emerges in the elite politics of the Politburo. Some citizen intellectuals were very active in promoting Bo Xilai's populist and statist Chongqing model, while others advocated the more liberal "Guangdong model" that is credited to Wang Yang, who was the party secretary of that province. Certainly, Bo and Wang both proposed China models as part of the struggle to be promoted to the PBSC in 2012. But the Chongqing and Guangdong models also presented alternative directions for China's future. The founding editor of the Maoist website Utopia declared: "The Chongqing model is the only hope for China's future. Only Bo can save communism and save China." On the other hand, another commentator felt that China faced a choice between the Chongqing model's North Korea–style vision of the future and the Guangdong model's Singapore–style future of limited democracy.[37] Bo's replacement as party secretary of Chongqing seems to confirm this evaluation: Zhang Dejiang has a degree in economics from Pyongyang's Kim Il Sung University, and he is the Politburo's expert on North Korea. In the end, neither Bo Xilai nor Wang Yang made it onto the PBSC in 2012—both were sacrificed because the central leadership was threatened by their charismatic public media campaigns. The rather uncharismatic Zhang Dejiang, however, was appointed to the PBSC because he is a safe pair of hands.

These examples of citizen intellectuals' dreams show that China's new civil society is not necessarily liberal; rather, it contains a broad spectrum of activity that ranges from promoting the fundamentalism of the China model to more cosmopolitan views of China and the world. The "red line" that divides the work of citizen intellectuals and dissidents is not clear. In a controversial request to the party-state for cultural freedom, celebrity blogger Han Han gave his sense of both what is allowed and what is not allowed: "I will not try to settle old scores; I will look ahead; I will not discuss the sensitive issues

in history; I will not discuss or criticize the senior-level groups or their families and their relevant interests; I will only criticize and comment on current
social issues."[38]

Although people such as Liu Xiaobo choose to be dissidents to defend
their views, others such as Ai Weiwei are "dissidented" by officials as part of
the party-state's strategy of control. Yet, even the officials do not know where
the "red line" is—until they draw it to crack down on someone.

Rather than dealing with a progressively opening trajectory of political
reform, dissidents and citizen intellectuals have to negotiate Chinese society's
periodic openings and closings. Thus, people migrate between activities as
officials, dissidents, and citizen intellectuals. While I was writing this book,
Bo Xilai was removed from his official post and held incommunicado at an
undisclosed location (the fate suffered by many dissidents) in 2012. Ai Weiwei
went from citizen intellectual to dissident in 2011. And Lung Ying-tai, who
will be discussed in chapter 4, migrated from citizen intellectual to official
when she was appointed Taiwan's minister of culture in 2012.

While the PRC's favorite keyword is "stability," in this chapter we have
seen how everyone is changing: Chameleon-like officials adapt to each new
situation; artists and literary critics get politicized into dissidents because of
political oppression and social injustice; and academics became citizen intellectuals in order to persuade officials and the general public that their chosen
path is the correct direction for China's future.

Looking closely at what these three groups of people are doing can give us
a sense of China's current millenarian *zeitgeist*: Everybody knows that something is about to happen, but no one is quite sure what.

Three Scenarios

Officials, dissidents and citizen intellectuals can help us to think about
China's future role in the world in terms of three scenarios: (1) convergence
with international norms, (2) mixing of Chinese and Western norms, and
(3) divergence from Western norms.

Scenario 1: Convergence through Multipolarity
and Multiple Civilizations

China's goal, according to former president Hu Jintao, is to "build a harmonious world of lasting peace and common prosperity." In this new world
order, different civilizations would coexist in the global community, making

"humanity more harmonious and our world more colorful." I will discuss China's geostrategy in more detail in chapter 2, but at this point we should note that although it uses the exotic vocabulary of "civilizations," harmonious world policy deliberately avoids challenging the current international system. Here China is not a threat; world harmony is the cornerstone of Beijing's peaceful development strategy that promises win-win opportunities for everyone in the world.

Harmonious world policy thus is evidence of the "socialization" of China through its growing practice of multilateral diplomacy. Harvard University's Alastair Iain Johnston has shown in his research that Beijing is learning the rules and norms of international society as its economy and society become more integrated into the international system.[39] Rosemary Foot and Andrew Walter even argue that China is more of a status quo power than the United States[40]—at least during the George W. Bush administration.

Harmonious world policy thus is not controversial: It employs mainstream diplomacy to protect China's national sovereignty by working within the UN system. Xi Jinping's intemperate statement in Mexico actually fits in with this view of foreign affairs: China is a responsible power not in the positive sense of seeking to lead the world but in the negative sense of not trying to disorder the world.

Yet, not challenging the system does not mean that China accepts U.S. unilateral power. Rather, the talk of multiple civilizations underlines how China prefers a more multipolar world order. In this sense, Beijing wants to make the international system work *better* to build a more orderly and prosperous world.

On the other hand, Liu Xiaobo and China's liberals are pushing for a different kind of convergence when they call on China to join the global civilization of democracy and human rights.

Scenario 2: Combining Western and Chinese Values for a New World Civilization

Other citizen intellectuals say that the PRC's engagement with the world is not a process of "socialization" in which China gradually becomes westernized. Rather, they suggest that influence goes in both directions—or *should* go in both directions. While Beijing learns international rules and norms, China's soft power will also influence the world, gradually changing international norms by adding Chinese ideas to Western ones about world order.

The question then becomes: which Western values, which Chinese values, and how will they be combined?

China's harmony vocabulary is catching on around the world: President Barack Obama used it to talk about human rights when Hu Jintao visited Washington in 2011. Harmony is prominent in the Asian Development Bank's *Asia 2050* report (2011) and the World Bank's *China 2030* report (2012). Many foreign pavilions at the Shanghai World Expo (2010) also used the "harmony" concept to present their nations to the Chinese people: "Harmonious relations" (Pacific joint pavilion), "Feel the harmony" (Austria), and "Harmony of the heart, harmony of the skills" (Japan).[41] On his blog supporting "Charter 08," the Dalai Lama even declared that "a harmonious society can only come into being when there is trust among the people, freedom from fear, freedom of expression, rule of law, justice, and equality."

A harmonious world promotes an egalitarian view of the world that will "democratize" international relations, which, of course, is in China's interest as the most populous nation in the world. But many of the citizen intellectuals are illiberal in the sense that their new/old norms promote elite views of society and hierarchical views of international relations. While anti-imperialism used to be the cornerstone of Chinese nationalism, authors such as Yan Xuetong see the imperial concept of the Kingly Way (*wangdao*) as China's contribution to world order theorizing.[42] Chinese intellectuals are also fascinated by illiberal, militarist, and imperialist values from the West. Many strategists look to the rise of Europe's and America's global empires for ideas: Bismarck's unification of Germany is a popular model for China's rise within the system; American admiral Alfred Thayer Mahan's theory of sea power (1890) is revived to justify China's naval expansion;[43] and the Monroe Doctrine is used to justify carving out China's own sphere of influence in Asia.[44]

This combination of Chinese and Western values appears in Beijing's popular press and official foreign policy statements. In 2010, Chinese foreign minister Yang Jiechi declared to his Southeast Asian neighbors, "China is a big country and other countries are small countries, and that's just a fact." A *Global Times* editorial fleshed this out when it warned "small countries"—South Korea and the Philippines—to stop challenging China in the Yellow Sea and the South China Sea: "If these countries don't want to change their ways with China, they will need to prepare for the sounds of cannons."[45]

Scenario 3: Divergence: From Westernization to Easternization

While the first scenario socializes China into international society, the third scenario reverses this logic to socialize the rest of the globe into the Chinese world order. Here China's rise to global power is not just a story of economic success or military modernization. The PRC's success is normative because Chinese ideas, we are told, are *better* than Western ideas. As we saw with Pan Wei's China model and Zhang Wei-wei's civilization-state, this scenario asserts a uniquely superior system of economics, politics, and society, one that is presented as the complete opposite of capitalist democracy.

Rather than hope that Chinese civilization will add to global diversity, many of the citizen intellectuals examined in this book dream of a "World of Great Harmony" that is unified around Chinese values—to the exclusion of other values. The international system of equal nation-states, thus, will be replaced with China's hierarchical Sinocentric tributary system. Chinese thinkers explain that China's exceptional civilization will make the PRC a peaceful and harmonious superpower—but when probed for details, it turns out that even extreme violence can be taken as "peaceful" in China's new world order. China's historical experience shows that in this Sinocentric system, people—and countries—that don't fit in will be "harmonized" and "pacified."

Beijing often says that the PRC will be a moral power as opposed to a "hegemonic" one, such as the United States. Yet, when Chinese leaders tell us that the PRC will never be "hegemonic," they are not saying that China will not dominate; they are merely saying that the PRC will never see itself as immoral, which, as experience shows, few countries do. To be fair, the United States often makes the same arguments—but this suggests that China will not be a different kind of world leader if and when it gains global power.

In this way Eurocentrism is replaced by Sinocentrism, Westernization by Easternization, and American exceptionalism by Chinese exceptionalism. Other possibilities for China's future—and the world's future—are largely crowded out of this fundamentalist view of global politics.

Chapter 2 will discuss in more detail the dreams of a post-American world order that have been formulated by a range of officials and citizen intellectuals.

2

Strategic Futures and the Post-American World Order

ALTHOUGH WE DID not recognize it at the time, Beijing's current assertive foreign policy started in September 2005 when Chinese president Hu Jintao delivered a major speech to a global audience at the United Nations. From the podium of the General Assembly, Hu introduced "Harmonious World" as a new way of thinking about global politics, explaining that his goal was to "build a harmonious world of lasting peace and common prosperity." In this new world order, different civilizations would coexist in the global community, making "humanity more harmonious and our world more colorful."[1]

To see how proclamations of building a harmonious world led to China's current tensions with its Asian neighbors and Western powers, it is necessary to trace how Beijing's foreign policy encouraged China's officials and its citizen intellectuals to talk about new post-American world orders. To explore this debate, we will compare Beijing's official view of "building a harmonious world" with two citizen intellectuals' views of China's future—and the world's future: Zhao Tingyang's *The Under-Heaven System: The Philosophy for the World Institution* (2005) and Senior Colonel Liu Mingfu's *The China Dream: The Great Power Thinking and Strategic Positioning of China in the Post-American Age* (2010).[2]

The Under-Heaven System uses traditional Chinese ideas to craft a new world order; *The China Dream* argues that the People's Republic of China (PRC) needs to undertake a military rise to guard its economic rise. These two books are of particular importance because they show how popular voices increasingly influence debates among foreign policy experts. They each became social phenomena and the occasion for media events, provoking debates that spread their influence far beyond their core audiences of philosophers and military officers, respectively, into China's broader civil society. The work of citizen intellectuals can give us a sense of the parameters—ranging from *The Under-Heaven System*'s idealist world society to *The China Dream*'s realist power politics—of the discussions of China's proper role in the world that are increasingly popular in Beijing.

While many assert that China will be a different kind of world leader, one that appeals to non-Western norms, these debates about future world orders show how China's officials and citizen intellectuals are reproducing familiar themes, namely the liberalism of multilateral diplomacy, the idealism of a perfect word order, and the realism of political and military competition. Indeed, in many ways it is best to understand these themes in terms of Deng Xiaoping's slogan from the early reform era: "socialism with Chinese characteristics." Many think that China's ideology has shifted from "socialism" to "Chinese characteristics." However, we will see how these three alternative world orders each entail a productive tension between "socialism" and "Chinese characteristics."

Socialism is not dead in China; although its power as a revolutionary ideology is weak, it is thriving as a life style and a way of thinking that continues to inform discussions of issues such as the "China model" and the "Beijing Consensus."[3] Even with its many problems, the Chinese Communist Party (CCP) is not about to collapse: It is the wealthiest political party in the world, has 80 million members, and is growing. While Chinese nationalism is strong and Confucianism is a growing force, Chinese tradition does not dominate the discussion of "Chinese characteristics" as much as people in the West might think.

It is necessary, then, to pay attention to the nuance of foreign policy discussions in China to see how realism, idealism, and liberalism are combined in a range of different ways. Rather than building a harmonious world, it is important to understand how these texts are harmonizing socialism and Chinese characteristics. Ideas are, thus, very important as Beijing faces what Chinese strategist Shi Yinhong calls its "era of many troubles" as the PRC's fifth-generation leadership takes control in 2012–2013.[4]

I should be clear that I am not arguing that a direct link exists between citizen intellectuals and official foreign policymaking. Since the opaque nature of Zhongnanhai (China's Kremlin) obscures the dynamics of foreign policymaking, citizen intellectuals are interesting because they can give us a strong sense of the parameters within which foreign policy discussions take place. While many dismiss citizen intellectuals as irrelevant because they are not "part of the foreign policy establishment,"[5] their status as relative outsiders actually gives them more leeway to think about China's alternative futures. These new voices are challenging the foreign policy establishment's monopoly on discussion of China's place in the world. This chapter will explore their writings to see how China has multiple strategies and multiple futures—for many Chinas. Citizen intellectuals such as Zhao Tingyang and Liu Mingfu are important because they take advantage of the openings provided by vague government policy to nudge China's geostrategy in new directions.

As we will see below, all three proposed world orders—harmonious world, the Under-Heaven system, and the China dream—are not only vague, but are also unlikely to be actualized in the next few decades. In other words, although declarations of American decline are popular in China, the United States is still likely to dominate global affairs far into the 21st century. China's strategic futures are important, however, because they show how Chinese officials and citizen intellectuals are starting to think beyond the current world system to craft post-American world orders. Their impact thus may simply be destructive of the status quo: even if such alternative world orders are not realized, they still can serve to delegitimize American-influenced global norms.

This chapter will argue two points: first, Hu's harmonious world foreign policy has had unintended consequences by creating opportunities for citizens to talk about a wide range of possibilities for China's future, including a range of post-American world orders that produce different combinations of socialism and Chinese characteristics; and second, although these strategic dreams often come from unexpected quarters, citizen intellectuals are growing in influence, due in part to the commercialization of old media and the spread of new media. While Party Central is still very strong, citizen intellectuals can no longer be written off because they have become significant sources of ideas about China's future—and the world's future.

In this sense, I am treating China like any other great power. While much has been written about the impact of neoconservative ideology on U.S. foreign policy, very little work has been done on the impact of ideas on the foreign policy of the world's most important rising power, China.

Hu Jintao's Harmonious World

Before looking at Beijing's alternative world orders, it is helpful to get a better sense of how Hu Jintao's harmonious world would work. Although Hu has now retired, harmonious world is still important because it will continue to define China's foreign policy while President Xi Jinping develops his own policy narrative over the next few years.

FIGURE 2.1 Hu Jintao announcing
Harmonious World at the United Nations
Source: Courtesy of William A. Callahan

After Hu announced harmonious world at the United Nations in September 2005, the concept was explained in two official documents: the "China's Peaceful Development Road" White Paper (2005), and Hu Jintao's "Report to the 17th Party Congress" (2007).[6] A harmonious world will be built, according to "China's Peaceful Development Road," through "mutual dialogues, exchanges and cooperation" that lead to "mutual benefit and common development." The White Paper explains that "upholding tolerance and opening to achieve dialogue among civilizations" is necessary because the "diversity of civilizations is a basic feature of human society, and an important driving force for the progress of mankind." China will lead this dialogue because "opening, tolerance and all-embracing are important features of Chinese civilization." The goal is to build a harmonious world that is more "democratic, harmonious, just and tolerant." Hu's harmonious world will be peaceful because "the Chinese nation has always been a peace-loving one. Chinese culture is a pacific culture. The spirit of the Chinese people has always featured their longing for peace and pursuit of harmony."

Thus, China's foreign policy, according to the White Paper, is more than simply policy. It presents a new way of thinking about the world—and about the future: "Peace, opening-up, cooperation, harmony and win-win are our policy, our idea, our principle and our pursuit."

Here harmonious world expresses the ideals of the official version of Chinese exceptionalism, which sees China as an inherently peaceful civilization—as opposed to what is seen as Western civilization's inherent violence. Actually, Chinese history—like most countries' histories—has involved many periods of violent expansion and contraction.[7] According to China's Academy of Military Science, in its long imperial history (770 BC–1912 AD) China engaged in 3,756 wars,[8] for an average of 1.4 wars per year. Against this historical evidence, however, official texts promote harmonious world policy by telling us that China has never invaded any country—and never will. To support this narrative, officials switch from the messy events of history to the pure ideals of philosophy, underlining how in classical Chinese language, the character *he* means both "harmony" and "peace." Beijing's recent White Paper, "China's Peaceful Development" (2011), thus can declare: "Under the influence of the culture of harmony, peace-loving has been deeply ingrained in the Chinese character."[9] Chinese civilization, then, is idealized as "exceptional" because it provides a peaceful alternative model of a harmonious world.

Hu Jintao confirmed harmonious world as China's official foreign policy when he invoked it at the Chinese Communist Party's (CCP) 17th Party Congress in October 2007. Whereas Hu spoke to world leaders at the UN General Assembly, here Hu was reporting the country's recent progress and future plans to a domestic audience of 2,217 party delegates assembled at Tiananmen Square's Great Hall of the People.

As at the UN, Hu stressed that building a harmonious world was necessary because of the "ever closer interconnection between China's future and destiny and those of the world.... The Chinese people will continue to work tirelessly with the people of other countries to bring about a better future for humanity." Hu stressed that China's goal was to build a more democratic and egalitarian harmonious world because "We maintain that all countries, big and small, strong and weak, rich and poor, are equal."

The importance of harmonious world was proclaimed in a characteristically Chinese way: at the end of the congress the assembled party members adopted an amendment enshrining "the building of a harmonious world characterized by sustained peace and common prosperity" in the CCP constitution. In adding harmonious world to the pithy slogans of Mao Zedong, Deng Xiaoping, and Jiang Zemin, Hu Jintao aimed to ensure his strategic legacy.

Yet harmonious world's laudable goals are hardly earth-shattering—who would argue against global peace, prosperity, and harmony? Hu's methods for building a harmonious world are not very innovative either. In both his UN speech and his "Report to the 17th Party Congress," Hu stressed that China would use multilateralism, the UN Charter, international law, and universally recognized norms of international relations to build a harmonious world. Yet, China is hardly alone in pursuing liberalism's mainstream diplomacy; actually, the European Union's robust multilateralism is much more effective than China's rather limited multilateralism.

To fully appreciate the impact of Hu's harmonious world policy it is necessary to examine it in the context of China's domestic politics and its international affairs. When we remember what was going on in 2005—the U.S.-U.K. war in Iraq was spiraling into insurgency and civil war—it is easy to see why global opinion may well have welcomed Hu's new concept. Hence, to a world weary of American unilateralism and incensed at the Bush Doctrine of regime change, Hu's policy of world harmony was compelling. In outlining this strategy, Hu Jintao did not even need to mention George W. Bush, the United States, or Iraq; it was enough simply to criticize "hegemonism" and "power politics" while supporting multilateralism, international law, and the United Nations. Beijing had been trying to change China's global image for years; Hu was finally successful because he was able to draw a clear distinction between a bellicose America and a peace-loving China.

Thus, the PRC was able to take advantage of U.S. overcommitment in Iraq and Afghanistan to assert itself as an alternative center of power in Asia. Hence, we should not be surprised at Beijing's lack of enthusiasm for the Obama administration's pivot back to Asia in 2011.

However, the domestic context for China's harmonious world foreign policy is more complex. As in many rapidly developing countries, China's dramatic transition to a market economy has created a new set of winners and losers. Urban areas on China's East Coast have benefited much more than rural areas and the interior, and the educated have benefited much more than the less educated. While Deng Xiaoping's economic reform policies have lifted hundreds of millions of Chinese out of absolute poverty since 1979, the PRC has become increasingly polarized between wealthy urban elites and impoverished residents of rural areas. One of the enduring concerns of the Chinese Communist Party is national unity, and these economic reforms still risk tearing the country apart at the seams.

The domestic equivalent of harmonious world is "harmonious society," which appeared as a policy narrative in 2004 to address the negative fallout from China's spectacular economic growth. It describes a set of government policies that seek to rebalance China's economic and social polarization. New funds have been made available, for example, to provide free public education and subsidized health care to disadvantaged people, especially those in rural areas. Harmonious society thus is a very detailed set of policies that look to the party-state to solve China's economic and social problems. Therefore, harmonious society's state-centric intervention into society appeals to a particular blend of socialist modernity and Chinese tradition. While English-language descriptions of the policy stress its Confucian roots, in Chinese it is called "harmonious socialist society."

What can Beijing's experience of building a harmonious society in the PRC tell us about China's goal to build a harmonious world on a global scale? A strong state is necessary to build China's harmonious society at home. Although it is common for Chinese writers to proclaim "Harmonious society to be [a] model for the world,"[10] Hu was not clear about whether a strong state is necessary to build a harmonious world abroad. Just before the 17th Party Congress in 2007, the PRC-owned Hong Kong newspaper *Wen Wei Po* certainly thought so; it urged Hu Jintao to take the lead as the "'formulator, participant and defender of world order', in order push the entire world toward harmony."[11]

Since 2005, harmonious world has come to define Beijing's foreign policy narrative; whenever President Hu or Premier Wen Jiabao talked to foreign leaders or foreign audiences, they repeated the "harmonious world of lasting peace and common prosperity" mantra.[12] Unfortunately, neither leader discussed in detail how China would build a harmonious world. Even the three main documents describing harmonious world are filled largely with discussions of other things: harmonious world is only one of four points discussed in Hu's UN speech, it is one of five points raised in the "China's Peaceful Development Road" White Paper, and it is briefly mentioned in only one of the twelve sections of Hu's "Report to the 17th Party Congress." The most that we can say is that Hu's harmonious world follows harmonious society policy in mixing a state-centric top-down notion of "socialism" with "Chinese characteristics" that point to the traditional ideal of harmony.

It is deliberately ambiguous because the more Beijing clarifies its vision of a harmonious world, the more this policy concept will necessarily exclude nation-states and peoples that have different ideals of world order. This bland evocation of harmonious world is effective simply because, again, who could argue against global peace and prosperity?

While official descriptions of harmonious world lack substance, the concept has generated huge interest among China's official intellectuals and citizen intellectuals. Before 2005, only one discussion of China's international politics used the phrase harmonious world; the phrase was more often used to describe events like a Buddhist world conference. The article entitled "Light and Shadow in a Harmonious World" (2003) is not a sophisticated theoretical discussion of world order; rather, this essay in *Beijing Real Estate* magazine offers advice about lamps and lampshades to the capital's elite interior designers.[13]

After Hu introduced harmonious world at the United Nations, however, thousands of commentators and academics have used it to describe not just Beijing's foreign policy, but also a new model of world order. Rather than focusing on how China would use the UN and international law to build a harmonious world, these citizen intellectuals are more interested in how Chinese ideals—both Confucian and socialist—can help shape the post-American world order.

Soon after Hu's UN speech, the CCP's official newspaper *The People's Daily* asked three well-known public intellectuals—the Chinese Academy of Social Sciences's Wang Yizhou, Renmin University's Jin Canrong, and the Central Party School's Men Honghua—to explain this new diplomatic concept to the general public. They largely repeated Hu's formula of "building a harmonious world of lasting peace and common prosperity" through the UN and international law. But they also stressed how Beijing would use ideals from traditional Chinese culture to "restructure the world." In this formulation, China would be not only the "initiator of a harmonious world," but also "a major practitioner of it."[14]

This is a good example of how citizen intellectuals can help the state while still maintaining a measure of scholarly independence and integrity; in a sense, they are behaving like public intellectuals in more liberal countries as the Chinese state becomes more open to expert advice and public opinion.

Over the next few years, citizen intellectuals also invoked harmonious world to develop new ideas of world order, especially post-American orders that look to a combination of socialist and indigenous Chinese ideals. China's interlinked domestic and foreign policies of harmonious society and harmonious world, which appeal to Chinese values like harmony over "Western" values like freedom, thus have opened up space for a wide debate about China's future.

Certainly, it is easy to dismiss harmonious world as simply propaganda. As we saw in chapter 1, since Beijing now vigorously employs "harmony" to explain domestic and foreign policy, China's netizens now use it ironically to criticize the party-state: "*bei hexie le*-been harmonized" is slang for being censored on the web or otherwise harassed for expressing your views. But we should take harmonious world seriously simply because many Chinese intellectuals do—both to support official policy and to suggest policy alternatives. In this way, the deliberate ambiguity of official harmonious world pronouncements has created a strategic vacuum that is being filled by a range of official, unofficial, and quasi-official theories, concepts, and grand strategies for the Chinese century.

Idealistic World Society: Zhao Tingyang's Under-Heaven System

Although it sounds exotic, harmonious world foreign policy is an important part of China's quest to be a modern nation that is influential in international society. Yet, in the past decade a group of theorists has emerged that looks beyond the pursuit of modernization—which they criticize as "westernization"—to see how Chinese concepts are necessary for the 21st century. Zhao Tingyang's book *The Under-Heaven System: The Philosophy for the World Institution* (2005) is a prominent example of this trend.[15]

Zhao works in the Philosophy Institute of China's largest think tank, the Chinese Academy of Social Sciences; but his goal is to reach beyond intellectual circles to appeal to a broad audience to tackle problems not only in political philosophy, but also in public policy. And Zhao has been very successful both in China and abroad: Officials now use similar concepts to talk about China's harmonious world foreign policy, and the World Security Institute, a think tank based in Washington, D.C., commissioned Zhao to write for the "Debating China's Future" section of its *China Security* journal.[16] *The Under-Heaven System* thus dramatically shifted discussions of Chinese-style world order from the margins to the mainstream and from philosophy to security studies. This can be seen in the new 2011 edition of the book, which includes critical commentaries from public intellectuals in China and abroad.[17]

Chinese people need to discuss China's worldview, according to Zhao, because to be a true world power, the PRC needs to excel not just in economic production, but also in "knowledge production." To be a knowledge superpower, China needs to stop importing ideas from the West, because it needs to exploit its own indigenous "resources of traditional thought." To be a world power, therefore, China must "create new world concepts and new world structures."[18]

Thus, it is not surprising that Zhao praised the Chinese government for "utilizing the resources of China's traditional thought" in its twin policies of building a harmonious society and building a harmonious world.[19] But as a citizen intellectual, Zhao uses this opening to propose a model of world

FIGURE 2.2　Zhao Tingyang
Source: Courtesy of Zhao Tingyang

order that challenges harmonious world's support for the current international system.

To do this, Zhao looks to the traditional concept of *tianxia*, which literally means "Under-Heaven," but also means "Empire," the "World," and even "China" itself. Zhao aims to use Under-Heaven to solve global problems in a global way, namely thinking *through* the world in an "all-inclusive" way rather than thinking *about* the world from national or individual perspectives, which he sees as problematic.[20] Zhao appeals to Chinese philosophy for answers, and he bases his argument on a passage from chapter 54 of the ancient Daoist classic the *Daode jing* (6th century BC): "use the world [*tianxia*] to examine the world [*tianxia*]." World unity, for Zhao, leads to world peace and world harmony. Under-Heaven thus is a utopia that sets up the analytical and institutional framework necessary to solve the world's problems.

Chinese words like *tianxia* are difficult to translate into English. "Under-Heaven" sounds exotic—and even mystical—to people unfamiliar with classical Chinese philosophy. Yet, confusion about this vague concept is shared by Chinese people too, and even experts debate about what it really means. Zhao is trying to redefine Under-Heaven for the 21st century; but he is also drawn to Under-Heaven precisely because it is exotic and hard to translate into English. He and others see this incommensurability as part of Chinese exceptionalism. Another strategist even argues that the untranslatability of classical Chinese concepts is a strength for the PRC because Westerners will

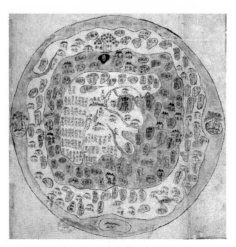

FIGURE 2.3 Map of Under-Heaven (Ch'onhado)

Source: © British Library Board, Maps.33.c.13

have to rely on Chinese experts to define and implement this post-American new world order.[21]

Zhao's defines Under-Heaven as a unified global system that is geographical, psychological, and institutional. Since there are no physical or ethical borders in Zhao's Under-Heaven, the main task in this holistic system is to use Confucian ethics to transform enemies into friends, "where 'transformation' seeks to attract people rather than conquer them."[22]

Since it is a Utopia, Zhao does not provide many details of his holistic Under-Heaven system. Like in Hu Jintao's harmonious world, Zhao looks to civilizations to understand global politics. But rather than different civilizations coexisting on the world stage, Zhao defines world order in terms of one unified Civilization with China at the apex.

Here Zhao's Under-Heaven system looks back to imperial China's tributary system, which governed China's relations with its neighbors before the 20th century. The best way to understand the tributary system is to look at the maps of Under-Heaven that were popular in late imperial China (1300–1900). The "Under-Heaven-style" map in Figure 2.3 presents China at the center of the world, and often as the world itself. This is not a UN-style world map of equal nation-states; rather, the Under-Heaven map and the tributary system are both organized around a hierarchy of concentric circles where civilization is strong in the center but diminishes as you travel away from China's imperial capital out to the periphery of provinces, vassal states, and finally the barbarian wilderness. On such maps, foreign countries—even Vietnam and India, let alone Portugal, England, and America—often appear as small and insignificant islands off China's coast.

Within the tributary system, we are told, early modern East Asia (1300–1800) was remarkably stable and peaceful, especially in comparison with a bellicose Europe. Likewise, the Under-Heaven system stresses the values of peace and order as opposed to Western strategic theories that are based on threats and conflict.[23]

The Under-Heaven map does not simply describe relative power and influence in premodern East Asia. It is normative, showing how imperial China's goal was to "civilize" its neighbors. The map itself is evidence of imperial China's cultural power because this Sinocentric map was made in Korea, not China: "Ch'onhado" is Korean for "Under-Heaven map." Although "mutual benefit" is one of the catchphrases of Hu's harmonious world, it is also often used to describe the benefits of the hierarchical tributary system.

Zhao tells us that the Under-Heaven system's assimilation policy was useful for transforming enemies into friends not only in the past, but it will be useful in the future as well. In his later book, *Investigations of the Bad World* (2009), Zhao feels that the goal of Chinese philosophy is to improve all the nations and peoples of the world; against the liberal ethic of "live-and-let-live," Zhao promotes what he calls the Confucian ethic of "improve-if-let-improve."[24] Rather than allowing space for different ways of life, according to this logic it is the duty of Chinese to "harmonize" the world's people so they can better fit into the Under-Heaven system.

Although many Chinese commentators stress that Beijing will not re-create the tributary system, recent discussions with public intellectuals in Thailand and Singapore confirm that many of China's smaller neighbors take for granted that China is trying to rebuild the tributary system. This is not to say that Southeast Asians see it as an ideal world order; although they do not like China's hierarchical world order, many felt that they would have to adapt to it.[25]

Throughout his discussion, Zhao plays with the definition of this ancient and often vague term, at times reading Under-Heaven as "the World" and at other times understanding it as "Empire." Either way, Under-Heaven is presented as a legitimate world order. Although it sounds similar to European, American, and Japanese imperial ideals, Zhao insists that his "Empire" is very different from Western imperialism. Zhao thinks that the Roman Empire, the British Empire, and America's new "empire" of globalization all have fatal flaws; thus, he concludes that the Under-Heaven system is the "acceptable empire" for the 21st century because its benevolent system of governance is "reasonable and commendable."[26] In other words, the problem with "Western imperialism" is not "imperialism" itself, but only its Western form; the solution is not universal equality or justice, but Under-Heaven's Chinese-style benevolent empire.

Zhao thus presents the Under-Heaven system as the solution to the world's problems; it is a new interpretation of Confucianism's hierarchical system that values order over freedom, ethics over law, and elite governance over democracy and human rights. Rather than looking to the United Nations as a liberal model for building world order from the bottom up, such as in Hu's harmonious world, Zhao thinks that global peace and prosperity can be guaranteed only in a top-down manner through a single world government institution.

Zhao's arguments are very popular, especially among officials promoting harmonious world policy and scholars who are developing Chinese-style worldviews.[27] Yet, Zhao has his critics in China, too; one reviewer described his arguments as "pale and weak."[28] While Zhao presents himself to international audiences as the "Chinese Perspective," his critics in the PRC argue that this Under-Heaven system is merely his own individual perspective, which actually is full of errors.

But such criticisms miss Zhao's point. *The Under-Heaven System* is both an ambitious and an ambiguous work. Zhao is very clear that he is *not* interested in joining the standard philosophical debate about the true meaning of ancient texts. Rather, his project is to "transcend the historical limits" of Chinese tradition in order to explore how Chinese thought can help us address contemporary problems. His goal, therefore, is to "rethink China" in order to "rethink the world."[29]

Consequently, Zhao is part of a growing group of citizen intellectuals who look to the past for China's future strengths. Zhang Yimou's blockbuster film *Hero* (2002), for example, concludes with the assassin being transformed into a hero when he decides *not* to kill the emperor, which is much like Zhao's goal of transforming enemies into friends. The lesson drawn from this historical parable is that the individual has to sacrifice himself and his kingdom for the greater good of the Under-Heaven empire because, as the hero reasons, "Only the King of Qin can stop the chaos by unifying Under-Heaven through conquest." Zhao's book is part of the broader discussion of *how* China will be a world power in the 21st century.

Many government officials and international relations scholars are also fascinated with the idea of making China's Under-Heaven a universally valid model of global order. In the early 20th century, imperial China's hierarchical world order was seen as the problem; however, now many Chinese intellectuals see it as the solution to the world's ills. They feel that imperial China's Under-Heaven system of governance worked very well in creating a stable, prosperous, and peaceful East Asia until it was destroyed by Western imperialism in the 19th century. The destruction of that system forced China in the 20th century to build a modern nation-state to defend itself from these foreign challenges. The question that many Chinese citizens and officials are now asking is whether it is time for China (which now has a strong nation-state) to engage in promoting, establishing, or constructing Under-Heaven.

Although it may seem obvious to people outside China that Under-Heaven is an empire, it is difficult for most Chinese intellectuals to understand Under-Heaven in this way because one of the key ideas of 20th-century Chinese thought is "anti-imperialism." But now that China is strong again, ideals that can explain and justify Chinese power on the world stage are back in vogue.

As with harmonious world policy, people use Under-Heaven to promote both more benevolent and more aggressive foreign policy narratives. On the one hand, Yu Keping, who was a close adviser to Hu Jintao, sees the tolerance and equality of harmonious world as a "new take on the development of the ancient Chinese dream of Tianxia [Under-Heaven] Datong (the great harmony of the world)."[30]

On the other hand, top strategist Yan Xuetong argues that the Chinese world order is superior because it involves "voluntary submission" to an international power that "owns the world [Under-Heaven]." This is part of "the rejuvenation of China" in the 21st century, in which the goal is to "restore China's power status to the prosperity enjoyed during the prime of the Han, Tang and early Qing dynasties" when it was at the center of a hierarchical world order.[31]

In both its modest and its aggressive forms, the Under-Heaven system is promoted not just for China's benefit, but also for the world's benefit. Since Chinese culture is assumed to be superior, many feel that it is the duty of patriotic Chinese to spread Chinese values, language, and culture not just in Asia, but also all over the world. Drawing inspiration from the British Empire's concept of the "white man's burden" to "improve" Asians and Africans, some Chinese now speak of China's global mission as the "yellow man's burden" to pacify and civilize the world.[32]

While Beijing says that China will peacefully rise as a responsible power to build a harmonious world within the present international system, the success of *The Under-Heaven System* shows that there is a thirst in China for

Chinese solutions to world problems. Zhao engendered a wave of interest in policy circles because Under-Heaven combines the seemingly contradictory discourses of nationalism and cosmopolitanism into a new form of "patriotic cosmopolitanism."

Still, Zhao's plan for the future is quite vague, telling us how China and the world *should* be rather than what Beijing *will* do. Both "the present" and China's party-state are clearly missing from Zhao's mix of ancient ideas and utopian futures, which fails to tell us how to get from here to there. In this way, it is similar to the deliberate ambiguity of Hu's harmonious world. Yet, not surprisingly, it has a different combination of socialism and Chinese characteristics. Zhao's Under-Heaven system is based in Chinese tradition; but, it actualizes these norms through a top-down global institution reminiscent of China's socialist party-state.

Strategic Competitor: Liu Mingfu's The China Dream

Liu Mingfu's *The China Dream: The Great Power Thinking and Strategic Positioning of China in the Post-American Era* generated major local and global interest when it was published in 2010. In contrast to Beijing's policies of peaceful rise and harmonious world, Liu tells us that to guard its economic rise, China needs to have a "military rise" to contest American hegemony. He warns that China should not follow the Japan model to become an economic superpower because this would make China a "plump lamb" that other military powers might gobble up. To be a strong nation a wealthy country needs to convert its economic success into military power. Rather than follow Deng Xiaoping's peace and development policy of beating swords into ploughshares, Liu tells us that China needs to "Turn some 'money bags' into 'ammunition belts.'"[33]

Yet, *The China Dream* does not see conflict with the United States as inevitable: "China's military rise is not to attack America, but to make sure that China is not attacked by America." Liu uses the logic of deterrence to stress that China must seek peace through strength: Its peaceful rise to great power status must include a "military rise with Chinese characteristics that is defensive, peaceful, limited, necessary, important and urgent." If the United States chooses to accommodate China's rise rather than challenge it, then "China's dream need not be America's nightmare," he tells us. The goal of this peaceful military rise is "to grasp the strategic opportunity for strengthening the military" in order to surpass America to become the world's number one military power.[34]

Why should we care about *The China Dream*? Liu is Senior Colonel in the People's Liberation Army (PLA) who teaches at China's National Defense University (NDU) and so it is reasonable to think that the book reflects some part of the military's views. Yet, since Liu is a political officer who deals with ideology rather than a field officer who leads the troops, it is necessary to question whether *The China Dream* is actually that important. Liu himself stresses that his book is not a reflection of official policy: It was written for a mass-market audience and published by a commercial press. Nevertheless, even Liu admits that his book "reflects a tide of thought."[35]

Although some commentators warn us not to exaggerate Liu's "extreme" views,[36] *The China Dream* constitutes an important part of the conversations about China's strategic future taking place in the barracks, on the web, and among citizen intellectuals. In response to the book, more than 80 percent of the netizens polled by *Global Times* agreed that China should pursue global military supremacy.[37] The Maoist website Utopia reported, with glee, both this popular support and—more importantly—how foreigners felt threatened by *The China Dream*.[38] Indeed, Henry Kissinger, in his book *On China*, analyzes Liu's work as a key example of China's "Triumphalist View."[39]

The book also has served as a source of debate among China's military intellectuals. Some have depicted Liu's China dream as a "fantasy," while others, such as the widely quoted PLA strategist Colonel Dai Xu, are even more pessimistic about the likelihood of conflict between China and the United States.[40] Indeed, compared with the conspiracy theories that characterize much of China's strategic thought,[41] *The China Dream* is quite reasonable. This debate about the direction of China's future is likely to continue, and, for this reason, we should value *The China Dream* in the same way as *The Under-Heaven System*: It is important because people are talking about it- and influenced by it.

The China Dream thus is a key example of Chinese citizen intellectuals' plans for the future, in which Beijing successfully converts economic resources into enduring global political power. Liu builds on the line of argument first broached in the celebrated Chinese television documentary *The Rise of Great Powers* (2006). This popular series was pathbreaking because it challenged China's official historiography; rather than taking the Maoist line of seeing world politics as a contest between Western imperialism and China's anti-imperialist nationalism, *The Rise of Great Powers* studied how Western countries conquered the world to define the modern age. *The China Dream* quotes liberally from Western futurologists: John and Doris Naisbitt's *Megatrends China* (2010), Martin Jacques's *When China Rules the*

World (2009), Goldman Sachs's Jim O'Neill, as well as other forecasters of Chinese boom and Western bust. Liu's core message is that Beijing needs to take advantage of the current "period of strategic opportunity" to become the global "champion" that is "world number one."

Although it draws on China's dynastic history and contains dashes of exotic Chinese culture, including discussions of Du Fu's medieval poetry, the Kingly Way (*wangdao*), and Sunzi's *Art of War*, *The China Dream* is not really interested in classical Chinese thought. Liu's book primarily employs familiar geopolitical concepts to craft China's grand strategy: deterrence, balance of power, and peace through strength. Moreover, in addition to looking to China's dynastic history, Liu uses socialist history and concepts to argue that "building socialism" in China is a part of "building a harmonious world." In particular, he is fascinated by the Great Leap Forward (1958–1961), seeing the outrageous ambition of this Maoist mass movement as the key to China's success in the 21st century.[42]

Mao is described here as a top ideologist of "world number one-ism" because he dared to craft a grand plan to surpass America, stating that beating the United States would be China's greatest contribution to humanity. As recent studies have documented, the Great Leap Forward led to the world's worst famine with a death toll of more than 30 million people.[43] Liu admits that the Great Leap Forward "suffered defeat" and that "a large population met an irregular death."[44] But Mao's key mistake, Liu tells us, was that he got the timetable wrong: rather than fifteen years, China would need ninety years to become the world's number one power. Liu thus understands Deng Xiaoping's post-Maoist reform and opening policy as a continuation of Mao's Great Leap Forward plan. China's current (and future) success, in this telling, is the upshot of Mao's ambitious aspirations.

What are Liu's goals once his China dream comes true? In the book's conclusion he tells us that Beijing will make three major innovations to guarantee China's long-term peace and security:

- Create the miracle of a hierarchical Chinese-style democracy that is better than the egalitarian American-style democracy
- Create the miracle of "wealth distribution" that is fairer than the "welfare state"
- Create the miracle of "long-term honest and clean governance" in a single-party state that is more effective than "multiparty competition"[45]

Thus, Liu's three major innovations are ideological and bureaucratic rather than technological. He views world politics as essentially a battle between the

China model and the American model. *The China Dream* is intertwined with the American dream of democracy and prosperity. Yet, he celebrates only a certain type of competition: competition between great powers is natural and good, while competition between political parties is a problem. His China model thus looks to the CCP as the source of ideas for a better, stronger, and more creative country that would be a model for the world.

For all the optimism that he displays, Liu still nurses various national anxieties. Like many Chinese strategists, he is convinced that Washington is actively conspiring to contain the rejuvenation of the Chinese nation. He sees competition with the United States as a zero-sum game of total victory or total defeat: "the distance between the rise of a great power and collapse of a great power is only one step."[46] In this way, Liu's book shows the uneasy combination of ambition and anxiety that is common among China's citizen intellectuals. He frames China's ambition in simple terms: to be the world's number one superpower. Like many other speeches, books, articles, blogs, and films, *The China Dream*'s optimism about China's future is infectious. It oozes confidence by presenting China's rise as inevitable: It is a matter of when—not if.

How do these ideas relate to Hu Jintao's concept of harmonious world? Rather than follow Hu's advice to build a world that tolerates different social systems and civilizations, Liu explains that "in order to build a harmonious world, [China's] competitive spirit must be strengthened." China's competitive spirit is not just economic, but also militaristic: "To rejuvenate the Chinese nation, we need to rejuvenate China's martial spirit."[47] Rather than talk about China's strategic industries as "national champions," Liu stresses how China needs to become the "champion nation." In this way, Liu refocuses China's ambitions from economic growth back to political-military power.

However, Liu looks to ideas associated with harmonious society as the ultimate challenge to a bold Chinese strategic future. In his view, China's own internal problems present the greatest challenge to his vision. Rather than constituting a crisis of governance or institutions, Liu sees China's problems as a leadership crisis of civilian cadres who are corrupt, mediocre, and inflexible. After a detailed discussion of how civilian corruption brought down the Communist Party of the Soviet Union, Liu proposes that Beijing solve its leadership crisis through better "knowledge planning" and better cadre training. Liu's latest book, *Why the PLA Can Win* (2012), stresses that corruption in China has now become a major problem for military officers as well as civilian cadres.[48]

Although Liu feels that Chinese power will benefit the world, his main goal is not to build a harmonious world or the Under-Heaven institution for the benefit of humanity but simply to strengthen China's party-state. Liu thus appeals much more to the socialism element in "socialism with Chinese characteristics"; however, it is necessary to note that Liu employs China's dynastic history and civilization in his arguments for a strong leadership.

Tensions among Competing World Orders

As suggested above, Deng Xiaoping's 1982 slogan "socialism with Chinese characteristics" can help us understand how alternative world orders are conceptualized in China. Hu's harmonious world contains a balance between socialist construction and harmonious culture. Zhao's Under-Heaven system is based on Chinese tradition; however, it actualizes these norms through a state-centric institution. Liu's goal in *The China Dream* is to complete Mao Zedong's Great Leap Forward to surpass the United States to become world's number one power—an argument that he, like Zhao, frames in terms of Chinese history and civilization.

These three views of the world's future show the range of commentary produced by the opportunities opened by harmonious world discourse. All are very optimistic about China's future: They assume that China's success will continue and that the rejuvenation of the Chinese nation is inevitable. Many hypernationalist books in China are boiling with righteous rage about American conspiracies and an unfair world system. But Hu's harmonious world, Zhao's Under-Heaven system, and Liu's China dream all express more pity for America than anger at it: The greatest concern of these authors is that the United States will have a rocky and violent decline into obscurity. The proper resolution of America's global problems, they each suggest, would be for Washington to recognize China's universally valid ideals of world harmony, Under-Heaven, and/or the China model. While they pity America, these three worldviews largely ignore Japan, Europe, and the rest of the world altogether. In this odd way, the American nightmare is the China dream.

They all agree that China needs its own worldview, which for them is, by definition, different from European and American world orders. In different ways, they all feel that China has a moral mission to improve the world, either through its peaceful civilization or through its martial spirit. Otherwise, all three are quite vague about the details of their world orders; Zhao and Liu, in particular, are much clearer about what they do not like—America and the West—than they are about what they do like. Thus, their impact may be more negative—to delegitimize the current U.S.-guided world order—than positive in the sense of promoting a coherent post-American world order.

Alongside these shared themes, there are tensions between Hu's, Zhao's, and Liu's visions of the future, which offer different concepts and different methods for ordering the world. Hu's harmonious world employs mainstream liberal views of international politics: equal nation-states engaging in multilateral diplomacy toward positive sum win-win solutions of mutual security and prosperity. But Hu quickly switches to see world harmony as the tolerant interaction of discrete, but still equal, civilizations. Likewise, Zhao's Under-Heaven system focuses on civilization. However, his world harmony is holistic and hierarchical: one singular global civilization-state harmonizes all the peoples of the world. Rather than a positive sum win-win strategy, the Under-Heaven system exemplifies a universal WIN strategy, which does not allow much space for diversity. Liu's China dream, on the other hand, is not about diplomacy or harmony—it entails a zero-sum great power competition that produces clear winners and losers. But as with the other two worldviews, Liu's nations quickly become civilizations and then races: he sees world politics as a competition between the "yellow race" and the "white race."[49]

There is also a tension between the centralized planning of the future and multiple dreams about it. Harmonious world is part of China's Leninist tradition of centralized planning, including Five-Year Plans for economic development and reports every five years to the party congress. *The Under-Heaven System* and *The China Dream*, however, mix planning and dreaming. They both break free of official rules and slogans to dream of different futures for China as the seat of a utopian global system or as the global champion nation. Yet, both Zhao and Liu still express their dreams in terms of industrial planning: Zhao urges China to upgrade its "knowledge production" while Liu concludes that China's fight against corruption requires better "knowledge planning." This focus on knowledge and ideas reveals the tension between soft power and hard power in China. As the examples offered above graphically show, we cannot understand China's dreams unless we understand its economic and military power.

There are unexpected crossovers: although Hu presented harmonious world as a diplomatic strategy, citizen intellectuals also try to recruit the military into their harmonious world. In October 2010, for example, UN Undersecretary-General Sha Zukang gave General Chi Haotian the World Harmony Award for his contributions to world peace. Many viewed Chi as a controversial choice: this former defense minister ordered the military assault on protesters in Beijing in June 1989, which killed, at a minimum, hundreds of citizens. Although the Chinese press announcement suggested that this was a UN award, it actually came from the World Harmony Foundation, which is the pet project of a Chinese businessman.[50] The World Harmony Award, which was created in response to dissident Liu Xiaobo's Nobel Peace Prize, highlights how citizens and officials think that world harmony, diplomacy, and the military are intertwined in China. It also suggests that world harmony is not necessarily peaceful.

This was confirmed when China's new Confucius Peace Prize was given to Russian prime minister Vladimir Putin in 2011 primarily for his decision to go to war in Chechnya in 1999. As the award committee explained, Putin's "iron hand and toughness revealed in this war impressed the Russians a lot, and he was regarded to be capable of bringing safety and stability to Russia."[51] While Confucianism generally talks about peace coming from harmony, here peace is the result of violence.

Hence, a tension is found in all three scenarios between the more modest goal of fostering world harmony and the more aggressive project of harmonizing the world—by force, if necessary.

Conclusion

How can we explain Beijing's recent turn from a modest foreign policy to a more assertive global stance? While there are economic sources of this change, this chapter has shown how we also need to pay close attention to how ideas shape opinion-makers' and policymakers' views of the world. Alongside China's current "era of many troubles" in East Asia, Europe, and America there is a growing unrest among China's citizen intellectuals; new voices are challenging the foreign policy establishment's monopoly on discussion of China's place in the world. Indeed, prominent strategist Yan Xuetong recently lamented the declining status of professional strategists in the face of popular (and populist) views from outside the security studies fraternity.

However, we have seen how it is necessary to recognize that China has multiple strategies and multiple futures—for many Chinas. Citizen intellectuals such as Zhao Tingyang and Liu Mingfu are important because they take advantage of the openings provided by vague government policy to develop China's geostrategy in new directions. Such citizen intellectuals engender interest and gain influence because as relative outsiders they can give us a sense of the parameters within which official policies (like harmonious world) are formulated, implemented, defended—and rejected. Together with Hu's harmonious world, they provide a range of views—from idealist world society to realist power politics—that help us to better understand the range of possibilities for China's post-American world order.

What they do not provide is clear answers about China's future foreign policy; but, such arguments beg the question of whether Beijing actually has a clear foreign policy to begin with, which then could be discovered through Kremlinological methods. My argument is that rather than search for a clear unified foreign policy, it is more productive to analyze a range of views and catalogue the possibilities that are being discussed in China while noting both their negative and their positive influences.

It is common for Chinese thinkers to assert that China will be a different kind of superpower that offers more peaceful, moral, and harmonious norms as its contribution to world civilization. This should not be surprising; rising powers typically promote their unique values as the moral model for a better world order: Europe's *mission civilisatrice*, America's free world, Japan's economic miracle, and so on. Certainly Hu, Zhao, and Liu would agree that China is exceptional. But rather than promote Chinese exceptionalism, the examples in this chapter suggest that Chinese strategy is better understood as a response to global debates about international relations; instead of being a unique alternative, the nation's strategy is *intertwined* with the dominant schools of realism, liberalism, and idealism. Although they are not exactly the same as theories in Europe and America, the difference is a matter of degree rather than of kind: a Chinese-inflected realism, for example.

Citizen intellectuals also remind us that analysis of Chinese foreign policy still needs to take socialism seriously. While its power as a revolutionary ideology has declined, socialism as a way of thinking (especially in its Leninist-modernist form) still informs the way that problems and solutions are formulated in China. This helps to explain the enduring influence of top-down centralized planning in China's various dreams of the future.

Lastly, although official and unofficial Chinese texts speak as if China's victory is imminent, in fact the PRC is unlikely to catch up to the United States economically, politically, culturally, or militarily in the next few decades. This disjuncture between grand ambitions and middling capabilities could lead to conflict because Beijing is promising its citizens much more than it can deliver in terms of global power and influence. A "propaganda gap" of this kind is likely to increase tensions between China and the West in the next few years; populist voices demanding a post-American world order are growing louder with Beijing's long transition to the fifth generation leadership.

3

The China Model and the
Search for Wealth and Power

SHENGSHI, THE GOLDEN Age: This ancient term encapsulates China's dreams of its future. While in 2011 the European and American economies teetered on the edge of a double-dip recession, the Chinese economy grew at the enviable rate of 9.2 percent. The People's Republic of China (PRC) thus has emerged as an economic superpower.

Since 1978, Beijing's economic development policy has pulled over 300 million Chinese out of extreme poverty. China's economic success, however, does not just benefit its citizens; the PRC is now the main engine of global economic growth. Its economic ideas that look to both the authoritarian state and the free market are gaining prominence among those who proffer policy advice in international institutions such as the World Bank as well as among those who craft policies in many African countries. In 2009–2010, the PRC actually lent more money to developing countries than the World Bank.[1]

To understand how the PRC's growing economic power impacts people around the world, it is necessary to understand the secret of China's success, variously known as the "China miracle," the "China experience," and the "China model." Discussions of China's distinct economic development model actually originated in the West with Joshua Cooper Ramo's "The Beijing Consensus" (2004) think tank report, which challenged the dominant neoliberal view, summarized as the "Washington Consensus." It was followed by Martin Jacques's book *When China Rules the World* (2009), which encouraged Chinese officials and academics to value their own "unique" approach to politics and economics.[2] Hence, especially since the Great Recession erupted in New York in 2008, discussions of the China model are now very popular in the PRC.

It is important to probe Chinese understandings of the PRC's economic success because analysis in China mirrors the trends discussed in the introduction: the shift from the future situated outside China to China itself as the future and the shift from Beijing centrally planning the future to various citizen intellectuals dreaming about China's future.

The China model is often summarized as a unique combination of "authoritarian state + free market." Yet, this is not a new issue. Since Adam Smith's revolutionary book *The Wealth of Nations* (1776) founded the discipline of political economy, theorists in the West have been talking about the correct relationship between the government and the market. This conversation has deep roots in China as well: The "Debates on Salt and Iron" (*Yantie lun*, 81 BC) were between advocates of a free market and of an interventionist government.[3]

But China's political-economy debate began in earnest at the turn of the 20th century when young translator Yan Fu began his search for wealth and power. To find the "secret" of Europe's and America's success, Yan translated Smith's *The Wealth of Nations* as well as a host of other European economic, sociological, and philosophical texts. This citizen intellectual, who wasn't tied to any institution, transformed the role of intellectuals in China from defending Confucianism's universal morals to defending the modern Chinese state in its dog-eat-dog geopolitical competition with the West and with Japan.[4]

Since the turn of the 21st century, a number of new books on China's economic future have been published on the mainland. Like Yan Fu, everyone is searching for the secret of success. According to the chief theorist of the China model, Pan Wei, many people asked him, "Since today's West is China's future, why strain yourself making a China model?"[5] But as the enthusiastic response to Pan's edited volume *The China Model* (*Zhongguo moshi*) shows, rather than looking to the West for models, now most Chinese intellectuals find the correct path to "wealth and power" in their own country. The PRC has changed from student to teacher, whose China model can contribute to global prosperity.

The China model, as we will see, is not simply about economic growth; it inspires a millennial mission that celebrates what many call "the rejuvenation of the Chinese nation" as a global power. British economist Angus Maddison's research that shows China leading the global economy before 1820 inspires China's top economists for more than academic reasons: It sets the goal for China's reemergence as a new kind of superpower.[6] Maddison's global economic pie graphs have a popular following as well; one pie graph showing China having 33 percent of global GDP (and the United States less

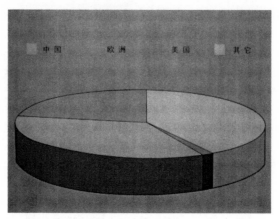

FIGURE 3.1 Maddison's pie at Beijing's Confucius Temple (2012)

Source: William A. Callahan

than 1 percent) in 1800 is even displayed at the Confucius Temple in Beijing. (Fig. 3.1)

The sense is that China will soon return to its "natural place" at the center of the world. Economic success, in both the past and the future, thus is located in China.

This chapter will examine how China's top economists and political scientists are dreaming about China's economic future. To get a sense of how China achieved its current success and its future direction, the work of rural development economists Justin Yifu Lin and Hu Angang will be compared. To understand the broader political and cultural goals of the China model, the writings of political scientists Pan Wei and Cui Zhiyuan will be compared. Lastly, radical challenges to the China model will be considered by examining *The Golden Age: China, 2013* (Shengshi: Zhongguo, 2013 nian), a science fiction novel by Chan Koonchung that sparked vigorous debate in the PRC. In this way, the second trend of the shift from officials planning China's economic future to citizen intellectuals dreaming about it will be explored.

To grasp the impact of debates about the China model, we need to put China's economic dreams in the context of tensions between state planning and free market, between political-economic convergence and divergence, between Western and Chinese models, and between universal values and Chinese exceptionalism. Rather than being a simple either/or choice between, for example, state planning and the free market, we will see how these ideas are joined on a continuum: more or less state planning and more or less free market. As in chapter 2, "socialism with Chinese characteristics" is a major theme; as we will see, socialism is still quite strong and Chinese characteristics include both Confucian tradition and socialist ideology.

Thus, we will see how innovation in China is not simply technical: All of these citizen intellectuals highlight the power of China's "fresh ideas" and its growing "discursive power" on the world stage. The China model is about much more than economics: It is about how China can and must regain what advocates see as its natural place as the center of the world. At the end of the chapter, we will consider how China's various plans and dreams for the future will impact the economic fortunes of the United States and Europe.

To get a sense of the role played by the China dreams of the country's citizen intellectuals, it is important first to look more closely at the goals of Beijing's official economic China dream.

The Official Dream: Eleventh and Twelfth Five-Year Plans

China's five-year economic development plans show the second trend noted in the introduction: the shift from official centralized planning to the decentralized dreaming of multiple citizen intellectuals. After three decades of reform that has marketized and liberalized China's economy, one could be forgiven for thinking that the era of Soviet-inspired five-year economic plans that began in 1953 had passed. However, the PRC launched its 12th Five-Year Plan (12FYP) in March 2011. This ambitious plan to restructure China's economy is certainly triumphalist, proclaiming "We successfully held the Beijing Olympic Games, the Shanghai World Expo and the Guangzhou Asian Games. We have achieved the major objectives set in the 11th Five Year Plan...writing a new chapter of socialism with Chinese characteristics." Indeed, using the same language of "strategic opportunities" that we saw in chapter 2, the 12FYP highlights the tension between "precious historic opportunities" and "unforeseeable risks and challenges."[7]

But it would be a mistake to write off China's Five Year Plans as a propaganda exercise. The 12FYP is actually another expression of Beijing's official China dream for 2015 and beyond. Its aim is to create a more sustainable, balanced, and innovative development that is "people-centered." It is a blueprint for expanding both economic growth and social welfare programs, thereby building what it calls a "moderately well-off" society by 2020. As the results of the 11th Five-Year Plan (2006–2010) show, Beijing is good at achieving its targets: It often overachieves them.

More importantly, the 11FYP marked a watershed in Beijing's formulation of China's economic and social development plans. Before Deng Xiaoping's reform and opening policy started in 1978, China's production and distribution activities were determined by a centralized planning process that issued detailed targets. With economic reform, "planning in China has shifted from a process characterized by highly centralised and interventionist methods towards one whose intent is to guide, but not dictate, economic decision-making."[8] The 11FYP was a milestone in the shift from central planning to policy guidance: even its Chinese-language title changed from "plan" to "guideline program." The 12FYP continues this shift by having fewer binding targets and more aspirational targets.

While the targets of Beijing's five-year plans have shifted from centralized government intervention to aspirational guidelines, the planning process itself also has been opened up to citizen intellectuals. China's top economists, Justin Yifu Lin and Hu Angang, are part of this shift. Both formerly worked for the official planning body, China's National Reform and Development Commission, and both are now external consultants. For example, Hu's Tsinghua University think tank, the China Studies Center, was commissioned to make policy recommendations for the 12FYP; the results were later published as *China: Moving Towards 2015* (2010).[9]

China's economic future thus is shifting from a Eurocentric focus to a Sinocentric one and from official centralized planning to the decentralized dreaming of multiple citizen intellectuals. But as we will see, it is not a complete shift. China still appeals to Western measures of success (e.g., modernization theory),[10] and citizen intellectuals still work closely with the government.

In the 21st century, China has been facing the social and environmental costs of three decades of rapid economic growth: a polarization of income, especially between urban and rural areas and between China's interior and coastal provinces, and an environmental crisis: according to the World Bank, sixteen of the world's twenty most polluted cities are in China. Thus, both the 11FYP and the 12FYP seek to "rebalance" the Chinese economy. The main goal of the 11FYP was to build a "harmonious socialist society" by shifting priority away from rapid GDP growth to "sustainable" and "inclusive" growth and from an export-oriented economy fueled by foreign investment to one in which China's domestic market is the major engine driving growth.

Unfortunately, it failed: the 11FYP's target was 7.5 percent annual growth, but China's GDP grew at an average of 11 percent per year; the gap between rich and poor actually increased; and domestic consumption's share of China's GDP fell by 12 percent (2000–2010). Rather than continue the process of economic reform in which the state retreats from economic life as the private sector expands (*guotui minjin*), in 2009–2010 China's massive $586 billion stimulus package and generous loans to state-owned enterprises (SOEs) led to the expansion of the state sector and the retreat of the private sector (*guojin mintui*).

The global financial crisis is one reason for the 11FYP's problems. But as American economist Barry Naughton argues, there are deeper issues. China has been so successful, he explains, because Deng Xiaoping's economic reforms fundamentally "tailored, tuned, pruned, focused, and rebuilt" the PRC's political-economic system to single-mindedly concentrate on "the process of economic growth."[11] Retooling China's political economy again to rebalance the quantitative target of economic growth and the qualitative goal of sustainable and inclusive development is a huge challenge that the 12FYP continues to pursue. The objective is to successfully move from an economy based on export-oriented labor-intensive light industry to one based on capital-intensive high-tech industry. By 2020, the PRC plans to become a "moderately well-off" society that has the social and political stability of a harmonious socialist society.

Economists Chart China's Past and Future Success

When Justin Yifu Lin visited Beijing in autumn 2010, he was treated like an all-conquering hero. As vice president and chief economist of the World Bank, Lin was celebrated by his compatriots as the first Chinese to rise to the leadership of an international financial organization. The PRC harbors high hopes that Lin will be the first Chinese to win a Nobel Prize for something that the party-state is proud of.[12] Before he went to the World Bank, Lin was famous, according to Nobel Laureate Joseph Stiglitz, for bringing "market economics into China." Then as the World Bank's chief economist, Lin became the "global ambassador" for the Chinese model of economics.[13] Lin thus is a key figure who works at the center of both the Beijing Consensus and the Washington Consensus.

This straddling of worlds is nothing new for Lin. As we saw in the introduction, he is the most famous person to defect *into* China. In May 1979, just as the mainland was starting its "reform and opening" program, Lin decided to leave his charmed life as a member of the Taiwanese elite to seek his fortune in China. Although he seemed to be swimming against the tide of history (even as he negotiated the tides on his 1.5 mile swim from a Taiwanese army

FIGURE 3.2 Justin Yifu Lin
Source: Courtesy of the World Bank

base to the mainland), both Lin and China have been very successful over the past thirty years. The secret for both successes has been avoiding extremes to mix things that seem to be opposites: Lin's economic theory is a curious combination of Marxism and capitalism, while the PRC's economic reform program combines government intervention and free markets.

Lin's economic thought has been quite consistent, regardless of whether he writes in Chinese or in English, in academic monographs or on his World Bank blog "Let's Talk Development." Starting with his co-authored book *China's Miracle* (1994)—which has been translated into seven languages—Lin has argued that a country's development strategy needs to follow its comparative advantage and endowment structure.[14] Hence, developing countries that have abundant unskilled labor and scarce capital need to get foreign investment to develop labor-intensive light industries that make consumer goods for trade on the global market. Using the profits from this global trade to develop human capital (i.e., educate workers) and physical capital (i.e., build infrastructure), the country will be able to shift from labor-intensive industry to capital-intensive industry, thus making the transition from a developing to a developed economy that has an equitable distribution of wealth. In so doing, countries can move from an agricultural to an industrial economy and from a centrally planned economy to a free-market economy.

Lin's objective is to narrow the gap between developing and developed economies and, thus, between the Global North and the Global South. The goal of "catching up and building equitable societies," Lin tells us, is "a dream championed by many revolutionary leaders and social elites in developing countries, such as Vladimir Lenin, Sun Yatsen, Mao Zedong, Jawaharlal Nehru and Gamal Abdel Nasser."[15]

Lin argues that ideas determine developmental success. To explain his mix of industrial policy and free markets, he locates his advice in the historical context of the two "bad ideas" that dominated postwar social thought: import-substitution industrialization and the Washington Consensus. In the 1950s and 1960s, the new postcolonial states felt that to guard their hard-won independence they needed to rapidly develop heavy industry for armaments. To support this capital-intensive development program, many Asian, African, and Latin American countries adopted the policy of import-substitution industrialization, which involved state-led economic planning, the nationalization of strategic industries, subsidies for heavy industry, increased taxation, and protectionist trade policies.

This "leap-forward strategy" did not lead to sustainable economic growth, Lin argues, because capital-intensive development defied the countries' comparative advantage of abundant cheap labor. Since the government couldn't keep subsidizing heavy industry, economic growth stagnated, unemployment rose, and income distribution polarized. This strategy also led to humanitarian disasters. Mao's Great Leap Forward campaign (1957–1961), whose goal was to catch up to the United States in fifteen years, directly led to humanity's greatest famine, killing more than 30 million people.

The Washington Consensus, which was promoted by the International Monetary Fund (IMF) and the World Bank, was a direct response to the failure of the strategy of government intervention and import substitution. It instructed developing countries to privatize and liberalize their national economies; this "market fundamentalism" also became the consensus view for reforming socialist centrally planned economies. But the failure of the IMF's "shock therapy" in the Soviet Union and Eastern Europe convinced many that neoliberalism does not work either. Because Russia's state-supported firms were not strong enough to weather rapid privatization and liberalization, economic growth plummeted while unemployment skyrocketed. Lin concludes that such "shock without therapy" produced "economic chaos."[16]

Lin's economic theory is innovative because it employs elements from both failed economic models to argue for the importance of both government intervention and free markets. He looks to examples from East Asia, the only region to successfully graduate from developing to developed economies. While it is common to argue that Confucian civilization is the key to the East Asian economic model, Lin explains the model through economic theory, although at times with a cultural twist. Rather than discarding government intervention in favor of the market, or marginalizing the market to promote industrial policy, Lin argues that the East Asian experience shows that developing economies need both government intervention and free markets. Japan, South Korea, Taiwan, Singapore, and Hong Kong were each successful because their government's industrial policy correctly exploited their comparative advantage at every stage, enabling the economies to grow both quantitatively in terms of GDP and qualitatively in terms of transitioning from labor-intensive light industry to capital-intensive high-tech industry. Rather than submitting to shock therapy and rapid transition, East Asian countries shifted from centrally planned economies to market economies through a hybrid approach that gradually opened their economies to foreign competition. Lin thus subscribes to the standard view of "Reform China": Its economic success over the past three decades likewise comes from Deng Xiaoping's pragmatic and experimental approach of gradually opening the Chinese economy step-by-step.

Lin's main conclusion, then, is that ideas matter. But they cannot be dogmatic ideas like Mao's "leap-forward strategy" or the IMF's "one-size-fits-all" policies. The key to development, he argues, is to get the right mix of industrial policy and free markets. In a sense, the China model is that there is no model, no hard and fast prescription that every country can follow for success. Yet as British political economist Shaun Breslin explains, the China model is still important because it creates space for other countries to develop their own "indigenous strategies" of economic development.[17]

Lin's ideas impact debates both in China and in the West. His career trajectory is a mix of official policymaking and activities as a citizen intellectual who tries to shape public opinion around the world. In 1987, Lin was the first American-educated economics PhD to return to China since 1949. He was recruited into officialdom as a key adviser to the State Council's Development Research Center, where he brought capitalist economic theory to Beijing's five-year planning process. But, at the same time, Lin pursued an academic career at Peking University, where he co-founded the China Center for Economic Research, the PRC's top economic think tank.

In addition to his work as an economic adviser, Lin has taken on an important public role as a member of China's top political institutions: He was a representative at the 11th National People's Congress (2008–2013), and was vice chairman of the Committee for Economic Affairs of the Chinese People's Political Consultative Conference. Hence, Lin is an exemplary "scholar-official" who takes China's national destiny as his personal responsibility. As he wrote to his cousin soon after defecting to the mainland, "it struck me that it would be a waste of my life if I didn't devote it to pursuing the happiness of future hundreds and thousands of generations.... Let's work to achieve China's unity and prosperity!"[18]

Since 2008, Lin's most important impact has been on the international stage. When World Bank president Robert Zoellick hired Lin in 2008, he was encouraging China to be a "responsible stakeholder" in the international system—the policy Zoellick inaugurated in 2005 when he was deputy secretary of state in the administration of President George W. Bush. Yet, from the very beginning Lin and the Chinese leadership planned to use the World Bank to promote Chinese ideas to a global audience. By showing the utility of government intervention and industrial policy, Lin set a new research agenda at the Bank, which successfully challenged the Washington Consensus's market fundamentalism.

This should not be surprising; since the Great Recession started in 2008, even neoliberal powers such as the United States have been pursuing stimulus packages and other forms of government intervention. Since the Chinese economy is outperforming the American economy, the *China Daily's* columnist in New York proudly proclaimed that the United States needs to have a five-year plan like the PRC.[19] Even the bastion of liberal economics, *The Economist*, credits Lin for showing how industrial policy has trumped neoliberalism.[20] It will be interesting to see if Lin's arguments for government intervention continue to be influential after his departure from the World Bank in 2012.

Lin's China dream becomes clearer when we think of his work in terms of the distinctions outlined above: state planning/free market, political-economic convergence/divergence, Western/Chinese models, and universal values/Chinese exceptionalism. Lin's development model combines state planning and the free market to argue for the economic convergence of the developing world catching up to the developed world. Rather than contrasting "Western" and "Chinese" models, he combines features from the import-substitution and the export-oriented regimes. In this way, he uses examples from East Asia and around the world to argue for a general theory of development, which he calls "New Structural Economics." Certainly, Lin's goal is for China to catch up to the United States; he forecasts that China will become the world's largest economy by 2030.[21] But the United States is not the focus of his research: Lin's comments on global imbalances, reserve currency, and global economic governance are relegated to the appendix of his latest book: *Demystifying the*

Chinese Economy.[22] Not surprisingly, he supports Beijing's view that the global economy would benefit most from a gradual appreciation and international-ization of the renminbi.

While Justin Yifu Lin was busy in America challenging the Washington Consensus, Hu Angang has been fine-tuning the China model as a key government adviser and public intellectual. Hu, who teaches at Tsinghua University's School of Public Administration and Management and runs its China Studies Center, is known as "China's most versatile and pragmatic economist." According to former Goldman Sachs president John Thornton, Hu is influential because "no Chinese thinker is better at predicting the pace and direction of China's development."[23] Three of Hu's recent books attest to his influence: *2020 China: Building a Comprehensive Well-Off Society* was originally commissioned by the party to make policy recommendations for Hu Jintao's "Report to the 17th Party Congress" (2007); *China: Going Toward 2015* was commissioned by the National Development and Reform Commission as a policy study for the 12FYP; Hu's latest academic book, *2030 China: Towards a Common Prosperity* (2011), uses the data from these official projects to think about China's long-term future.[24] Hu is also well known for coming up with key ideas for policymakers, ranging from "comprehensive national power," which aggregates economic, military, political, and cultural factors to rate each country on a global scale, to "green GDP," which considers the environmental impact of China's development strategy.

What is Hu Angang's China dream? On the last page of *China in 2020: A New Type of Superpower* (2011), Hu states that Chinese need to "rethink"

FIGURE 3.3 Hu Angang
Source: Courtesy of Hu Angang

the "China Dream" beyond pure economics. Since China's success in the 21st century will be measured by its contributions to the world, Hu argues that "China's modern renaissance" will be shown through its "contributions to human development, science and technology, the green movement, and culture."[25] This progressive view of China's future role in the world is indicative of Hu's role as a social critic. As a citizen intellectual he is famous for pushing the government to address the problems of rural poverty and environmental degradation in order to make China's economic development inclusive and sustainable. His goal for 2020, which is taken from the communiqué of the Sixth Plenary Session of the Sixteenth Central Committee (2006), is to "build a wealthy and powerful, democratic, civilized and harmonious socialist modernized country."[26] Rather than conclude that Hu is parroting official views as part of a propaganda campaign, we should remember that Hu probably formulated this policy himself as a government consultant. It is significant, therefore, when Hu tells the world that the PRC will be a different kind of world leader, "predict[ing] that China will be a mature, responsible, and attractive superpower."[27]

But a closer look at Hu's work shows that tension exists between the qualitative human development goals and the quantitative goal of surpassing the United States. Simply put, both Hu's reports for the government and his academic work stress the quantitative target of catching up to and surpassing the United States. Like Lin, Hu is optimistic about China's prospects. To forecast China's future success, Hu looks to China's recent experience between 1978 and 2009, when its GDP grew 18.6 times larger, at an average rate of 9.9 percent per year. Since the country's fundamentals are still strong, Hu confidently forecasts that China's rapid economic growth will continue for another generation. He forecasts that by 2020 the PRC will surpass the United States to be the world's top economic power.[28]

More than Lin, Hu is concerned with the economics of catching up to the West. They are actually close colleagues, whose career paths as experts in rural development have followed a similar trajectory. They have abundant international experience: Both were postdocs at Yale University, are members of Beijing's elite "50 Chinese Economists Forum," and even hold appointments at the Chinese University of Hong Kong. But they come from different backgrounds: Lin is the son of a poor shopkeeper, while Hu's parents were academic "National Model Workers." More importantly, while Lin was a patriotic activist at Taiwan's top universities in the 1970s, Hu was sent down to the countryside during the Cultural Revolution to work on a collective farm, where he braved Heilongjiang's brutal environment for seven years. This "humbling experience" made Hu passionate about the issues of economic inequality, regional gaps, and urban-rural gaps.[29] It also, perhaps, explains his continued devotion to Mao (see below).

Lin argues that China will prosper by following its comparative advantage at every stage; catching up to the United States is an added benefit of this general process. Hu's argument is quite similar: He likewise praises Deng Xiaoping's pragmatic policy that gradually reformed China's political economy through a process of trial and error. The key, once again, is to develop China's infrastructure and human resources. Similar to the 11FYP and 12FYP, Hu argues that the PRC is shifting from an export-oriented economy to one in which the domestic consumption of China's growing middle class will drive development.[30] While Lin sees government facilitating the market, Hu was an early critic of market fundamentalism. Following this state-centric view, Hu thinks that China's SOEs are the key to its continued success.

Hu deviates from most economists' views, however, when he declares that we need to acknowledge the importance of the Maoist period (1949–1976) in China's economic development.[31] He challenges the popular notion that views the Cultural Revolution as "ten lost years," explaining that this "ten-year upheaval...made reform and opening possible. It provided the circumstances necessary for the last thirty years of progress towards increased unity, stability and prosperity." Hu credits Mao for creating "the strategic concept of catching up and then surpassing the U.S.," declaring that "it now seems that Mao's grand strategy for China is on the verge of being realized."

Yet, if we follow Lin's analysis, Mao's political campaigns to develop heavy industry actually retarded China's economic growth. In other words, Mao's grand political goal of beating the United States could be achieved only by discarding Mao's economic policies. In asides and footnotes, Hu acknowledges the problems with Mao's "leap-forward" economic theory—which he recently called the "Moscow Consensus"[32] (as opposed to the Washington or Beijing Consensus). Yet he still quotes Mao's aspirational statements throughout his work. In the end Mao's thought is useful, Hu argues, simply because it is Chinese: "Mao's thought and language may not have been the best in the world, but they were and remain the most suitable for China as well as the easiest for the Chinese people to accept."[33] Perhaps Hu also clings to Mao's capital-intensive heavy industry strategy for personal reasons: He was named after it—"Angang" is short for the Anshan Iron and Steel Factory, where Hu's parents worked.

Hu's arguments go beyond economic issues to target the United States not just as an economic or a political competitor, but also as a moral problem.

In *2030 China*, Hu states that the Washington Consensus's advice to "completely privatize the economy and democratize politics" is not just mistaken (as Lin argues), but it is also the "evil road."[34] Americans, he tells us, are selfish because their culture is "exceedingly individualistic." Chinese are "more tolerant" because their culture is guided by "the principles of harmony, peace, and cooperation." China thus will be a "mature, responsible, and attractive superpower," Hu explains, because it is *different* from the United States

Consequently, China's different style of economic power will transform the way the world works economically, politically, and culturally: "China can promote the reform of global governance systems, break the monopoly of the United States, and assert a greater influence in the world. This can also serve to break the western culture's long-standing monopoly over modernity and bring more diversified cultures and values to the world stage."[35]

To promote what he calls the "China Road," Hu provides an insider's view of the PRC that develops the "discursive power" of the "Chinese voice" and the "Chinese perspective."[36] Although he occasionally references China's classical culture, the Chinese perspective for Hu is guided by "socialism with Chinese characteristics." Rather than quote Confucian aphorisms, Hu cites Deng Xiaoping's "well-off living standard," Jiang Zemin's "well-off society," and Hu Jintao's "harmonious society" and "peaceful development" as "modern Chinese innovations that bear strong Chinese and socialist characteristics."[37]

To understand how Hu is developing a political-economic China model, it's helpful to compare his views with those of Justin Yifu Lin. While Lin seeks to balance government intervention and free markets, Hu argues that government intervention and SOEs are the key to China's economic success. China's successful economic path thus is different not only from that of the West, but also from those of Japan and the East Asian development model. Hu forecasts not simply a great convergence of developed and developing economies, but a "great reversal," one in which the Global South has more wealth and power than developed countries in the North.

While Lin analyzes China as a "developing country," Hu is shifting from a general view of "China in the world" to a more specific view of China as a unique case, which other countries can follow if they choose. Lin appeals to the neoclassical economic theory of comparative advantage; but Hu declares that due to its unique "national conditions" China "cannot be interpreted using existing economic growth theories or models."[38] Lin works to solve the problem of poverty shared by China and the developing world, while Hu focuses on forecasting when China will become a superpower and when the Global South will seize power from Western countries. Lin looks to Deng's economic reform and to its opening to the West, and Hu cheers Mao's challenge to the West. While Lin explores how the rise of China will usher in a multipolar world, Hu concludes that, by 2030, China will guide a Sinocentric world order to establish the "World of Great Harmony" (*datong shijie*), which is not only "China's dream," but also the "world's dream."[39]

Thus, Hu is moving from general arguments about global developmental economics to a specific argument about the PRC's unique "China road," which is one that, as we will see in the next section, is popular with many political scientists in China.

Political Scientists Promote the China Model and the Chongqing Model

Although Justin Yifu Lin and Hu Angang offer sophisticated explanations of China's hybrid strategy of economic development, to many the China model is still simply shorthand for "authoritarian state + free market capitalism."

However, Pan Wei, the director of Peking University's Center for China and Global Affairs, is not satisfied with this description. In the long introduction to his popular edited volume, *The China Model* (*Zhongguo moshi*, 2009), Pan argues that Western social science concepts such as "authoritarianism" and "the free market" cannot explain China's unique experience. China's experience thus "challenges the 'market/state planning dichotomy' of Western economics, the 'democracy/autocracy dichotomy' of Western political science, and the 'state/society dichotomy' of Western sociology."[40]

These concepts are not "universal," he argues, because they grew out of Europe's (and then America's) particular historical and cultural experience. Since China has a radically different historical experience, one that is entirely unique, Pan says that it can be judged only by its own set of concepts. Pan here is doing more than describing the Chinese experience. Through his books and speeches in China and abroad, Pan is building his unique China model to challenge the very idea of "universal values" such as democracy and human rights. This is part of Pan's shift in the mid-2000s from social science methods to cultural explanations that we discussed in chapter 1.

Pan explains the China model in terms of three "indigenous" Chinese submodels—public/private (*guomin*) economics, people-based (*minben*) politics, and organic (*sheji*) society—that are contrasted with "Western" approaches to order and governance. Mainstream Western philosophy generally recognizes the diversity of interests in modern society, and it sees order in terms of balancing competing interests through "checks and balances." Chinese philosophy, Pan tells us, starts from the assumption of unity, and it sees order as a process of integrating divisions into an organic whole, ultimately into the "World of Great Harmony" (*datong shijie*). While Western economics sees a struggle between free markets and state intervention, China's public/private economic model harmonizes both sectors. While Western politics looks to legalistic concepts of competing rights, China's people-based political order is based on mutual responsibility. While Western sociology sees a battle between the state and civil society, China's economic development and political stability are based on organic society's integration of officials and the people.

Public/private economics, people-based politics, and organic society are all new concepts; but Pan looks to China's two traditions—ancient Chinese culture and modern socialist ideology—to argue that they are an integral part of Chinese civilization. He quotes many passages from classical Chinese philosophy to show how the "China model is the 21st century's new edition of the Chinese system." Pan also looks to socialism to describe his public/private economy, which he concludes is the same as what CCP "officials call the 'socialist market economy with Chinese characteristics.'" Like Hu Angang, Pan reclaims the Maoist period (1949–1978) as part of the China model's "60 years of achievement" because "our country's state-owned sector was built in [the PRC's] first 30 years." The economic, political, and social submodels all rely on a strong CCP, which Pan describes as "an advanced, neutral, united ruling group."[41]

The China model is famous for building China's ultramodern cities—Shanghai, Shenzhen, and Beijing—and the 12FYP seeks to speed up China's urbanization process. Pan, on the other hand, appeals to traditional Chinese village life to explain the organic social model. *Sheji* is an interesting term because it refers both to a whole society and to the local village shrine where officials and common people pray for "prosperity and harmony" by making offerings to ancestors. Pan develops *sheji* society's focus on ancestors by explaining that Chinese society is based on a "family theory" that values responsibility—unlike Western society that is based on individual rights. Organic society, according to Pan, is the bedrock of the success of China's political and economic models: SOEs and private companies are all run like small family businesses; the party loves the people like a caring father, while the masses are loyal, grateful, and respectful, like good children.

Although Pan's description of public/private economics seems to balance the two sectors, he is very clear that the state is in control in China. As he puts it: "The West and China have taken two different roads: in one, capital [i.e. the private sector] has captured the state, in the other the state surrounds capital." Leaders are selected from among "sages" instead of through competitive multiparty elections. In Pan's view, China is neither a democracy nor an autocracy because the PRC is a "meritocracy." It has the rule of law and an independent judiciary, he explains, but little room for open debate in "civil society," which Pan sees as a battleground of special interests that divides the organic whole.[42]

In this formulation, Chinese society is configured as a conflict-free organic whole that must be defended from Western attack. According to Pan, Chinese critics who advocate deeper political reform really want "to demolish the Forbidden City in order to build the White House" in China, so "foreign forces can control China's military, politics, economy and society." China thus is at a "crossroads": "In the next 30 years; which direction will the Chinese nation take? Will it preserve China's rejuvenation? Or will it have superstitious faith in the Western 'liberal democracy' system, and go down the road of decline and enslavement?" Chinese people, he tells us, should celebrate the China model simply because it is not "foreign" or "imported."[43]

To put Pan's China model in context, it's helpful to think of it in terms of the conceptual distinctions mentioned above: state planning/free market, political-economic convergence/political-economic divergence, Western model/Chinese model, and universal values/Chinese exceptionalism. Although Pan stresses harmony and balance as Chinese values, his model very clearly advocates government intervention in place of the free market. It sees Chinese political-economic-cultural trends diverging from Western hegemony, and he pits the China model against what he calls the Western model to promote Chinese exceptionalism against universal values. Like Hu Angang, Pan argues that the China model is different from the East Asian development model that Lin supports. Even more than for Hu, the West is for Pan a source of conspiracies to keep China down, including "booby traps" like liberal democracy. While Hu insists that China needs to enhance its "discursive power" so the world can hear the "Chinese voice" and appreciate the "Chinese perspective,"[44] Pan argues that Chinese scholars need "to be confident about their own native civilization to promote the formation of 'Chinese discursive power' and the rise of the 'Chinese school.'"[45]

One of the main goals of China model discourse thus is to affirm and support Beijing's current system of governance that is dominated by the CCP. The China model involves tight state control of politics, economy, and society to promote the key values of stability, unity, and statism. Pan's expression of "Chinese exceptionalism" justifies the status quo of authoritarian rule because China's uniqueness shields it from criticisms that look to values that Pan would dismiss as "foreign."

Pan Wei's definition of the China model is quite precise, and his economic, political, and social submodels are explained in elaborate detail. But Pan's description of an ideal Chinese society lacks the support of hard evidence because he sees the China model less in terms of a set of policy prescriptions than as the sign of China's "cultural renaissance." However, the "Chongqing model," especially as narrated by Tsinghua University political scientist Cui Zhiyuan, can give us a better sense of how a "third way" of equitable development that is neither capitalist nor socialist is developing in China.

The Chongqing model, of course, was the signature project of Bo Xilai, the princeling who was ejected from the CCP in 2012 amid scandals about his corruption and violent abuse of power. After his demise, many of Bo's key officials in Chongqing were purged, and the "Red Culture" ideological program was quickly dismantled. But the Chongqing model's economic policies have largely survived, as has the city's mayor, Huang Qifan, who was also a key figure in Chongqing's economic success in the 2000s. The egalitarian economic policies remain popular among leftists, including both elite economists such as Cui and broad social movements represented by Maoist websites such as Utopia, before it was shut down. It is important, then, to understand how the Chongqing model works before considering if and how it can survive Bo's fall, and how it can perhaps influence China's national development plans.

While Shenzhen was the symbol of economic reform in the 1980s, and Shanghai's Pudong district was the symbol of economic growth in the 1990s, we should remember that Chongqing became the symbol of the possibilities for equitable development in the first decade of the 21st century. Chongqing was successful because it took advantage of various opportunities. In 1997, Chongqing was separated from Sichuan Province to become an autonomous city like Beijing and Shanghai. In many ways, Chongqing already looked like a province: it is the size of Austria, has 33 million people, and has a similar demographic mix to China as a whole: 30 percent urban, 70 percent rural. Thus, Cui Zhiyuan describes Chongqing as "basically a microcosm of China," whose "experience could serve as a mirror of national development."[46]

Chongqing's experience is noteworthy because it addressed many of the problems that plague the "China miracle": rural/urban and regional inequalities, inflated housing costs, forced relocation, and so on. Chongqing aimed to solve these problems by encouraging economic growth in both the public and the private sectors (over 15 percent annual growth since 2001), while also delivering welfare programs to better integrate poor and rural people into urban life, thus creating a more equitable society. The dream is to build a Chongqing that is "liveable, smooth flowing, green, safe, and healthy."[47]

The Chongqing government pursued this dream through two major social welfare programs: allowing peasants to register as urban residents and launching a large-scale public housing project. The PRC's economic miracle has been built with the labor of the floating population of migrant workers who leave rural China to work in the cities. Unfortunately, Beijing still enforces a household registration system (hukou) under which this floating population is treated as second-class citizens when they move to the city, where their access to public services, including health care and education, is limited.

Since Hu Jintao designated Chongqing a "National Experimental Zone for Integrating Urban and Rural Development" in 2007, more than three million peasants have reregistered as urban residents. The long-term plan is to give urban residence status to 10 million peasants by 2020, and thus not only reduce the rural/urban gap, but also expand domestic consumption as these urbanized peasants spend their new wages. Chongqing's experiment in integrating rural and urban development, according to Cui, "has national significance."[48] To house these new urban residents, Chongqing is building 40 million square meters of low-cost public housing by 2013. Chongqing's housing strategy, likewise, is a "national model" for the 12FYP's target to build 36 million affordable apartments for low-income people by 2015.

Chongqing's welfare projects are quite expensive, and, according to Cui, the city's real innovation has been in funding them. Rather than relying on laissez-faire capitalism's "invisible hand" of the market or the "visible hand" of socialist state planning, Chongqing has used the "third hand" of its profitable public sector companies to finance government spending on welfare programs and infrastructure projects. These companies have been successful in the market as well; Chongqing's state-owned assets have had an eightfold appreciation in value, "from 170 billion yuan in 2002 to 1,386 billion at the end of June 2011."[49] The city also created an innovative "land certificate" system to ensure that the public would benefit from the rapid increase in land value that accompanies urbanization and industrialization.

To many, Chongqing's public sector–led development model is a prime example of the "advance of the public sector, retreat of the private sector" (guojin mintui) that China has experienced since the global financial crisis of 2008. But Cui argues that the Chongqing model balances public and private to promote a healthy private sector; Chongqing has attracted flagship multinational corporations to invest in the city: Hewlett Packard, Foxconn, BASF, BP, Acer, and Chang'an/Ford Motors. Chongqing's low-cost public housing for workers attracts this foreign investment, as does its low corporation tax.[50] The private sector thus is growing even faster than the public sector. Chongqing's economic growth and urbanized peasant population are designed to create a vibrant domestic market in China, thus "making possible a shift from an export-driven pattern of growth to a domestic consumption–driven pattern."[51] This, Cui reminds us, will be good for both China and America.

The Chongqing model thus provides a cogent example of the harmonious society theorized in Pan Wei's *The China Model*. Its mix of socialism and capitalism, Cui explains, "gives some substance to this concept of a socialist market economy…[which] used to be just a slogan."[52] Chongqing was able to simultaneously pursue economic growth and welfare programs because these policies are designed to be "complementary and mutually reinforcing." Thus, Cui concludes that the Chongqing experience has "universal significance" as a model of development.[53]

At times it is hard to separate the Chongqing model from its chief promoter: Cui Zhiyuan, the "red professor" who teaches at Tsinghua University's School of Public Policy and Management, alongside Hu Angang. Like the other citizen intellectuals, Cui has abundant foreign experience: He received a PhD in political science from the University of Chicago in 1995, and he taught at MIT for six years. Even while in the United States, Cui was very active in mainland China's intellectual discussions, which were critical of the spread of neoliberal reforms in the PRC. He returned to take up his position at Tsinghua in 2004 because he wanted to be more directly involved in shaping the PRC's future direction.

Curiously, Cui first encountered the Chongqing model by chance; while attending the Chinese economic association's 2008 convention in Chongqing, Cui was invited to meet Bo Xilai and Chongqing mayor Huang Qifan. Fascinated with what he saw in Chongqing, Cui returned to the city eight times in 2009 to study the Chongqing model. His goal was to provide "theoretical justification" for Chongqing's "co-development of both public and private enterprises." In 2010, Cui was recruited by Bo and Huang to take leave from Tsinghua to serve as the deputy director of Chongqing's State-Owned Assets Management and Supervision Commission for a year. In this capacity, Cui's job was to "publish articles about Chongqing's experience" to "communicate both internally to government officials, and to the general press."[54] Cui enjoyed working with officials in the Chongqing government as an "engaged academic"; however, some worry that working so closely with officials in Chongqing has damaged Cui's academic credibility—especially in light of the Bo Xilai scandal.

FIGURE 3.4 Cui Zhiyuan
Source: Courtesy of Cui Zhiyuan

Even so, Cui's work is interesting because it anticipated the post-Bo Xilai separation of the ideological and economic strands of the Chongqing model. As we saw in chapter 1, Bo worked hard to link the "Red Culture" and "Strike-hard on Organized Crime" mass campaigns to his egalitarian economic policies. According to *The Chongqing Model*, a book by academics working at Chongqing's Communist Party school, the "sing red songs" campaign reconstructed the Communist Party's "core values and social basis" that were damaged by China's rampant pursuit of the free market. Bo's military-style anti-mafia campaign was likewise praised for both promoting law and order and cleaning up government.[55]

Cui Zhiyuan, on the other hand, mentions the Red Culture campaign only in the last paragraph of his key "Chongqing model" essay, and he does not talk about the Strike Black anti-mafia campaign at all.[56] Although Cui is a founding member of the nativist New Left, his explanations of the Chongqing experience stress how it resonates with the ideas of foreign theorists (Henry George and James Meade) and a pre-communist Chinese leader (Sun Yatsen). It seems that Cui was employed by Chongqing to promote the economic aspects—rather than the ideological ones—of the Chongqing model to domestic and international audiences. He has been successful: Cui's key article on the Chongqing model was published in one of China's top ideological journals: the *Journal of the Central Party School*, and China's main newsweekly, *Outlook* (*Liaowang*), ran a special issue on the Chongqing model, as did the American academic journal *Modern China*.[57]

But, as Bo's high-profile fall from the CCP leadership demonstrates, there is trouble in Chongqing. Cui stresses how the city's policies are "complementary and mutually reinforcing," producing a virtuous cycle that benefits urban and rural, public and private, and foreign and domestic. But the inner workings of the Chongqing model, which were revealed only after Bo's removal, actually show a vicious cycle at work. It turns out that Chongqing's generous social welfare programs were funded by a massive public debt that will soon come due.[58] Moreover, a major source of state-owned assets' spectacular growth was property seized in the anti-mafia campaign. As Australian journalist John Garnaut's investigative reporting shows, Bo Xilai's strike-hard crackdown missed Chongqing's chief mafia boss, who was an integral part of the Chongqing system. As the head of one of the city's public companies, the Chongqing International Trust, he received "billions of yuan in seized gangster assets, including the Hilton Hotel."[59] The anti-mafia campaign thus simply replaced one mafia with another that was more loyal to Bo Xilai. This leads Chinese critics to see Chongqing as a dark version of their country's future: China as a mafia-state.[60]

Still, it's not clear whether the Chongqing model will suffer the same fate as Bo Xilai. Its egalitarian policies continue to draw both elite and mass support. Either way, the experience of the Chongqing model shows the conditional status of "models" in China: The rise and fall of a model is dependent on the messy personal politics of its elite suppporters.

To summarize, Cui's Chongqing model seeks to create a Third Way that transcends Left/Right ideology by balancing the public and private sectors and integrating state planning and the free market. His goal is the economic convergence of both China's rural and urban populations and its interior and coastal regions. Politically, the Chongqing model is diverging from the West, like Pan's China model. Yet, unlike Pan's *sheji* organic society that cherishes traditional family values, the Chongqing model sang red songs to promote "socialist spiritual civilization" for China's "socialist market economy." While Pan's China model is a unique alternative to Western liberal democracy and neoliberal capitalism, Cui is not really concerned with global politics: For him, the Chongqing model is an alternative *within* China. Cui's goal was to "nationalize" the Chongqing experience so that other cities, provinces, and regions could likewise successfully develop in a way that is "liveable, smooth flowing, green, safe, and healthy." While Cui is suspicious of the "universal values" of democracy and human rights, he certainly sees the universal significance of the Chongqing model. Although Bo Xilai is gone, many of the economic ideas of the Chongqing model remain influential.

From Political Economy to Wealth and Power

Our survey of the work of these four citizen intellectuals shows that at least four China models exist—not to mention other variations, such as the Wenzhou model, in which the private sector dominates the public sector, and the Guangdong model, which is more open to civil society, if not liberal democracy.

The analysis has also focused on people who are crafting an alternative to the West. Certainly, there are critics of the China model within the PRC. Yao Yang, who became the director of Peking University's China Center for Economic Research when Lin went to the World Bank, argued in *Foreign Affairs* that the present China model no longer works, even for the PRC; He concludes that "ultimately, there is no alternative to greater democratization if the CCP wishes to encourage economic growth and maintain social stability."[61]

Tsinghua University historian Qin Hui criticizes Lin's comparative advantage argument in saying that, in fact, China's real comparative advantage is "poor human rights"; yet, rather than exploiting this comparative advantage, Qin argues that economic advancement requires the protection of Chinese people's human rights, including the rights of workers and peasants.[62] Others look beyond Lin's critique of Mao's "great-leap strategy" to criticize China's recent "great leap forward mentality," which demands rapid and glorious achievements such as the PRC's high-speed rail network. This rush to greatness, they argue, has led to a rash of accidents, including a major train accident in 2011, as well as to broader social and environmental problems.[63]

Thus, many prominent citizen intellectuals are concerned that the China model's stress on the material factors of economic development is warping Chinese values into "money-worship." Shanghai historian Xu Jilin sees this as a problem of "wealth and power" discourse. He feels that since China already has arrived as an economic power, the main question should not be how can China accumulate more wealth and power; rather, it should be "what kind of civilizational values will it show the world?"[64] But unlike Pan, who looks to the exceptionalism of China's ancient values, Xu looks to the future, arguing that China needs to pursue the global mainstream universal values of liberal democracy, human rights, and social justice.

Among the China model's supporters and detractors, the key issues, however, remain the same: What is the proper relation between the government and the market, divergence and convergence, the China model and the Western model, and Chinese exceptionalism and universal values? Justin Yifu Lin's explanations of the China miracle generally lean toward the side of this

conceptual continuum that values the market, convergence, Western economics, and universal values—his goal is to move from developing to developed
economy and from state planning to a full market economy.

Hu, Pan, and Cui, however, see China's goal as a combination of government intervention and markets. These three citizen intellectuals are also much
more interested in political, cultural, and social explanations of China's success. Their explanations shift not just from developing to developed economy,
but also from economics, first to political economy and then to the search for
China's road to wealth and power.

Lin is critical of Mao's early heavy industrial strategy, which he calls the
"leap-forward strategy" after the failed Great Leap Forward mass movement.
He argues China's success started with the economic reforms of 1978. The other
three citizen intellectuals each date China's emergence as a great power to 1949 in
order to reclaim the experience of the PRC's first thirty years. Rather than criticizing Mao's leap-forward strategy, they see it as the secret of China's success.

Although these four citizen intellectuals differ about the past, there is a
consensus about China's long-term objective: Great Harmony (*datong*). Hu
and Pan specifically mention "Great Harmony World" as their goal for China
and the world. This utopian ideal, which comes from China's two millennia
old *Book of Rites* (*Liji*), describes a happy, conflict-free, organic society—which
will be considered in more detail in chapter 4. Lin, who brought a calligraphic
scroll of the Great Harmony passage with him to Washington, D.C., explains
that "it advocates a world in which everyone trusts each other, cares for others
and not only for himself.... This was my vision for the World Bank.... We try
to work on poverty reduction and promote sustainable growth."[65]

As for the near and medium term, all four citizen intellectuals share
concerns about China's leadership and succession. Since they credit China's
leaders with the great ideas that inspired economic success—from Deng's
pragmatic ideas for the PRC to Bo Xilai's radical ideas for Chongqing—they
wonder how China's political-economic success can continue after these
leaders move on (either to a better job, to jail, or to the grave). Discussing
the Chongqing model before Bo's demise, Philipp C. C. Huang asked: "The
Chongqing populace thus far has certainly benefited from having two leaders
who seem genuinely to have the people's interests at heart, but in the longer
view, the question must be raised: what happens in the absence of such exceptional leadership?" Like the citizen intellectuals, Huang argues that the CCP
must continue to follow its "mass line" policy, while wondering how China
can "find a way to develop institutionalized and genuinely powerful structures of popular supervision."[66]

An obvious answer to questions of leadership selection and public accountability is "liberal democracy." But Lin, Hu, Pan, and Cui all agree that democracy is the problem rather than the solution. Cui tells us that the CCP "is determined not to surrender to the competitive, multiparty system."[67] Pan is particularly defensive, seeing democracy as a conspiracy, a booby trap, that the West wants to use to enslave China. At times, China model discourse seems to boil down to Occidentalism: For China to be good, it needs to understand all Western things as "evil" (and all evil things as "Western").

As we can see, China's economic development and discussions of the China model both take place in a global context. It is not surprising that Western commentators called on China to use its massive foreign exchange reserves—over $3.3 trillion in 2012—to save world economy when the Great Recession started in 2008, and then to rescue the euro in 2011–2012. Beijing disappointed many when it refused to institute a Marshall Plan–style bailout. But President Hu Jintao responded in November 2008 that the best way for China to help the global economy was for the PRC to take care of its own economic situation, which is now Beijing's response whenever Western leaders come begging.

Yet, even the prospect of China aiding the West in this way fundamentally misunderstands how the global economy works: China's foreign exchange reserves exist only because of the large trade imbalance. Beijing can't "lend" the reserves to help Europe or America because that would undermine China's managed exchange rate regime, which helped to create the trade imbalances in the first place.

Hence, the three main issues that vex Western policymakers and opinion-makers—the exchange rate, the trade imbalance, and the political ramifications of China holding Western sovereign debt—are all interlinked.[68] Most warnings of an impending trade war focus on Beijing versus Washington: Paul Krugman's biting commentaries in the *New York Times* frame the currency issue as a Sino-American problem. Yet, the problem is much broader; Beijing's management of the U.S. dollar/Chinese yuan exchange rate impacts other countries' exchange rates and trade balances as well. Britain's pound sterling and the euro are also inflated. Even Beijing's BRIC* ally Brazil now complains about Beijing's unfair economic policies. Southeast Asian countries likewise are worried about their own growing trade imbalances with China. As a *New York Times* editorial declared: The China model may be good for the PRC, but "it isn't working for anyone else."[69]

---

* Brazil, Russia, India, and China.

China's citizen intellectuals present two scenarios for solving global economic imbalances. If Beijing achieves the targets set in the 12FYP, then it will be able to move to an economy that is less dependent on foreign exports and investment to one that is driven more by domestic consumer demand. In this scenario, it would be in China's interest to let the renminbi float on the international currency market. A sudden liberalization of China's currency would likely lead to depreciation as wealthy Chinese try to get their money out of the PRC to safe havens. But the renminbi would soon rise, allowing the Chinese people to purchase more imports, thus balancing international trade. A tradable renminbi would internationalize China's currency, one of Beijing's policy goals. Once the renminbi rose in value, China's GDP would rise in value as well, thus hastening China's emergence as the number one economy in the world.

The trick is to move from the export-led model to a domestic consumption-led model; all of the economists and political scientists see this as their goal. None is very clear about how China will achieve it; Beijing tried to switch to a domestic demand economy during the 11FYP, but it was unsuccessful, largely because vested interests (banks, SOEs, the military, planning bureaucracies, coastal provinces, etc.) slowed the reforms. *China 2030*, a report jointly written by the Chinese government and the World Bank and supported by Justin Yifu Lin, endorses this shift to a new economic model that relies more on the service sector and domestic consumption.[70] There is much hope that the new leadership will push through the necessary economic reforms—but it will be difficult.

In the other scenario, China will continue to muddle through without making the major structural reforms necessary for building a high-tech industrial economy and service economy. Part of the muddling through is to have a gradual appreciation of the renminbi, while still under Beijing's control. From this Chinese perspective, Chinese policy is not the problem—it is American and European policies that need to be changed. Lin makes this argument in the appendix to *Demystifying the Chinese Economy* (2012). He tells us it is a mistake to blame East Asian countries' export-led growth strategy or China's foreign exchange management policy. Global imbalances come from American problems: the U.S. dollar as the global reserve currency, poor financial policy regulation, and the Federal Reserve's low interest rate policy, which encouraged bubbles in housing and equity markets. Lin's "win-win solution for a global recovery" is to dethrone the dollar as the global reserve currency and change the rules of global economic governance. Unfortunately, he does not give many details of his plan. As these citizen intellectuals show, little sympathy exists in China for the United States and Europe. They are seen as "rich countries" that are mismanaging the "blood and sweat money of the Chinese people" (slang for China's foreign exchange reserves).

Conclusion: China's Golden Age

One of the best descriptions of China's economic problems—and clearest advice on how to solve them—does not come from an economist. Chan Koonchung's science fiction novel about China's near future, *The Golden Age: China, 2013* (2009), provides a fascinating alternative scenario for the China model.[71] As we saw in the introduction, *Shengshi* is a classical term describing the height of Chinese civilization when the country enjoyed both wealth and power during the Han and Tang dynasties. Chan, who was born in Shanghai, grew up in Hong Kong, and now lives in Beijing, noticed that *Shengshi* was making a comeback in 2008 as a way of describing the PRC's growing prosperity, power—and confidence. The English translation of the title, *The Fat Years*, conjures images of crass materialistic excess. But it really doesn't capture the moral sense of *Shengshi*: China here is not simply wealthy; it is morally *good*, an example of a virtuous society, economy, and polity.

Chan's *The Golden Age* is a fascinating mix of fact and fiction that reproduces many of the arguments about the China model popular among citizen intellectuals over the past few years. Published in Hong Kong, it is officially banned on the mainland. Yet, the book filtered through China's various restrictions to become an underground bestseller, and it really took off when a free digital version appeared on the Internet. On her popular blog, a mainland journalist gushed: "Starting from today, I have no friends and I have no enemies. I now divide people into two categories—those who have read *The Golden Age* and those who haven't."[72]

The novel starts by following the Taiwanese writer Chen, whose greater China experience seems remarkably similar to Chan's, as he goes to a reception for the Chinese literary magazine *Reading* (*Dushu*), which, in fact, really is China's top intellectual journal. Chen remarks at how happy and satisfied everyone is in 2013: "Now everyone's saying there's no country in the world as good as China."[73] (By the end of the story we find out that this overwhelming sense of contentment is too good to be true: The party-state has been secretly drugging the entire population of China—except the elite leadership—much like in Aldous Huxley's *Brave New World*.)

In *The Golden Age*'s blissfully conflict-free society, which is much like the World of Great Harmony envisioned by Pan Wei, there are no citizen intellectuals; critics have been either bought off with generous research grants or totally marginalized as dissidents. This scene is indicative of the novel's surreal quality for Chinese readers: It describes familiar places (and even familiar people), but with strange twists. Since, in the story, Starbucks has been bought out by the Wantwant China Group, Chen drinks their new signature tea: Lychee Black Dragon Latté.

Not only is China the most prosperous country in the world; the West, especially the United States, is caught in a deep downward spiral of stagflation. In a section of the novel called "The China Model," a high-ranking party official named He Dongsheng describes how the CCP used its top-secret "Action Plan for Achieving Prosperity amid Crisis" to save China from economic and political disaster. Although this novel was published in 2009, we should note that China's 12th Five-Year Plan (2011) contains a long chapter on setting up an "Emergency Response System." 12FYP's goal is not just natural disaster relief; its new focus on "social management" means that it is designed to address what the party-state sees as possible social and political disasters.[74]

Back in *The Golden Age* a fictional second global economic crisis erupts in early 2011 when the U.S. dollar loses one-third of its value overnight. The He Dongsheng character explains how Beijing's secret "Action Plan" created prosperity in China amidst this global chaos through five economic policies.

The party-state's first policy, He explains, was to radically restructure the Chinese economy from export-oriented production to domestic consumption. To do this, Beijing instructed China's banks to convert 25 percent of all savings accounts into vouchers that are valid only for purchasing Chinese goods and services. One-third of these vouchers had to be spent in the first ninety days and the remaining two-thirds within six months. After six months, the vouchers would be worthless. Thus, in one fell swoop, the party-state was able to solve China's twin problems of "excessive savings" and a weak domestic market by jump-starting domestic consumer demand. In ways reminiscent of the Chongqing model, He tells us that this experience shows the benefit of dictatorship in China because the policy employed "coercive measures of the sort Western countries would not dare dream of."[75]

The second policy was designed to stimulate production to satisfy China's new consumer demand. To do this, Beijing repealed "over three thousand regulations governing the manufacturing and service sectors, making it easier for private capital to invest in business." While Beijing's response to the first economic crisis in 2008 entailed the "advance of the state sector, retreat of the private sector," *The Golden Age's* deregulation policy is described as the "retreat of the state sector, advance of the private sector." China's export-production hubs were able to quickly retool to produce for domestic consumers, transforming the economy in six months. This shift from the export market to the domestic market had the added benefit of solving China's unemployment problem.

In other words, what two official Five-Year Plans failed to accomplish, the Action Plan's "extremely effective" policies were able to do in only half a year. "The Chinese people," He proudly tells us, "just give them a chance to do something and they can make a great success of it."[76]

The first two policies deal with China's urban industrial economy. The third policy addresses rural issues because peasants are seen as the top source of social instability in China, either as the floating population of migrant workers or as the victims of land-grabbing local officials and property developers. The Action Plan's third policy is "to enhance peasants' property rights to their farmland." When peasants are busy taking care of their property, He reasons, they will no longer protest against the government. He quickly moves on to the fictional Action Plan's fourth policy: a crackdown on (1) official corruption, (2) manufacturing unsafe products, and (3) spreading misinformation. Once Party Central has taken full control of China's economy and society, it is able to put the fear of God into everyone—including the CCP's local cadres.[77]

The Action Plan's last policy, according to He, is its most controversial: price controls. He gives a long lecture on economic history to show that Western countries—including Nazi Germany—have implemented price controls in times of crisis. The market fundamentalism of the Chicago School of economics thus is the exception rather than the rule of economic policymaking, he tells us. Like many of this chapter's citizen intellectuals, He argues that it is perfectly rational to combine capitalism and a planned economy: Price controls make the real prices transparent, and thus they discourage profiteering. Luckily for him, the older generation of cadres did not question the price control policy because they had fond memories of China's socialist command economy. The key, for He, is timing: Party Central "needed to relinquish control at just the right time"—which, in the novel anyway, it did. China's success—and the rest of the world's failure—is proof that the country is on the right track.[78]

While Pan Wei criticizes those who call China "authoritarian," He Dongsheng unapologetically describes how China was able to create prosperity and stability amid chaos because of its own unique dictatorial system: "In the world today…China is the only country that could accomplish all five of these policy chances at the same time."

The Golden Age's five fictional policies are interesting because they deal with many of the issues raised by economists and political scientists in this chapter: the correct balance of the state and the private sector, the shift from an export-oriented economy to one driven by domestic consumption, rural land policy, the value of traditional Chinese culture, and so on. But these five fictional economic policies are actually the final phase of China's "Action Plan for Achieving Prosperity amid Crisis." The first two phases are much less attractive: phase one is anarchy, and phase two is a broad ruthless crackdown.

How does one plan anarchy, you may ask. Carefully, would be He Dongshang's answer. When the collapse of the U.S. dollar sparked the second global economic crisis in 2011, Beijing saw that trouble was in store for China as well. Just as in 2008, factories that produced exports quickly closed, throwing many people out of work and provoking a steep decline in China's stock market. Unrest was brewing in the cities, but rather than take control of the streets, Party Central ordered China's police and army to stay in the barracks. Fear, hoarding, and anarchy grew for seven days. But the security forces waited until wide-scale riots erupted on the eighth day to step in to restore order. When the PLA finally marched in to take control of more than 600 key cities, soldiers "were welcomed with open arms by the local population"—as expected according to the Action Plan. As He explains, "Only a major crisis could induce the ordinary Chinese people to accept willingly a huge government dictatorship."[79]

The party-state thus was able to turn the danger of global economic crisis into an opportunity to reestablish centralized control of the country. *The Golden Age*'s He Dongsheng follows China model theorist Pan Wei to justify his own organic conflict-free society with classical Chinese concepts: He's pet name for the emergency plan is "Action Plan for Ordering the Country and Pacifying the World," which comes from a famous passage in the Confucian classic, the "Doctrine of the Mean" (*Zhongyong*).

But curiously, to explain his ruthless plan He keeps returning to Western examples and European political theory. In a section called "The Chinese Leviathan," the novel offers a long discussion of Thomas Hobbes's landmark work *Leviathan* (1651), which was written during the English civil war. He looks to this Western classic to explain Chinese people's collective fear of chaos and acceptance of totalitarian order. He explains that when offered the Hobbesian choice between anarchy's "war of all against all" and the order of absolute dictatorship, the Chinese people always pick the Leviathan: "The machinery of the state was waiting for the people of the entire nation once again to voluntarily and wholeheartedly give themselves into the care of the Leviathan."[80] Against his critics who argue that there are preferable options between widespread chaos and total order, He agrees with the China model theorists who tell us that the iron rule of the CCP is the only path for China.

After the military took control of the cities, the second phase of the "Action Plan for Achieving Prosperity amid Crisis" kicked in: the violent crackdown. This crackdown targeted anyone who didn't fit it; thousands were arrested, tried, convicted, and executed—often on the same day—simply because they were at the wrong place at the wrong time. Whenever China faces economic crisis, such as in 1983 and 1989, He explains that it needs a political crackdown to assert complete control over society. The minimal resistance to the Action Plan's five economic policies, for He, confirms the utility of political violence. While the five fictional economic policies entail the "retreat of the state and the advance of the private sector," the Action Plan's two political policies show that Party Central is not willing to allow a "retreat of the state" in terms of political power. He thus tells us that democratic reform will lead to chaos.

Stability is the number one priority, He explains. But the ultimate goal is for China to accomplish "big things" (*dashi*), such as the Olympics, the Shanghai Expo 2010, China's first space walk, and the high-speed rail network. Recall that such "big things" were celebrated in the introduction to Beijing's 12FYP, and they are at the heart of China's debate over the "great leap forward mentality." According to *The Golden Age*, to accomplish such grand feats, China needs a strong party-state; He explains that the violence of the Action Plan's anarchy and crackdown is the inevitable cost of China's economic and social "progress."[81]

Chan's China model sounds much like the Chongqing model, whose magnificent economic success depended on a harsh crackdown on organized crime and a few corrupt officials, on the one hand, and the massive red culture propaganda campaign on the other. The reaction to *The Golden Age* among Chinese readers is also interesting. Liberals certainly saw it as a harsh critique of China's Leviathan, the CCP, thus confirming the necessity of political reform. But others had a different reaction: A friend who is a Chinese-language teacher read the whole novel in one night and wondered why it was banned at all. She took the necessity of strong state power for granted, and she was happy with China's growing prosperity and what *The Golden Age* calls "90% freedom." The China model, for her, was a success; and China's *Shengshi* age of peace and prosperity certainly is preferable to the economic crises that continue to dog Beijing's political critics in the West.

Still, *The Golden Age*'s story of China's rise doesn't just depend on the fall of the United States. As Chan's novel narrates, China's economic golden age depends upon chaos and state violence in China as well. This is certainly an argument for the utility of creative destruction for developing China's wealth and power.

But since *Shengshi* ideally describes a virtuous kind of prosperity, we have to ask: Does the China model present a superior model of moral order as well?

4

Cosmopolitan, Fundamentalist, and Racialist Dreams

HOW TO GET wealth and power is the main issue in China. But this is not merely an economic concern. The issue of wealth and power, as we saw in chapter 3, infuses all other aspects of Chinese life in the 21st century. The goal of catching up to and surpassing the United States motivates not only the developmental economists Justin Yifu Lin and Hu Angang. In chapter 2, we also saw how it also motivates military strategists: Senior Colonel Liu Mingfu likewise dreamed of China's 21st century destiny according to Mao Zedong's "leap-forward strategy" to surpass the United States.

This diverse group of citizen intellectuals exhibits what can be called a "catch-up mentality." They measure China's success in terms of accepted international standards: GDP, human development index, steel production, Transparency International, foreign futurologists, and so on. The catch-up mentality is permeated by status anxiety, sees international politics as a competition between great powers, and crafts familiar strategies of national development (for the economists) and "peace through strength" (for the strategists) to build the PRC's international stature. Although Liu's martial dream of China's future and Hu's "great reversal" of the world economic order may sound disturbing, in another way they are familiar: Liu and Hu actually are arguing for the convergence strategy in which China beats the West at its own geopolitical and geoeconomic game.

Alongside this catch-up mentality there is a "new era mentality" that stresses China's uniqueness, superiority, and exceptionalism. Liu repeatedly tells us that China's rise cannot be a copy of the experience of the Western great powers; Hu and Pan Wei argue that the People's Republic of China's (PRC) success thus must be judged according to Chinese characteristics and Oriental civilization because China is fundamentally different from the West. Against what Liu sees as Western fears that China's rise is the new "yellow peril," he argues that we are entering the new "Yellow-Fortune Era" that heralds the rejuvenation of the Chinese nation to what he sees as its natural place at the center of global politics.[1] Rather than a security dilemma, geopolitics here is an identity dilemma of competing civilizational models.

But this is more than the standard culturalist argument that we saw in Pan's China model. Liu's Yellow-Fortune Era highlights the georacial politics of what could be called "yellow supremacism"; he stresses that the Chinese "race" is the "most excellent race," the "superior race," that is "even better than the white race."[2] He Dongsheng, the high-ranking official in Chan Koonchung's novel *The Golden Age*, likewise argues that China's strategic goal should be to create a "new world order...a new post-Western, post-white era."[3]

How are we to understand such statements? Do they represent a minority view in the PRC, which sees itself as an inclusive and tolerant multiethnic nation? Or are they evidence of an enduring problem in China? As a Chinese-American blogger has asked: "Are Chinese racist or simply politically incorrect?"[4]

As we will explore in more detail below, Liu is actually quoting revolutionary leader Sun Yatsen (1886–1925), the Father of Modern China, who was fighting against the Western anti-Chinese racism that was prevalent in the late 19th and early 20th centuries. The Chinese Exclusion Acts (1882–1943), which used racialist arguments to prohibit ethnic Chinese from immigrating to the United States, is a case in point; the U.S. Senate apologized for this racist policy only in 2011.[5]

According to its constitution, the PRC is a "multinational nation-state" that includes both Han Chinese and fifty-five officially recognized national minority groups. Beijing has generous affirmative action–like policies that benefit non-Han Chinese minority groups such as Mongolians, Tibetans, and Uighurs. Thus, in 1988 CCP general secretary Zhao Ziyang—the liberal leader who was put under house arrest after he tried to negotiate with student demonstrators in 1989—famously declared that racial discrimination is common "everywhere in the world except China."

But is tolerance Chinese exceptionalism's guiding value, as citizen intellectuals ranging from Zhao Tingyang to Pan Wei argue? China's racial harmony was tested in 2009 on the DragonTV network's *Go! Oriental Angel* program, the Chinese version of *American Idol*: one of the contestants was Lou Jing, a young woman whose mother is Han Chinese and father is African American.

FIGURE 4.1 Lou Jing and her mother at *Go! Oriental Angel*
Source: AllVoices

Lou's mixed-race background was a media phenomenon in the PRC, making many people—including Lou herself—wonder just what it means to be "Chinese."

Individual Chinese express a wide range of attitudes about race; the TV program thus sparked a spirited debate in the Chinese blogosphere. Some of China's netizens were cosmopolitan, declaring that "love conquers all" and commending Lou's mother for her bravery in bringing up Lou alone. (Lou's father returned to the United States before she was born.) The phenomenon could even be seen as progressive: DragonTV certainly chose Lou as a contestant because she was a different kind of Chinese (we should remember that until the 1970s black women were not allowed to compete in the Miss America pageant).

But many other netizens understood Lou, and blacks in general, in starkly racist terms: Lou was called a "black chimpanzee," a "zebra," whose mixed Chinese and black parentage was an ugly "mistake." One netizen stated that it is "common knowledge" that "mixing yellow people and black people together is very gross." Others cursed Lou's mother as a "shameless bitch" and her father as a "black devil" who "after fucking ran back to his home in Africa." While recognizing that the fascination with "foreigners is indeed a fad," one person reminded Lou's mother that "you still can't pick blacks!"

In a statement posted on the Internet, Lou tearfully replied that

1. My father is American, not African.
2. I am a born and bred Shanghainese person.
3. I should not have to bear my parents' mistake, I am innocent!
4. I sternly but strongly protest some people's racism, my skin color should not become a target of attack!

Lou finished her statement by "reserving the right to take legal action!"[6]

Although China's official documents and public intellectuals see racial discrimination as a Western problem, Lou's experience shows how race is an issue in the People's Republic of China. Many people in China and the West argue that racism is something new in China—another lamentable legacy of Western imperialism. Yet Dutch Sinologist Frank Dikötter's *The Discourse of Race in China* (1992) does an excellent job of tracing how race-like ideas have informed Chinese identity and politics for thousands of years.[7]

Dikötter's research is interesting and helpful because, from the very beginning, he is clear that the "race" category itself is highly problematic. It is based on the pseudo-scientific argument that skin pigmentation defines all other aspects of one's life: intelligence, morality, physical strength, and so on. The problem with discussing "race," according to British sociologist Paul Gilroy, is that it is "fissile material" that not only is explosive, but also radioactive. Even those who seek to critically discuss "raciology"—the science/ideology of race—risk contamination, and they even run the risk of being denounced as "racists" themselves. Because the topic is so problematic, Gilroy advises us to stop thinking in terms of "race" in order to pursue freedom, democracy, and justice through "planetary humanism."[8]

While sympathetic to Gilroy's arguments—even more so as a "white man" writing about race discourse in China—I feel that it is necessary to consider how China's raciology shapes broader issues in the PRC—especially since Chinese intellectuals are so deafeningly silent on this issue.

To put it another way, Lou Jing's uncomfortable situation can tell us about more than racial politics in China. Her mix of Chinese and black parents and Liu Mingfu's mix of internationalist and racialist arguments both show the tension between fundamentalism and cosmopolitanism that characterizes China's dreams of the future. With its economic success, China does not just "go out" to the world; the world's citizens are increasingly coming into China. We usually think of mixed-race in terms of Chinese/Caucasian children, but the southern metropolis of Guangzhou (Canton) hosts Asia's largest community of Africans; more than 300,000 Africans live in a neighborhood that Chinese call "Chocolate City." Alongside Shanghai's countless multinational corporations, there are more than 3,000 mixed-race marriages every year. The story of foreign multinational corporations opening offices in China is a familiar part of our understanding of Beijing's economic reform program. The growth of mixed-race marriages has been equally dramatic, especially when we realize that Deng Xiaoping had to personally approve the first such marriage after the Cultural Revolution.[9] Most Chinese take their identity as self-evident: They are the descendants of 5,000 years of civilization. However, the recent influx of foreigners from the West, Asia, and Africa is challenging what it means to be Chinese.[10]

In the last chapter, we looked at the contest between the China model and the Western model in terms of the tension between (Chinese) exceptionalism and (Western) universal values. The tension between fundamentalism and cosmopolitanism works in similar ways. We usually see them as complete opposites: fundamentalism as an inward-looking, pure, and exclusive idea of community and cosmopolitanism as an outward-looking, nonexclusive ideal of humanity. But here I will show how they are intimately intertwined in China, often in peculiar ways to create patriotic cosmopolitans and global fundamentalists. We will also see how the grand ideals of Chinese "civilization" can be reworked into the daily practices of democratic "civility."

Previous chapters have offered grand geopolitical and geoeconomic scenarios that chart China's future and its impact on the world. This chapter, however, will consider citizen intellectuals' plans for the future in terms of a specific people-to-people scenario, asking "where does Lou Jing fit into their ideal worlds?"

Chinese Fundamentalism (I): Race-Nation

Fundamentalism takes many forms. In the last chapter, we saw Justin Yifu Lin and Hu Angang criticize the "market fundamentalism" of the Washington Consensus. Here fundamentalism means that the market—rather than the state—is the ultimate arbiter of value—and even truth. They cogently argued that this kind of fundamentalism was inappropriate for China, and that it had warped the European and American economies as well.

With the "War on Terror," we are used to understanding fundamentalism in terms of the religious beliefs of Islamic and Christian fundamentalists. But in China fundamentalism is a question of exceptionalist identity: an essentially unique, fixed, separate, and pure entity called the "Chinese race" (*Zhonghua minzu*) that needs to be defended against impurities both local—e.g., mixed marriages—and global, in the sense of Pan Wei's grand battle between the Chinese model and the Western model.

Sun Yatsen's *Three People's Principles*—nationalism, people's livelihood, and democracy—inform the work of many citizen intellectuals in the 21st century: Sun's idea of "people's livelihood" actually inspired Pan Wei's and Cui Zhiyuan's dreams of China's future prosperity that were examined in chapter 3. Sun's idea of democracy likewise inspires many liberals in China.

Yet, as mentioned above, Liu Mingfu's ideas about China as a "race-nation" (*minzu*) also come from Sun Yatsen. Hence, it is helpful to examine Sun's racial ideas because they were indicative of how Chinese intellectuals—and elites around the world—thought about politics and community in the early 20th century. In the "First Lecture on Nationalism" that opens Sun's magnum opus the *Three People's Principles* (1924), he states that China has uniquely "developed a single state out of a single race." The Chinese race here is defined by five factors: blood kinship, common language, common livelihood, common religion, and common habits. But for Sun, the key factor for China is common blood: "The greatest force is blood. The Chinese belong to the yellow race because they come from the bloodstock of the yellow race. The blood of ancestors is transmitted down through the race, making blood kinship a powerful force."

When Sun made these statements, China was in disarray, divided by powerful warlords and foreign imperialists. Sun therefore stressed that if China's leaders didn't promote nationalism, the country would face a national tragedy: "the loss of our country and the extinction of our race." The Chinese race-nation thus was understood as a biological organism that was united by a common origin and a pure continuous bloodline. It was strong for thousands of years, but in modern times China had become the world's "weakest and poorest" race-nation, which faced life-threatening challenges.[11]

Sun's idea of the Chinese race-nation, which as Liu Mingfu's discussion shows is still popular today, is the product of China's long transition from empire to nation-state. The idea of race became popular in China at the end of the 19th century as a way of uniting and mobilizing the Chinese people, first, against the Manchurian rulers of the Qing empire, who were seen as "internal foreigners," and, then, against European imperialists, who were seen as "external foreigners." In the turmoil at the turn of the 20th century—Japan's humiliating defeat of China (1895), the failed 100 Days Reform movement (1898), and the Boxer Uprising (1900)—Chinese intellectuals shifted the way they defined "China" from the traditional cultural distinction of "civilization" to a new biological distinction of the "Chinese race" (*Zhonghua minzu*) and the "yellow race" (*huangzhong*). Thus, their goal changed from "protecting Confucian tradition" to "protecting the Chinese nation."[12]

Minzu is commonly translated as "nation," as in the "Chinese nation." But the meaning of this term, which became popular at the turn of the 20th century, is quite broad and ambiguous, ranging from ethnicity to nation to race. In all these variations, Chinese identity is understood as pure, unique, ancient, and superior. (Nationalism in Japan and Korea takes similar forms; blood kinship is even more precise in Japan, where identity is subdivided according to blood type.) In its racial nationalist form, Chinese identity is part of a hierarchy, with Han Chinese at the top and blacks at the bottom: Intellectuals commonly spoke of the "black slave race" until the 1920s, and Africans are still colloquially called "black devils" in southern China.

Chinese identity here is based on genetic heritage rather than cultural heritage. While Sun Yatsen is the "Father of the Country" in China, the Yellow Emperor (Huangdi, c. 2600 BC) was reinterpreted in the 20th century to be the Father of the Yellow Race. According to China's official Xinhua news agency, the Yellow Emperor is "credited with introducing the systems of government and law to humankind, civilizing the Earth, teaching people many skills and inventing all manner of items."[13]

Before the 20th century, the Yellow Emperor was an imperial symbol, China's first sage king whose tribe settled the Yellow River valley, the cradle of Chinese civilization, in the third millennium BC. Starting in the Ming dynasty (1368–1644), Chinese emperors sought dynastic legitimacy by sponsoring sacrifices and inscribing eulogies at the Yellow Emperor's tomb in northern China's Shaanxi Province. In the 20th century, China's top three political leaders—Sun Yatsen, Chiang Kai-shek, and Mao Zedong—all continued this tradition, except their goal was to gain legitimacy for their rule of the Chinese race-nation.

The Yellow Emperor is a unifying symbol because he combines cultural and racial identity. Sun's eulogy at the tomb is "Among all the civilizations in the world, ours is the best,"[14] and Chinese people around the world see themselves as "descendents of the Yellow Emperor." Since the CCP instituted its patriotic education campaign in the 1990s, the PRC's top leaders have gone on pilgrimages to the tomb of the Yellow Emperor. In 2009, Ma Ying-jeou became the first Taiwanese president to pay homage to the Yellow Emperor in a ceremony at Taipei's Martyrs' Shrine, thus demonstrating his "commitment to maintain an umbilical relationship between Taiwan and the People's Republic."[15]

But this is not simply a cultural ritual; it reaffirms shared blood ties and the importance of preserving the "yellow race." Even China's liberals, such as the now-exiled Su Xiaokang, take such racial discourse for granted. Su's critically acclaimed popular television series *River Elegy* (*Heshang*, 1988) begins by proclaiming,

> This yellow river, it so happens, bred a nation identified by its yellow skin pigment. Moreover, this nation also refers to its earliest ancestor as the Yellow Emperor. Today, on the face of the earth, of every five human beings, there is one who is a descendent of the Yellow Emperor.[16]

Thus, Chinese are Chinese by virtue of their skin color and their pure bloodline. Although racial discourse comes from pseudo-science in the West, "racial discourse thrived" in China, Dikötter concludes, because it resonated with "folk models of identity, based on patrilineal descent and common stock."[17]

In the 1930s, these folk models of identity were given scientific legitimacy in China through the new disciplines of archaeology, anthropology, and paleoanthropology. The Peking Man was unearthed in 1929, and, since then, the origins of Chinese civilization—and the Chinese race—have been pushed back from 5,000 years to several million years. Against international mainstream views of human development that argue that *Homo sapiens* emerged from Africa, the mainstream view in China is that the Chinese race emerged separately from the rest of humanity. Here Sinocentrism takes on a racial character in a biological division between Chinese and non-Chinese, yellow and non-yellow. This view, which has little support outside China, is promoted by the PRC government through key state-funded research projects that are tasked with building a unique and pure "Chinese school of archaeology." Rather than explore the origins of humanity as a whole, this project promotes China as the exceptionalist "homeland for the yellow race."[18]

The goal of this appeal to the Yellow Emperor and Peking Man is to legitimate the current regime (whichever regime that is) as the natural successor to thousands—or millions—of years of cultural, political, and racial continuity. These two figures are the founding heroes of a genealogy that directly connects today's rulers with sage kings from ancient history and race-nation progenitors from prehistory. The most interesting continuity here, however, is not between Peking Man and the Yellow Emperor but between officials and public intellectuals in Qing dynasty, the Republic of China and now the PRC, all of which have used racial discourse "to construct a myth of national belonging deeply rooted in the perception of a common history, soil and blood."[19]

China's netizens' harsh comments about Lou Jing (and her mother) thus follow the PRC's mainstream raciology: Lou is problematic first because she is "black" and then because mixed-race children are seen as compromising the "purity" of the Chinese race-nation.

Chinese Fundamentalism (II): Race-State

The controversy surrounding the Chinese school of archaeology graphically shows how racial discourse does not work in a vacuum referring only to insiders, whether they are "white supremacists" in America or the Yellow Emperor in China. These raciological discussions typically concern struggles between different races in a hierarchical world system. The Chinese school of archaeology's Chinese fossils thus struggle against African fossils to prove that the Chinese race-nation has its own pure, ancient, and unique genealogical line. The discourse of race in China is part of the broader social Darwinist movement that was popular in the West from the late 19th century through to the 1930s: The main issue is not racial difference but racial competition. Here we move from ideas of the origin and descent of the race-nation to the life-or-death struggles between race-states (*guozu*).

The main promoter of social Darwinism was Yan Fu, the citizen intellectual from the turn of the 20th century who translated key European philosophical, economic, and sociological texts into Chinese. In the last chapter, we saw how Yan's translation of Adam Smith's *The Wealth of Nations* (1776) created the field of political economy in China. After the shock of Japan's defeat of China in 1895, Yan became fascinated with Herbert Spencer's application of Darwin's evolutionary principles to international society. Spencer's biological struggle demands that the race-state bolster its national health and national spirit to successfully compete with other race-states. International society here is recast as a hierarchy of races and international politics as "race war."

Social Darwinism's doctrine of survival of the fittest made sense to Yan Fu because its struggle between superior and inferior races resonated with traditional Sinocentrism, which saw superior Chinese civilization battling inferior barbarians.[20] In this fundamentalist hierarchy, the "black race" is the lowest, referring to China's historical neighbors (now called national minorities) and, later, to Africans, who were known as the "black slave race."

Yan concluded that social Darwinism was not just the best *description* of the struggle among societies; he also took the survival of the fittest of race-nations as his *normative* goal. His primary objective was to strengthen the Chinese race-state (against other race-states). He and other Chinese intellectuals felt that the yellow race was in a "perpetual state of war" against the "superior" white race and "inferior" red, brown, and black races.[21]

The stakes were high: as we saw in Sun Yatsen's *Three People's Principles*, the phrase "lose the country and extinguish the race" was popular to describe the risks faced by China. It is difficult to understand how one-fifth of humanity could be wiped off the face of the earth. Yet when we consider how Chinese intellectuals saw "racial extinction" in terms of the common problem of "lineage extinction"—the end of a clan when there is no male heir—their apocalyptic anxiety makes more sense.[22] The guiding idea of social Darwinism's struggle between race-nations helps to explain why, even in the 21st century, citizen intellectuals still see international politics as a life-or-death issue, where the Chinese race continues to risk extinction.

China's new leaders share this concern about "losing the country and extinguishing the race." While he was governor of Fujian province, Xi Jinping edited a book, *Science and Patriotism*, where he argues that "Today, Yan Fu's scientific and patriotic thought is still not out of date."[23]

The survival-of-the-fittest anxiety also motivates internal politics in China. The PRC divides its population into fifty-six official ethnic groups: the majority Han constitute 90 percent of China's population, while the fifty-five ethnic minorities, including Tibetans, Uighurs, and Mongolians, make up the remaining 10 percent. Since the 1950s, Beijing has implemented a progressive policy that grants affirmative action–style benefits to these ethnic minorities. Yet, in the past decade there has been a Han backlash (similar to the white backlash against affirmative action in the United States). Han supremacist groups have appeared, largely on the Internet, to fight for Han rights and even Han survival. This unofficial social movement takes odd forms: The main Han supremacist website emerged to promote pride in authentic Han clothing (as opposed to the Manchu garb that many (mis)take as "traditional Chinese"). But as historian James Leibold describes, this movement is sometimes violent and often very negative. Like Sun Yatsen and most Chinese nationalists, Han supremacists see blood as the most important marker of their identity. The group's more hard-core members "argue that the Manchu and other minorities are 'parasites' or 'garbage worms' looking to bore into the superior blood of the Han."[24]

If the Han are not careful, these conspiracy theorists tell us, their 1.2 billion strong ethnic group will disappear, slowly but surely to be assimilated by the "enemy within," namely the Manchus and other ethnic minority groups. Those Han who cooperate with this conspiracy are condemned as traitors, actualizing the common Chinese word for "traitor-*hanjian*," which more literally means "traitor to the Han."

While in Europe and America such social Darwinism is deeply discredited as antiscientific except among a fringe minority, in China it is still very popular. With this in mind, we can read the various meanings of Ren Yanfei's political cartoon "How much longer can America lead the world?," which is found at the beginning of Liu Mingfu's *The China Dream* (see fig. 4.2). On the face of it, the cartoon figures global politics as a marathon race between nation-states; China has just passed Germany and is quickly gaining on Japan and the United States. This Olympic competition thus marks how China's GDP passed Germany's in 2007 and how it would soon pass Japan to become the world's number two economy, which it did in July 2010. The cartoon exemplifies the "catch-up mentality," with China outcompeting its national rivals according to the global norm of international economic standards. The

FIGURE 4.2 "How much longer can America lead the world?"
Source: Ren Yanfei in *The China Dream*

cartoon thus drills home Liu Mingfu's message: China must "sprint to the finish" to be the "world number one" great power.

But Ren's cartoon also exhibits the "new era mentality" that sets China off as a uniquely healthy race-state that is outperforming weak foreigners: China has just passed a Germany that is balding and flabby. Japan is a sweaty blonde that frantically declares, "What is China eating to make it run so fast!" America is even more frazzled than Germany or Japan; although the U.S. economy is still nearly three times as large as the PRC's, China's rapid and determined approach makes America declare with fear and confusion, "My God, the Chinese are coming! The China threat is coming!"

If you think that this is an over-interpretation, then consider Chinese runner Liu Xiang's reaction when he won the 110-meter hurdle race at the Athens Olympics (2004): He declared that his victory "is a kind of miracle. It is unbelievable—a Chinese, an Asian, has won this event." Liu thus proclaimed that his Olympic victory "is a proud moment not only for China, but for Asia and all people who share the same yellow skin color."[25] This was not simply an adrenalin-fueled statement delivered in the heat of the moment. Similar statements were echoed in China's official press. A few weeks later, Liu's coach told Hong Kong's *Ta Kung Pao* newspaper that the runner's gold medal "shows that among athletes from the yellow race, some are top sprinters, who are able to beat black athletes."[26]

Such pop raciology is not uncommon in the West—but it is usually met with public condemnation. In China, Wang Meng, a former minister of culture, was one of the few to criticize Liu's racialist view of sports. China's netizens, however, responded to Wang with "a barrage of flaming retorts."[27] Hence, the lack of self-reflection and self-criticism among Chinese intellectuals is one of the defining features of the discourse of race in China.

Lou Jing would be excluded from this race-state.

Cosmopolitan Fundamentalism (I): Kang Youwei's Book of Great Harmony

Like fundamentalism, cosmopolitanism takes on many different shapes. Traditional cosmopolitanism, seen in ancient Greek philosophy and the work of Immanuel Kant, was a transcendent critique of the small-mindedness of local attachments. The goal was to see everyone around the globe as equal "world citizens," as Rousseau put it. In the past few decades, however, the focus of cosmopolitanism has shifted from the pursuit of equality to figuring out how different peoples can live together in productive harmony.

But when we look at prominent examples of cosmopolitanism in China, we see the limits of trying to find a single overarching definition because there is often a dynamic tension between fundamentalism and cosmopolitanism that joins these opposites together: patriotic cosmopolitanism and global fundamentalism, for example. In this section and the next section, I will compare two popular books that use "raciology" to plan a cosmopolitan world: Kang Youwei's *The Book of Great Harmony* (*Datongshu*) from the turn of the 20th century and Jiang Rong's *Wolf Totem* (*Lang tuteng*) from the early 21st century. Even more than with fundamentalism, we will see how China's cosmopolitans are constantly thinking of America as a resource for ideas—both good and bad—about cosmopolitan life.

The main source of Kang's ideal of Great Harmony is a famous passage from the two millennia old *Book of Rites* (*Liji*):

> When the Great Way prevails, the world will belong to all. They chose people of talent and ability whose words were sincere, and they cultivated harmony. Thus people did not only love their own parents, not only nurture their own children.... In this way selfish schemes did not arise. Robbers, thieves, rebels, and traitors had no place, and thus outer doors were not closed. This is called the Great Harmony (*datong*).[28]

Great Harmony thus describes an overarching unity: The "*tong*" in *datong* also means sameness. This sameness is seen as harmonious because it describes a universal Utopia.

The Great Harmony passage is one of Chinese philosophy's key visions of a perfect world. Kang's *Book of Great Harmony* is important because it revived this ancient concept and used it to solve the problems of modern society. In 1926, Guo Moruo continued this trend in his short story about Marx and Confucius discussing their shared utopian goal of Great Harmony.[29] Great Harmony still inspires utopian China dreams among citizen intellectuals in the 21st century; to get a sense of what they yearn for, it is necessary then to explore Kang's ideas in more detail.

Kang Youwei (1858–1927) is a fascinating figure who transcends his era. As we saw in the last chapter, China's top economic and political thinkers of today—Justin Yifu Lin, Hu Angang, and Pan Wei—all dream of the World of Great Harmony. As the direct descendent of thirteen generations of scholars, Kang was steeped in imperial Chinese tradition; after years of study, he passed the highest level of China's official examinations and took up a post in government.

FIGURE 4.3 Kang Youwei in America, 1908
Source: Library of Congress

But Kang was also an active citizen intellectual. In 1898, Kang was thrust into public life as the intellectual leader of China's 100 Days Reform movement. Because he had the Guangxu Emperor's ear, Kang actually became a practical politician, writing many of the laws that the reformers hoped would modernize Chinese society, much as the Meiji reforms had modernized imperial Japan. Yet after six months, the Empress Dowager Cixi seized control from the Guangxu Emperor, and she ordered the execution of many of Kang's fellow reformers. Escaping Beijing, Kang fled into exile; he traveled around Asia, Europe, and America for fifteen years. Kang returned to China only in 1913, after China's 1911 republican revolution.

While in exile, Kang kept gathering information and impressions about other countries and other systems; he finally finished *The Book of Great Harmony* in 1902 when he was in British India. But Kang never allowed the whole volume to be published. He felt that the ideas were "too advanced" for the time; Kang wouldn't let it be translated into English either. The book was finally published in 1935, eight years after his death.[30]

Although *The Book of Great Harmony* wasn't officially published in Kang's lifetime, it circulated like a *samizdat* among Chinese around the world as one of the most controversial books of the early 20th century. It is easy to see why Kang felt that it was "too advanced" for a general readership; it provides a detailed plan to radically transform the world for the common good. While

Pan Wei's China model presents a detailed plan that is inspired by China's traditional hierarchical society, and Zhao Tingyang's *The Under-Heaven System* gives a vaguely conservative sense of future possibilities, Kang's *The Book of Great Harmony* is both futuristic and radically egalitarian.

Surveying the world around him, Kang saw enormous human suffering. He explains that this suffering stems from inequality and division, and that the solution is equality and unity for all humans. Kang thus sees the boundaries that divide people as humanity's main problem; this division leads to fierce competition, which results in inequality, selfishness, and suffering. Kang proposes a plan to abolish all borders to create the One World of Great Harmony.

Kang starts this project by criticizing the territorial boundaries that have created competing nation-states, and he argues that after disarmament, states can build alliances with other states, eventually unifying first into grand federations and finally into a single unitary state. He takes the evolution of power in the United States as a positive example of this process: The individual states gradually allied to pool their power in a united federal government. Once nation-states are gone, Kang reasons, wars will cease. Kang was thus one of the first people to think about a single world government, and he anticipated regional organizations, such as the European Union, and international organizations, such as the United Nations.

But Kang does not stop with a world institution (as does Zhao Tingyang, as we saw in chapter 2). He thinks that abolishing territorial boundaries is just the start. In the balance of his book, Kang gives a detailed description of the problems created by the social and economic boundaries that divide classes, races, genders, families, and species. For each of these problems, he proposes a solution that will lead to total equality, freedom, independence, and, ultimately, "utmost happiness." Overcoming these divisions is a matter of principle: "Inequality is not only contrary to the universal principles of nature, but is actually detrimental to the progress of humanity."[31]

While Kang's contemporary Yan Fu reasoned that social Darwinism's "survival of the fittest" was both an accurate description of the world and a normative goal for global order, Kang felt that since human nature is essentially good, people should rise above their animal nature to cooperate rather than compete. Kang thus proposes ideas that were radical in 1902 and are still quite progressive today. They include equality between women and men, a cradle-to-grave welfare system, gay rights and gay marriage, economic equality, and so on. This is not a revolutionary program; according to Kang, over the next few centuries humanity will gradually evolve from the present "Era of Disorder," first, to the "Era of Increasing Peace-and-Equality," and, finally, to the "Era of Complete Peace-and-Equality."

But Kang's plan for the One World of Great Harmony runs into problems because he has such a hard time imagining racial equality. He agreed with other European and Chinese intellectuals that the world was divided into a hierarchical system of races: white, yellow, brown, and black. The "silver-colored race" and the "gold-colored race" are superior races for Kang because Europeans and Chinese have "occupied the whole world." To solve the problem of racial inequality, Kang doesn't propose that we value diversity or celebrate difference. Rather, he gives a detailed plan of how the white and yellow races can "annihilate" the black and brown races through a process of "smelting and amalgamating."

Following what he calls "natural evolution's theory of survival of the fittest," Kang is very Darwinian—if not Spencerian: Since white and yellow are the stronger races, he assumes that their essence will prevail in children from intermarriage with brown and black people. Kang is not espousing yellow supremacy: He thinks that the white race will eradicate the yellow race as well: "Before the One World has been perfected, the yellow people will already have amalgamated into white people."[32]

Kang is very optimistic about his plans for overcoming the other boundaries (territory, gender, class, etc.); however, he is pessimistic about abolishing racial boundaries because "the most difficult to amalgamate and smelt are the races of men which are completely different skin color." While whites and yellows can easily intermarry, "black people are a really difficult problem," Kang tells us, "owing to their extreme ugliness and stupidity." Thus, white and yellow people who "mate" with blacks should be awarded the "Benevolent Person" medal, the highest honor in Kang's One World of Great Harmony. After a thousand years or so, he reasons, blacks will be transformed into whites. As Kang writes with excitement and anticipation, "by the time we have our One World, the people of all the earth will be of the same color, the same appearance, the same size, and the same intelligence."[33]

Thus, Kang Youwei would have a clear plan for Lou Jing and her mother: He wouldn't worry too much about mixed-race children and would honor Lou's mother with a "Race Improver" award.

What is the cost of Kang's grand pursuit of equality? While he explains that Darwin's law of natural selection does not apply in his harmonious world, Kang does rely on a deeply problematic understanding of racial hierarchy. Like others at the time, he sees identity in terms of blood, lineage, and genealogy, and he even discusses the "Yellow Emperor race." Regardless of his flawed understanding of genetics, Kang's concept of equality is problematic because it sees equality in terms of sameness: recall that the "*tong*" in Great Harmony-*datong* means harmony—but it also means sameness. Yet this new purity of a fundamental "equality as sameness" leads to a grand genocidal plan to wipe out brown and black people, who, according to Kang, cannot enter the One World of Great Harmony.

When we go back and read *The Book of Great Harmony* with this in mind, we see that "equality as sameness" inspires his other solutions as well. The abolition of nation-state boundaries is not a bottom-up democratic process; rather, it is due to "natural selection, the swallowing up by the strong and large and the extermination of the weak and small may then be considered to presage One World." Kang solves the gender inequality problem by turning women into men: "clothing and ornaments should be the same for women and men."[34]

Perhaps I am demanding too much from a late-19th-century citizen intellectual, since racial equality was unthinkable for most people until recently. Kang had many radical ideas, but when it came to race he was a man of his time. But Kang's *The Book of Great Harmony* remains interesting because it graphically shows the tension between racialist fundamentalism and an idealistic cosmopolitanism that values equality, freedom, and independence. Kang's rancid raciology is not a quaint exception to his otherwise progressive plans for the future; it is an integral part of his cosmopolitan quest that seeks unity over diversity. Kang's book is also important because it has been very popular for over a century, inspiring each generation's reformers and revolutionaries, from Mao Zedong to Zhao Tingyang. What is curious is that few—if any—Chinese intellectuals offer a critical view of this Chinese-style Utopia's social Darwinistic plans for race annihilation, perhaps because in this global plan "yellows" are among the winners.

The Book of Great Harmony's enduring appeal also helps to explain the PRC's current ethnic policies that seek to meld non-Han ethnic groups, such as Tibetans and Uighurs, into the Han-dominated Chinese race-nation. It confirms that politics as a "racial struggle" is not seen as a problematic concept in China; rather, to many it is a self-evident fact.

Cosmopolitan Fundamentalism (II): Jiang Rong's Wolf Totem

Jiang Rong's novel, *Wolf Totem* (*Lang tuteng*, 2004) provides another example of how fundamentalism and cosmopolitanism can combine for a seemingly progressive project.[35] This fantastically successful book has sold more than

25 million copies since it was published in 2004, making it China's number two bestseller of all time—Mao Zedong's *Little Red Book* is number one. The novel is popular abroad as well: It has been translated into more than thirty languages, and its English edition won Britain's inaugural Man Asian Literary Prize in 2007.[36]

Wolf Totem is an autobiographical story about a Han Chinese student who leaves his intellectual family in Beijing to go to the grasslands of Inner Mongolia at the height of the Cultural Revolution. Chen Zhen, the main character, lives and works with nomadic Mongolians. As a shepherd, Chen becomes fascinated with wolves and the role they play in the local economy and culture of the grasslands. He is drawn to the wolves' strength, cunning, and ferocity, and he adopts a wolf pup to scientifically study how wolves think. But, in the end, Chen has to kill the pup because it can't be tamed to live among humans.

Wolf Totem is lauded for its environmentalist sensibility, especially among foreign critics; the Man Asian Literary Prize judges praised the novel for giving a "passionate argument about the complex interrelationship between nomads and settlers, animals and human beings, nature and culture." But *Wolf Totem*'s environmental message is wrapped up in a broader political message about China's national rejuvenation and international politics.

Actually, Jiang Rong is a pseudonym for Lü Jiamin, a political scientist who spent two years in jail for participating in the Tiananmen Square movement in 1989. He used a pseudonym because he feared that the party-state would censor his novel; in the 2000s, he was still prohibited—like Liu Xiaobo—from teaching and public speaking. In an interview with the *New York Times*, Jiang stressed that the Chinese needed to learn "freedom, independence, respect, unyielding before hardship, teamwork and competition" from the Mongolian nomads.[37] In the novel, Jiang stresses that his ultimate goals are freedom, democracy, and the rule of law.

This ideological program is detailed in the novel's sixty-four page appendix "Rational Exploration: A Lecture and Dialogue on the Wolf Totem," which is not included in the English translation.[38] While Chinese people generally fear wolves as forces of savage violence, *Wolf Totem* praises their ferocity, strength, and violence. Rather than seeing wolves as a problem that needs to be exterminated from the Mongolian grasslands, Jiang examines—in detail—how cultivating "wolf-nature" can aid China's future development.

Like many citizen intellectuals, Jiang stresses how "reform in China is not just about the transformation of the economic and the political system, but about the transformation of national character."[39] Many see Confucian civilization as the key to China's success; non-Han ethnic groups, whom Han supremacists characterize as "wild wolves of the frontier,"⁴⁰ are seen as even more of a threat than the cultural universals of Western "barbarians."

However, Jiang tells us that the Chinese people have been weakened over the centuries by a Confucian culture that only teaches them how to be followers. Rather than promote a China model, Jiang criticizes China's diseased mentality, which he calls the "China syndrome." Since "the root of the China syndrome is the sheep syndrome," he argues that the nomads' wolf-nature is the best model for China's national character. Thus, Jiang's argument is quite similar to Senior Colonel Liu Mingfu's in *The China Dream*, which sees Confucianism as a source of weakness, and which worries that without a strong "military rise" China risks being a "plump lamb" that militant countries might gobble up.⁴¹

To rejuvenate the Chinese race-nation, Jiang appeals to genealogy, bloodline, and social Darwinism's survival of the fittest. Here the Yellow Emperor is not the progenitor of the Chinese race-nation; rather, Jiang asserts that the Yellow Emperor is from a "nomadic race" from grasslands northwest of China. Because Han are soft and weak, Jiang explains, outsiders prey on them—just as wolves prey on sheep. He thus argues that, throughout history, fierce nomads from the North and the West have continually conquered and occupied China proper. This is not seen as a problem but rather as an important contribution to the greatness of the Chinese race. It is not simply a metaphor of nomadic cultural influence; one of Jiang's main arguments is that the soft "sheep-nature" of the Chinese race has been strengthened, again and again, through "transfusions" of nomads' ferocious blood.

Wolf Totem's revision of history explains why what Jiang calls the "Western race" was able to dominate China and become the most advanced civilization in the world. Europeans are ferocious, he explains, because they have wolves' blood from the same Inner Asian sources: Huns, Turks, and Mongols also attacked Europe. The Europeans' wolf-nature then was used to conquer Asia: "The Westerners who fought their way back to the East were all descendents of nomads.... The later Teutons, Germans, and Anglo-Saxons grew increasingly powerful, and the blood of wolves ran in their veins. The Han, with their weak dispositions, are in desperate need of a transfusion of that vigorous, unrestrained blood."⁴² As with nomadic Mongolians, Jiang revalues the "Western race" from "barbarian enemies" into "civilized wolves" who should serve as the model for China's national character.

Jiang's goal is to transform Han Chinese from being "civilized sheep," first, into "civilized wolves," and, finally, into "civilized humans" who have democracy and the rule of law. There are risks: "during World War II, the German, Italian and Japanese race-nations were unable to control their wolf-nature, thus fascism exploded causing a catastrophe both for those nations and for the world." Jiang cites the Red Guard's violent destruction during the Cultural Revolution as another example of unrestrained wolf-nature.

The main problem for Jiang is how to release and contain the power of what he calls the "thermonuclear reaction" of wolf-nature, whose ferocity not only can save a nation, but also can risk destroying the world. He argues that mixing wolf's and sheep's blood will produce the "modern Chinese civilized wolf," which is "a highly evolved 'world civilization people' that has an advanced level of liberal democracy."[43]

Rather than looking to international society's rules and norms, Jiang sees international relations as a series of social Darwinian race wars between wolf races and sheep races. In this racial struggle for the survival of the fittest, wolf-nature is worshiped for its strength, ferocity, and violence. This is an odd way to get to Jiang's goal of freedom, democracy, and the rule of law, and it provides a rather negative counterpart to *Wolf Totem*'s generally positive calls for environmental protection.

Jiang insists that his novel has a social democratic message. But the proof is in the pudding. The story's popularity in China comes from more than its nostalgic description of an exotic past; businesses and the military use *Wolf Totem* to train managers and officers in strategies for success in today's world of life-or-death struggles, and the Politburo has studied the book as a "significant work."

It's hard to say what Jiang would think of Lou Jing; since he likes Asian and Western "barbarians," it's likely that he would also see African blood as ferocious and applaud Lou's mother for adding a "transfusion" of vigorous foreign blood to the Chinese race.

Conclusion: Lung Ying-tai's Fundamentally Cosmopolitan World

Thus far all of this book's citizen intellectuals have been men. I will conclude the chapter by considering how a woman—Lung Ying-tai—creatively dreams of her own cosmopolitan world in a progressive and pragmatic way. Lung is interesting because she challenges exceptionalist ideas of Chinese civilization with the day-to-day practice of democratic "civility."

Lung was one of the people honored as a "China dreamer" by the *Southern Weekend* (*Nanfang zhoumo*) newspaper in August 2010; the other

FIGURE 4.4 Lung Ying-tai
Source: Courtesy of the University of Hong Kong

awardees were economist Wu Jinglian, artist Xu Bing, investigative journalist
Wang Keqin, actor John Woo, actor and director Jiang Wen, and diplomat
Wu Jianmin. Lung gave the keynote speech, "The Power of Civility: From
'Homesickness' to 'Formosa'" at a grand ceremony at Peking University.[44]

On the face of it, Lung was an odd choice for this prominent honor. She
was born in Taiwan into a family that had fled the mainland with the KMT
at the end of China's civil war. Although Lung is a famous cultural critic who
often writes for mainland newspapers, she is unpopular with the Beijing leadership: She committed the taboo of directly criticizing President Hu Jintao in
an open letter (2006), and her latest book, *Wide River, Big Sea: Untold Stories
of 1949* (2009), was banned on the mainland.[45] Mainland media were not even
allowed to discuss the book, and most of Lung's essays were scrubbed from
the web. Many hoped that Lung's invitation to speak at Peking University in
2010 was the sign of an opening—but unfortunately, the party-state clamped
down again in early 2011 in response to the Arab Spring uprisings.

In her acceptance speech, Lung creatively addressed the tension between
fundamentalism and cosmopolitanism by discussing what the "China dream"
means to her personally. She describes how her generation shifted from
big dreams about reconquering China to little dreams about democracy in

Taiwan. Lung's generation of intellectuals thus shifted from the fundamentalism defined by the Chinese race-nation's blood and soil to argue for the fundamental values, global values, and cosmopolitan values that grow out of shared experience. In this way, Lung criticizes the grand ideals of Chinese civilization in order to commend the everyday practice of civility.

Lung is a well-known social critic; but she is also a great example of a citizen intellectual. From her earliest essays in Taiwan in the 1980s, she demanded that intellectuals be socially and politically responsible. As we will see below, Lung is very critical of state power regardless of its ideology. But that doesn't mean that Lung won't work for the government if she thinks that she can make a difference. So when Taipei mayor (and now Taiwanese president) Ma Ying-jeou asked Lung to be the first director of Taipei's Cultural Affairs Bureau in 1999, she said yes. Over the next four years, she was successful not only in promoting Taiwan's cultural life, but also in energizing its broader civil society. At the end of her tenure, Lung returned to the life of a writer and a critic, showing how citizen intellectuals can be critical of the state while also working with the government for specific projects. Indeed, after nine years as a private citizen, Lung returned to government in 2012 when President Ma asked her to be Taiwan's minister of culture.

I am interested in what Lung did as a citizen intellectual between these two official posts. Curiously, after she left government in 2003, Lung also left Taiwan to take up a writing fellowship at the University of Hong Kong. Her career and life have been very cosmopolitan in greater China: She was born on Taiwan, worked in Hong Kong, and frequently publishes on the mainland. Lung is also cosmopolitan globally: she received her PhD in English and American literature from Kansas State University (1982); in 1987, she left Taiwan to spend an exile of thirteen years in Germany, where she married a German man and had three mixed-race sons. In ways similar to the web reaction to Lou Jing, some people claim that Lung's German experience makes her less Chinese: "Lung Ying-tai is a German citizen, where dual citizenship is verboten, but she profess to be Chinese. A hypocrite who intervenes in the internal affairs of other countries." Another comment was even more direct: "she is married to a caucasian and try to lecture Chinese about history. I guess she got some kind of superiority complex."[46]

Each of these experiences in greater China and the West have shaped Lung Ying-tai's ideas about fundamentalism and cosmopolitanism. Lung's speech at Peking University takes an interesting approach to the China dream. Its first section, "Our China Dream," actually lists six different versions of the China dream. By putting these different dreams in historical, social, and political contexts, Lung undermines any notion of a singular China Dream that is based on the exceptional fundamentalism of the race-nation and the race-state. The speech was a performance that combined Lung's spoken words, audio clips of popular songs, iconic pictures, and some videos. Curiously, Lung used these cultural artifacts, rather than scientific facts, to make her argument.

Lung's first three China dreams are interesting because they remind us of how people used to think. One of Lung's earliest memories is from her primary school days in the 1950s when she and her classmates dressed up in military uniforms, sported wooden rifles, and sang the patriotic song, "Recover the Mainland." This militarist China dream, which reflected Chiang Kai-shek's fantasy that the KMT would soon beat the "communist bandits" to reconquer the mainland, was shared by many people in Taiwan at the time. Lung's second China dream comes from memories of her parents' generation listening to a popular song "Homesickness." This sentimental song, which emerged in the political turbulence of the late 1950s and early 1960s, expressed the anguish of the 2 million people who were exiled to Taiwan by the Chinese civil war.

The exiles also survived by holding onto the fundamental Confucian values that supported the third China dream: propriety, justice, honesty, and shame. While Confucianism is characteristically illiberal, Lung recounts how reading classical Chinese literature in high school taught her how to be a critical intellectual. These four virtues still inform political movements in Taiwan: She recalls how a protest against corrupt government in 2006 included a blimp emblazoned with the words "propriety, justice, honesty, and shame." The lesson that Lung takes from this event was that each person "clearly knows what this society cares about." Thus, the China dream shifted, again, from returning to the mainland to the goal of clean and honest government.

Lung's fourth dream recounts how she, like much of her generation, awakened from Chiang Kai-shek's China dream to see Taiwan as her homeland; the great dream of reconquering China thus became the little dream of celebrating Taiwanese identity and the island's burgeoning democratic politics. Lung was shocked out of the "great China dream" by grand geopolitical events and intimate personal experiences. When Beijing took China's seat at the United Nations from Taipei in 1971, many Taiwanese felt abandoned by the United States—and by the world. The island's increasing isolation became a matter of survival. But rather than see this as the race-state's social Darwinian struggle of the survival of the fittest, Lung tells us how her generation turned "survival" into a question of cultural, social, and political identity.

Curiously, just as Justin Yifu Lin abandoned Taiwan to pursue his China dream on the mainland, Lung and other citizen intellectuals revised their ambitions and anxieties to focus on Taiwan's future. Rather than sing their parents' sad songs about a lost homeland, Lung's generation decided to "sing our own songs" about their homeland, Taiwan. Lung calls the popular song "Formosa" the "milestone of the Taiwan dream." It exemplifies the generational shift from the "great China dream" of reconquering the mainland to the little Taiwan dream of building an open and tolerant democratic society.

Lung herself was shocked out of her mainland identity by an experience in New York. The PRC started allowing its people to travel in 1979, so Lung recounts the shock of meeting her first real-life "communist bandit" in New York. The shock was not of ideology but of identity. She asked him where he was from, and he answered, in a thick accent, that he was Hunanese. Up until then, Lung had always followed the long-standing custom and said that she was from Hunan, since that was her father's home province. But when faced with a real Hunanese asking her where she was from, Lung was rendered speechless. She couldn't speak the Hunanese dialect, had never been to Hunan, and didn't know anything about the province. As she explains, "my personal China dream underwent a fundamental change." Torn away from a lifetime of thinking in terms of the mainland, Lung realized that she was Taiwanese.

Lung's shift from the China dream to the Taiwan dream is not based on a separate race-nation or a unique national genealogy (as it is for many in the Taiwan independence movement). It is a political dream of fundamental values rather than a biological dream of racial fundamentalism. Since the mainland audience sees democracy in Taiwan as chaotic and corrupt, Lung spends much time describing democratic change in Taiwan in terms of "dreaming together and learning together." While recognizing that serious divisions exist among political parties in Taiwan, Lung stresses that there is an underlying consensus about political values that encourages a critical view of both state power and corporate power. Since you can trust neither the government nor big business, Lung concludes that people have to fight for rights at all times and all places.

Her dream is that democracy will continue to blossom in Taiwan, and that it will also influence China as a "working model of democracy." As she told the *Wall Street Journal* in 2011: "The Taiwanese have a duty as world citizens to contribute to the progress of China, not just in terms of its economic prosperity, but also in how to help China become an open and civilized society."[47] Taiwan's 2012 presidential election, which was watched closely by the mainland's netizens for the first time, generally had this positive impact. A popular blog put it this way: "On the other side of the sea, Taiwan erected a mirror. And on this side of the sea, we saw ourselves in the future."[48]

Lung concludes her speech by thinking about what the China dream means to her now. What does the "China" in the China dream refer to? If it means the state or the government, Lung tells us that she's not interested; unlike Zhao Tingyang and Pan Wei, she does not dream of institutions. But if "China" refers to people—the Chinese dream—then "how could I not have a China dream?" she answers. Lung's Chinese dream is quite different from those that look to the PRC as a "rising great power" where all Chinese are joined by "blood ties." Rather than see the rise of China in terms of growing "wealth and power," Lung "hopes it is the rise of the power of civility."

The word "civility"—*wenming*—is usually translated "civilization," and characteristically refers to Confucianism and Chinese tradition. But Lung means something different here: rather than praising 5,000 years of Chinese civilization, she is describing the ethics of how people treat each other in everyday life:

> To see the degree of civility of a city, I look at how it treats its mentally ill, its services for the disabled, how it takes care of widows and the needy, how it treats the jobless rural workers who come to the city and the people at the lowest level of society. For me, this is a very specific standard of civility.
>
> For a country's civility, I look at how it treats its immigrants and how it treats its ethnic minorities. I consider how this country's majority treats its minority—this of course includes how 1.3 billion people treat [Taiwan's] 23 million people!

Civility here is a combination of traditional and modern values; it follows from China's four Confucian social values—propriety, justice, honesty and shame—and emerges through a democratic "dialogue about fundamental values" that cares for outsiders.

Lung finishes her speech by declaring:

> I deeply hope to see a China that dares to use the standard of civility to test itself; because it has self-confidence, this kind of China will be open; because it is open, it will be tolerant; because it is tolerant, its power will be more supple and strong, and more enduring. When it

has the power of civility's enduring flexibility, its crucial contribution to humanity as a whole will be peace.

Lung's work is compelling because she challenges the mainstream way of figuring politics in Taiwan (and China) as the struggle between diametrically opposed elements: Confucianism vs. liberalism, East vs. West, PRC vs. ROC, CCP vs. KMT, KMT vs. Taiwan's pro-independence Democratic Progressive Party, and so on. But Lung does not clearly identify with any party or place. As she wrote in her open letter to Hu Jintao (2006): "my homeland" will be whichever country that fits her "values identity," which includes "independence of character, the spirit of freedom, the rejection of wealth inequality, rejection of state violence, distrust of the rulers, respect for knowledge, sympathy for common people, tolerance of dissent, and contempt for lies." Lung thus unhinges homeland from the "scientific" issues of blood and soil to turn it into a cultural issue of values.

Her work is important because it consciously rejects the fundamentalism of exceptionalist national/cultural identity to pursue fundamental values that are both liberal and Confucian. The way Lung makes her points is important too: she is not a (social) scientist who seeks to discover the "scientific truth" of the race-nation or the race-state. Rather, she is a critical humanist who uses songs, poems and pictures to describe the ambiguities of values that grew out of the experience of learning democracy together with fellow Taiwanese.

Hers is a rational argument; but the appeal to tear-jerking personal stories and iconic songs shows that Lung knows how to use emotional arguments as well. Literary critic Leo Ou-fan Lee criticizes Lung for using personal stories to emotionally blackmail the reader, especially in her book *Wide River, Big Sea* (2009).[49] But it is also important to see how Lung shifts from simply collating the facts of a rising power's (economic) wealth and (military) power to see what ordinary people care about, which includes the fundamental values of democracy.

Rather than having to choose between the "catch up mentality" and the "new era mentality," Chinese models and Western ones, or Confucianism and liberalism, Lung offers her own personal mix. Through this process, Lung pursues global values as a citizen of the world without sacrificing her various local Chinese, Taiwanese, American and German experiences. Because Lung herself has mixed-race children, I think that Lou Jing would be welcome in Lung's dream homeland.

5

Shanghai's Alternative Futures and China's New Civil Society

SHANGHAI HAS ALWAYS been a dream city. As the country's first modern metropolis it has been China's center of commerce, culture, and industry since the late 19th century. But Shanghai's successes are bittersweet for many Chinese—the city was also the center of foreign empire: from 1843 to 1945 it was controlled by Western and then Japanese governments. It is a transient city full of economic, social, and cultural opportunities that mix East and West, traditional and modern, and rural and urban. This fast-changing cosmopolitan center thus presents an alternative vision of China.

To get a sense of Shanghai's mixed identity, all you need to do is go to the city's waterfront: The west bank of the Huangpu River is lined with the high modernist buildings of Western imperial capitalism, while the ultramodern skyscrapers of reform-era China line its east bank. These dueling skylines show how Shanghai has always represented "the future" in China. Even Beijing's central planners see Shanghai's knowledge economy as the epitome of not just Chinese modernization, but also global modernization.[1] While most take for granted that China's future is planned in Beijing, this chapter will examine how Shanghai dreams of—and thus creates—the future in alternative ways.

It will compare the Shanghai World Expo 2010's official view of the future with how citizen intellectuals worked both inside and outside this official space to craft alternative futures. On the one hand, the Shanghai World Expo's theme pavilions and corporate pavilions strove to build a harmonious, unified, and cosmopolitan world. Yet, in the Expo Culture Center, Jia Zhangke's film *Shanghai Legends* offered a nuanced view of the city's cosmopolitan past. Outside the Expo, Cai Guoqiang's Peasant da Vincis art exhibit celebrated rural ingenuity as a way of criticizing both the Expo theme—"Better City, Better Life"—and China's urban-focused development strategy.

The conclusion will examine how Shanghai blogger Han Han negotiates this terrain to build a new civil society in China. In this way, we will see how Chinese voices are questioning the China model of economics, politics, and society. While the party-state still tends to plan a centralized future, we will see how citizen intellectuals are multiplying and decentering what it means to be Chinese in Shanghai.

This chapter thus has two goals: first, it will contrast official constructions of a unified harmonious future with citizen intellectuals' multilayered (and often contradictory) views of Shanghai's past, present, and future. Second, it will explore if and how citizen intellectuals are creating new models of civil society.

Shanghai World Expo 2010

To introduce China to the world as a major power, Beijing recently choreographed three mega-events: the 2008 Beijing Olympics presented China as a soft superpower, the National Day military parade in 2009 confirmed that China also has hard power, and the Shanghai World Expo in 2010 was seen as "the Olympics for Culture, Economy and Technology."[2] All three were designed to show "The Real China" as a rejuvenated and unified nation that was returning to its rightful place at the center of world affairs: remember that "One World, One Dream" was the slogan for the Olympics.

Like previous expos, the Shanghai Expo was a dream factory that created various futures. The purpose of world expositions is both local and global: to showcase the host country's scientific, technological, and cultural power but to do so in a global context in cooperation with other nations. They are commonly seen as "coming out parties" for emerging great powers—the 1876 Centennial Exhibition in Philadelphia signaled the arrival of the United States on the international scene—and the Shanghai World Expo confirmed the rise of China.[3] The tension between nationalist pride and cosmopolitan idealism at the Shanghai World Expo thus was typical of its predecessors.[4]

The center of nationalist pride was China's national pavilion; it was striking both because it was huge and because it was elevated over the rest of the world to reign as the "Oriental Crown" (see Fig. 5.1).[5] Through films and exhibits, the pavilion celebrates China's past, present, and future—especially the achievements of Deng Xiaoping's reform and opening campaign since 1978. It explains that China has developed so quickly because Chinese people engage in a fruitful dialogue between the old and the young, the past and the future, traditional wisdom and scientific innovation, and the countryside and

FIGURE 5.1 China National Pavilion
Source: William A. Callahan

the city. The result of this conversation, the pavilion tells us, is the all-around development of a harmonious society that values tradition and the family. While the pavilion is full of Confucian aphorisms, China's dreams of the future clearly point to urban modernity: the World Expo's slogan, after all, was "Better City, Better Life."

The theme and corporate pavilions also explore the topics of balance and harmony. But rather than balancing China's past and future to build a harmonious society, they look to cosmopolitan themes to build a harmonious world. Intermarriage between Chinese and non-Chinese people in our future globalized world was a recurring topic in both theme and corporate pavilions. The "Future Cities Pavilion" (see Fig. 5.2) that was organized by the Expo committee explores how weddings will work in the future. A short video shows a wedding that joins a Chinese woman and an American man. Following Chinese custom, the groom organizes the nuptials; but, rather than having to spend months planning the wedding, he does it online on his wedding day. Choosing from a menu of global traditions (Christianity, Buddhism, Islam, etc.), he designs the cosmopolitan wedding of the future that integrates "Jewish" and "Chinese" clothes, rituals, and food. In addition to including family and friends in the lively wedding feast, they are even enabled to invite their favorite historical figures (he picked Attila the Hun). This video thus creates a future where East and West are in harmonious balance, at least at the microlevel of family relations. This virtual marriage of the future does raise another set of questions, though: since the bride was in Beijing and the groom in New York, how was the marriage consummated?

FIGURE 5.2　Future Cities Pavilion
Source: William A. Callahan

One of the corporate pavilions, called "We are the world" (*tianxia yijia*—Under-Heaven is one family), explores family life in such an intercivilizational marriage, this time between an Italian man and a Chinese woman. Like in the national and theme pavilions, this corporate pavilion (sponsored by the German multinational Siemens) explores "the life of an imaginary family in the year 2015"—i.e., at the end of China's 12th Five-Year Plan. In this three-generation family, the Chinese man lives in Shanghai and his sister lives with her Italian husband and their child in Milan, while the Chinese parents live in Beijing. The various exhibits highlight how a "globally networked and climate-friendly lifestyle" is the proper middle class dream.[6]

Communicating over 3D videophones, they discuss together how new technologies (provided, of course, by Siemens) make their daily life easier, healthier, and happier. The main message was that the green future will be full of comfort and luxury; for example, as part of the exhibit tour I was invited to drive a virtual version of the eco-sports car, the Ruf Greenster. At the end of this trip to the future, visitors are recruited into the cosmopolitan message of material prosperity: Videos of visitors shot at the entrance to the exhibit are used to show on the screen animated images of the current audience (including me) singing the happy song of high-tech global capitalism: "We are the world."

Thus, the Expo creates and manages cosmopolitanism by combining Chinese wives and Euro-American husbands, suggesting that this is the proper global harmony of East and West. Curiously, these mixed marriages repeat Kang Youwei's strategy for creating a world of Great Harmony.

The raciology of this preferred cosmopolitan match became clear with Chinese netizens' harsh reaction to Lou Jing, the young Shanghainese with a Han Chinese mother and an African-American father whom we discussed in the last chapter. The gendered and raced world harmony of the pavilions defines identities in terms of grand coherent traditions, which are chosen from a menu of cultural stereotypes. This logic certainly follows Hu Jintao's vision of a harmonious world in which different civilizations coexist, thus making "humanity more harmonious and our world more colorful."[7]

But this East/West cosmopolitanism, which ignores the rest of the world and fosters racialist views, often serves to solidify perceived differences between China and the world. By suggesting that the future reproduces high-tech forms of the past (i.e. Traditions), the theme and corporate pavilions do not allow much space for cultural diversity or innovation. As Shanghai blogger Han Han commented about the Expo: "when I tell people about my country, and they ask, 'What films has your country produced? What literature?' all I'll be able to come up with is Confucius. That's really boring."[8]

Many citizen intellectuals in Shanghai, then, found the Expo a disappointment. Its Five-Year Plan–style of cultural production was evidence of the "crisis of spirit among the Shanghainese," according to historian Xu Jilin.[9] Rather than showcasing Shanghai as a global city that transcends the Chinese nation, the Expo displayed the power of the central government in Beijing, "with the nation trumping the city in the end."[10]

Official messages here are not limited to China's national and theme pavilions: as a site of transnational capitalism, Siemens was happy to use the Michael Jackson song "We are the world" to reinterpret the classical Chinese idiom "*tianxia yi jia*" as part of its global marketing strategy. As Siemens CEO Peter Löscher confidently declared: "The entire Expo is our pavilion." This wasn't an exaggeration: Siemens helped Shanghai's application for the World Expo, won many of the contracts for enhancing the city's infrastructure, and was involved in more than forty projects on the Expo site itself, including China's national pavilion.[11]

Thus, the Shanghai World Expo constituted an expression of the China model on a global scale: It combined state planning, China's state-owned enterprises, and Western multinationals. China's future and the world's future here are co-created along the lines of Hu Jintao's harmonious world, a stable harmonious Utopia that combines global capitalism and Chinese civilization.

Jia Zhangke: Inside the System

To celebrate Shanghai as a global city, the World Expo management commit-tee commissioned famous director Jia Zhangke to make a film, according to the *Beijing Review*, to "introduce Shanghai's architecture, culture and life and explore the Expo theme, 'Better City, Better Life.'"[12] The result was *Shanghai Legends* (*Haishang chuanqi*), also known in English as *I Wish I Knew*. This film was shown at the Expo Culture Center ten times a day for 100 days.

To many in the West this came as a surprise: Jia is best known for his under-ground films that are censored in the PRC. Although Jia's films have evaded censorship, starting with *The World* (2004), it marked a big leap for him to work directly for China's propaganda officials.[13] Indeed, this issue came up while Jia was working on *Shanghai Legends*: to the disappointment of many Western commentators, Jia decided to follow Beijing's lead and withdraw his films from the Melbourne International Film Festival (MIFF) in 2009. China urged its directors to boycott the festival to protest the prominent screening of *The 10 Conditions of Love*, a documentary about Uighur dissident Rebiya Kadeer, whom Beijing sees as a terrorist who instigated July 2009's riots in Xinjiang. (There is no evidence to support this charge.) Jia's explanation for withdrawing his two films is indicative of citizen intellectual tactics:

> We have no interest in meddling with the festival's freedom of artis-tic exchange. Withdrawing from Melbourne is, rather, a kind of self-restraint. Xinjiang history is not something I'm well acquainted with, but the recent Urumqi violent incident was only two weeks ago, and I, at a minimum, should take a cautious approach. I don't want to do anything that would tarnish those who died.[14]

Here Jia is consciously asserting that he is not a dissident; he supports artistic freedom, but he is wary of being swept up into movements about which he knows little. There was little risk that Jia would be thrown in jail for com-menting on Kadeer's film; the risk was primarily to his career as a filmmaker who wants to showcase his work to Chinese audiences.

Rather than being negative in the sense of protesting against either the Kadeer film or China's censorship of it, Jia focuses on doing his own work—including preparations for the Expo film *Shanghai Legends*. In other words, although solidarity is an important value for citizen intellectuals, Jia wants to be able to choose his battles and, thus, avoid "being dissidented." Rather than understand this as "self-censorship," it is more interesting to consider how Jia was able to work with the party-state as a citizen intellectual. Even in this odd situation, he was able to make a docudrama that employs multiple voices to showcase Shanghai's ambiguous experience in the 20th century.

Jia was an odd choice for this official film for another reason; he does not come from Shanghai and is not known for making blockbuster commercial movies (like Zhang Yimou's *Hero*). Jia is from Shanxi Province in the inland North, and he is most famous for his artsy ethnographic films about poor people from rural areas. *The World* (2004) is a case in point; it shows how poor migrants from Shanxi deal with the rootless alienation of urban life while working at Beijing's Epcot Center–like "The World" theme park.

But Jia was a good choice because he was able to use this intimate aesthetic to see what makes Shanghai tick. While the rest of the Expo presents China as a unified civilization-state that is harmonious and strong, Jia's *Shanghai Legends* revels in the messy multiplicity of this cosmopolitan city that mixes the local and the global. Although the Expo maps a stable harmonious world in its shiny finished state, Jia's Shanghai is an overcast, polluted city that is engaged in a perpetual process of destruction and construction (see Fig. 5.3).

Rather than search for the core values of "The Real Shanghai," Jia highlights how motion and exchange are key to this global city's success. The film, for example, begins on a ferry crossing Shanghai's Huangpu River. The camera dwells on the passengers' faces as they prepare themselves for the hustle and bustle of the city; the tension produced by this combination of stasis and movement defines the film.

Rather than look to iconic buildings in the Expo, Pudong, or the Bund, Jia explores Shanghai's cityscape through a close examination of its people. Han Han (the last person interviewed in *Shanghai Legends*) agrees: "The people are the most *badass* exhibit the city has to offer. I suggest several Shanghainese should be chosen to be displayed as works of art in the China pavilion."[15] The

FIGURE 5.3 Screenshot from *Shanghai Legends*
Source: Jia, *Shanghai Legends*

film thus showcases eighteen individuals' intimate connection with Shanghai as patriotic capitalists, gangsters, communist revolutionaries, model workers, popular bloggers, reform-era tycoons, and so on. They describe events both momentous and banal, often showing how the grand struggles of war and revolution worked themselves out in the human relations of friends and family.

Chen Deqing, for example, describes how the grand politics of the Cultural Revolution shaped local struggles in his family's neighborhood. He recalls how his alley was polarized by the struggle of revolutionaries against "capitalists"—meaning his neighbors who had a few luxuries. But Chen's strongest childhood memories are of the gangs of little kids that took over his neighborhood. He had to carefully choose his playmates in order to join the correct gang; the Warring States–like battles between alleys amounted to a question of bully or be bullied. Chen's story alludes to ideology, but it is mostly concerned with personal relationships and local struggles.

Yang Huaiding, one of China's new-era tycoons, is interviewed in his office. As a self-made man who took advantage of the socialist market economy's new opportunities in the late 1980s, he made a killing buying and selling bonds. Curiously, Yang dwells on the logistical problems of his trade: the difficulties of carrying around his large investments when China's largest bill was the 10 RMB note and how he had to hire the police to protect him— otherwise he risked being arrested for being a gangster.

Shanghai Legends repeatedly returns to the struggle between the Chinese Communist Party (CCP) and the Nationalist Party (KMT), which culminated in the 1949 revolution. Just as with Chen's alley politics and Yang's investment schemes, ideology is rarely discussed; the political struggle is presented as a family squabble that led to a messy divorce that not only split up China, but fractured many families as well.[16]

While explaining how his father was assassinated by the KMT, Yang Xiaofo talks about his family's opulent lifestyle in 1930s Shanghai; he describes in great detail the luxuries of his father's chauffeured convertible before explaining how the KMT assassins killed his father while Yang was sitting in the back seat right next to him. Thus, Yang's memories are a combination of a specific horror enveloped in general nostalgia.

Ideas and ideology are certainly present. It is clear that Huang Baomei, the winner of the PRC's prestigious National Model Worker award who shook hands with Chairman Mao, supports the socialist system. After starring in her biopic "Huang Baomei" (Xie Jin, 1958) and attending Vienna's world youth festival (1959), she concludes "I felt very proud to be Chinese, and went back to put in all my efforts to increase production." Wei Ran is probably less sanguine about the party-state: He tells the horrible story of how the Cultural Revolution tore his family apart, making his mother commit suicide and ruining his sister's life. But we are not sure; Wei doesn't draw larger political conclusions.

Likewise, most of the film's subjects do not judge: when Du Meiru describes the life of her father, gangster Big-eared Du (Du Yuesheng), she doesn't mention that he controlled gambling and opium in Shanghai. Rather, she talks about his hard life as an orphan and his romantic courtship of her mother. The biggest tragedy is not Du's support of Chiang Kai-shek's massacre of left-wing activists in 1927; it is in 1949 when he didn't have enough money for his four wives and their families to buy their way into France.

Indeed, the fractured and complex family relations presented in *Shanghai Legends* directly contest the harmonious families of the China national pavilion, the Future Cities theme pavilion, and the Siemens corporate pavilion. In the film, the traditional Chinese family is not seen as a social model but as a social problem: Rebecca Pun explains that the "thing I don't like about old society" is how men flaunted their success by getting two or three wives. Everything changed in 1949, often splitting up these painfully extended families. Indeed, these stories suggest that while family is important, in the end we are all alone as individuals. Jia's direction stresses each subject as a loner: Each person is interviewed sitting alone in an empty office, restaurant, store, home, factory, race course, and so on.

Jia was able to work inside the system because he deals with momentous political events in this disjointedly personal way. It is up to the audience to make sense of these eighteen stories, which add up to a nuanced and decentered story of Shanghai itself. Hence, it is not surprising that *Shanghai Legends* revels in the uncertainty and anticipation expressed in the American jazz standard "I Wish I Knew," which is the film's alternative English title:

> I wish I knew, someone like you could love me....
> If you don't care, why let me hope you could love me.

The future here is not a shiny finished state, but the product of the past and present that is haunted with anticipation, uncertainty, and loneliness.

Outside the System: Cai Guoqiang

While Jia worked inside the system to produce "Shanghai Legends" for the World Expo, China's top global artist Cai Guoqiang worked outside the system to curate the Peasant da Vincis exhibit at Shanghai's new Rockbund Art Museum. This was a departure for Cai. He is famous in China for crafting spectacular pyrotechnic displays for the party-state's key international events, including the fireworks at the opening ceremony of the Beijing Olympics (2008). However, in 2010, as Cai explains, he was an outsider: "although this occasion is concurrent with the World Expo, I am participating purely in a private capacity."[17]

But Cai took this opportunity to comment on China's headlong rush for economic development. While the Expo's theme was "Better City, Better Life," Cai's theme was "Peasants—Making a Better City." His exhibit thus celebrated the ingenuity of rural people, whose hard labor as migrant workers actually builds China's cities, including the Shanghai Expo site itself. While Jia's film shifts from rural subjects to urban ones, here Cai does the opposite: His recent art, including pyrotechnic displays, has been very modern, high-tech, and urban. Cai thus sees Peasant da Vincis as an opportunity to shift gears and look for the future in the low-tech workshops of the countryside.[18]

Much like Jia's collection of eighteen portraits, Cai's exhibit offers a cornucopia of peasant inventions: a flying saucer, planes, helicopters, submarines, robots, and China's first aircraft carrier (see Fig. 5.4). These rusty industrial

FIGURE 5.4 Peasant da Vincis inventions (a) flying saucer (b) submarine, (c) Twilight No. 1 submarine, (d) flying machines and boats

Source: Images courtesy of Cai Studio

innovations are certainly anachronistic; rather than looking to the future, they seem to point to the past. Indeed, most of these inventions are made out of scrap.

However, these inventions are interesting because they present new takes on old themes: an airplane modeled on a pigeon, a helicopter that is a sedan chair with wings, submarines designed to swim like fish, and so on. By offering peculiar creations that do not quite fit in, these inventions offer a new approach to China's enduring unease about being a copy of Western technical and social models, which Cai calls "the anxiety present in Chinese society over its state of transition between 'made in China' and 'created in China.'"[19]

The exhibit thus is about more than boys and their toys: it explores the key issues that define China's intellectual discourse: what is modernity? Is it the same as Westernization? Can it provide spiritual excitement—or just material comfort? And just what is the China model?

Rockbund curator Liu Yingjiu feels that these Peasant da Vincis "have dreams, and pursue them however crazy they might seem. It shows how they have bigger dreams than city people who dream of getting a bigger house and a car. City people see the exhibit and are ashamed of their way of living, which is just materialist. The exhibit shows how the peasants are very smart and optimistic."[20]

Peasant da Vincis thus suggests that the China model's standards of economic success do not apply. Alongside the exhibit's peasant inventions are propaganda-style slogans written in bold characters: "What's important isn't whether you can fly" and "Never learned how to land." These inventors often talk about their work in terms of dreams, escape, and freedom. Technically, most of the inventions challenge gravity; these planes, helicopters, and submarines also pursue liberation from the shallow life of working for someone else in industrial society. Cai thus is drawn to these inventions because they are "born out of a desire to escape the gravity of one's circumstances."[21]

Xu Bin, a helicopter inventor from Jiangshan in Zhejiang Province, puts it well: "escaping the gravity of the ground is so difficult, but floating on the wind and spiraling in the air is so liberating." Xu tells us that flying is so "addictive" that he often forgets that he's running out of fuel: luckily his helicopter is able to "fall gently to earth."[22]

Wu Shuzai's goal is to escape the Wuyi Mountains that surround his village in Qianshan, Jiangxi. This sixty-nine-year-old man is alone with nothing to do; his five daughters are all married off and his wife passed away. When asked why he makes this sedan-chair helicopter, Wu answered that his real goal is to "fly it out of this mountain and see the world."[23]

Pursuing these dreams can have serious consequences: "A broken motor from a wrecked plane hangs from the ceiling" in the museum's foyer to commemorate the death of another Peasant da Vinci. While testing his fourth plane on April 8, 2007, Tan Chengnian crashed to the ground, dying on the spot.[24]

Peasant da Vincis thus are China's real risk takers. These loners want the freedom to succeed—which includes the freedom to fail. Actually, most of the inventions do not work: The pigeon planes and the flying saucers, for example, have never gotten off the ground. Many of the inventors' families think they are losers. Until he became famous when Cai "discovered" him, Wu Yulu's family thought he was a slacker for wasting his time building robots. Wu Shuzai's wife dismantled his sedan chair helicopter and used it for firewood. Cao Zhengsu's wife begged Cai not to buy her husband a more powerful engine for his pigeon plane: "The old man loves making planes. It's fine to play around, but if they actually flew, he'd be playing with his life!"[25]

The most successful "flight" of Xiong Tianhua's biplane was on the backs of a dozen men after it crashed. But as Figure 5.5 shows, this crash quickly transformed from a tragedy into a celebration of ingenuity and courage: "Spectators drawn by the excitement, swarmed over and helped them carry down the plane with its broken propeller."[26] Rather than disappointment, the men's expressions show joy.

After seeing a table-top model in Tao Xiangli's workshop, Cai specially commissioned Tao to build a 20-meter-long aircraft carrier in the museum during the exhibit (see Fig. 5.6). Not surprisingly, Tao came up with a unique

FIGURE 5.5 Joyfully salvaging Xiong's biplane
Source: Image courtesy of Cai Studio

FIGURE 5.6 Tao's aircraft carrier
Source: Image courtesy of Cai Studio

design, creating a catamaran carrier by placing the flight deck atop two submarines.

Rockbund curator Liu suggests that this invention exemplifies Cai's style of critical provocation: at the time, a Chinese carrier was a sensitive issue that was not much discussed in China. So Cai commissioned the aircraft carrier so people would have to talk about it—if only as a work of art. Cai thus concludes, "At a time when the first Chinese aircraft carrier is anticipated and feared by many, it seems that the peasants have already begun its construction."[27] (China's first aircraft carrier, the refitted Soviet-era *Varyag* that China bought from the Ukraine, was launched the following year in August 2011.) In this sense, Peking University's Zhang Yiwu is right when he describes Cai as a "dream magician," whose work "makes all Chinese people an important and essential part of the world's imagination."[28] The future here is created through the rural ingenuity of lone inventors who reframe the past as a means to escape physical and social gravity.

While the Expo's more official exhibits strive to build a harmonious world of respect for multiple civilizations, for Jia and Cai harmony grows out of messy combinations of odd experiences, which often provide uncertain messages. These parallel technologies are social innovations that develop a parallel society. The appeal to multiple meanings and uncertain endings explains how citizen intellectuals are able to be successful in China, both inside the system and outside it. Their work thus carves out an in-between space to explore the boundaries of what it means to be Chinese in the 21st century.

Conclusion: A New Civil Society

At the beginning of this book, I argued that we need to think about public space in China in new ways. Rather than being able to clearly label people as either "establishment intellectuals" or "dissidents" as part of the grand battle between state and society, I suggested that we need to have a more nuanced view of China's political geometry. The book has argued that a new group of people, whom I call citizen intellectuals, has been active in ways that blur the boundaries of any state/society distinction.

As the Shanghai Expo shows, the party-state still seeks to exert centralized control over Chinese identity and China's future. Yet, as Jia's and Cai's work shows, multiplying and decentering China's dreams is a popular strategy for citizen intellectuals. Since *Shanghai Legends* lacks both a central message and a clear moral conclusion, it would be hard for the officials to censor it-unless they wanted to scrap the whole project. Cai's critical method works in an analogous way: "Peasants—Making a Better City" does not directly challenge the Expo's "Better City, Better Life"; rather, Cai criticizes the China model by adding another element that twists the meaning of Shanghai's urban-themed event to include its opposite: multiple views of the future from the countryside.

Certainly, citizen intellectuals are playing with the red line that divides what the party-state will allow in Chinese society and what it won't. Rather than working in a civil society built on an open legal system of known rules and punishments, the party-state's red line is clear only when it is crossed: when artist-activists like Ai Weiwei are "dissidented" and "criminalized" by the authorities for directly challenging the Communist Party or the leadership. (The party-state doesn't know where the red line is, either—the authorities create it each time they arrest a dissident.) Most people focus on the self-censorship encouraged by the party-state's system of control that heavily penalizes such political critics. However, in this book we have been more concerned with the opposite: the opportunities for social activism that this caged bird system creates.

Jia's and Cai's appeal to a mix of lonely individuals, as opposed to the Expo's harmonious collective, has many parallels in the work of Han Han, whose style is exemplified by the title of his short-lived literary magazine, *A Chorus of Solos* (*Duchangtuan*), which was published during the Expo.[29] (Or to put it another way, a graduate student in Hangzhou admires Han Han for daring "to risk being alone," since people in China don't want to be around those who criticize the government.)

Han is a fascinating figure whose life embodies the tensions faced by
many Chinese people today: He grew up in the country but now lives in the
city; he dropped out of high school, but as a best-selling novelist he is part
of the cultural elite; although a serious writer, China's literary elite see him
as a mediocre dilettante; rather than limit himself to intellectual pursuits,
Han decided to follow his dream to become a professional race car driver—
where he has been quite successful (see Fig. 5.7). Han thus is seen by many
as the voice of the post-1980 generation of one-child policy children who
grew up in the economic reform era's environment of increasing prosperity
and freedom.[30]

This multimedia star is perhaps best known for his "TwoCold" blog,
which has received half a billion hits since it began in 2006; thus, it is the
most popular blog in China—and the most popular blog in the world. Using
the cultural technology of the blog, Han Han is able to build a parallel society
in cyberspace. The multiple decentered nature of blogs means that although
Han's posts are occasionally censored—or "harmonized"—they are always
available somewhere else. Just as with *Shanghai Legends*, the party-state could
censor his blog as a whole (as it did with Ai Weiwei); however, since Han is a
media darling even with the official press, the cost of pulling his wildly popular blog is still too high.

FIGURE 5.7 Han Han
Source: www.chinatibetnews.cn

As a writer, Han is particularly concerned with the shifting rules of censorship in China. In many of his recent blogs he has criticized—mocked, really—how official censorship produces absurd results: during the Diaoyu Islands controversy with Japan in September 2010, for example, his post was rejected because it used the phrase "Diaoyu Islands" which was censored as a "sensitive word" (*minggan ci*). Han solved this problem by using the Japanese name, Senkaku, which was strangely acceptable to the web filters even though it is anathema to Chinese nationalists.[31]

Although many of Han's blogs are overtly political,[32] his most effective commentaries are less activist. In three controversial posts—"Talking about Revolution," "Saying Democracy," and "Wanting Freedom" (2011)—Han actually argues against activism in the form of a dissident-led revolution against the CCP.[33] Like Lung Ying-tai in the previous chapter, Han sees politics at the local level of how people treat each other. The way to change the Party is through a reform of people, which, he concludes, will lead to a change in China's political institutions. Or as Han quips, "when Chinese drivers know to turn off their high beam lights when they pass each other, we can safely proceed with the revolution." Han thus questions the heroism of dissidents because he feels their revolution not only would lead to violence, but also would soon be taken over by "a revolutionary leader who is most likely going to be dictatorial, domineering, egotistical, presumptuous, venomous and incendiary." Reform, Han concludes, is better than revolution.

China's liberals and dissidents lambasted Han's three essays for selling out to the party-state. Ai Weiwei criticized Han's "tone as too orthodox, and his stance as too close to that of authorities." Perhaps the most damning comment came from Hu Xijin, the editor of the hypernationalist *Global Times*: "This is some real truth you rarely hear in China today!"[34] Han, however, explained that he was trying to avoid thinking about politics in the simplistic terms of "either this-or-that, either black-or-white, either right-or-wrong, either a pro-Western-traitor-or-a-government-paid-fifty-cent-gang-member." His point is that a Czechoslavakian-style "Velvet Revolution" led by intellectuals is unlikely in China. Yet Han's plans for building civil society in China through social and cultural activities have much in common with Vaclav Havel's method of social change that relies on people's "small-scale work" to build parallel cultures, parallel markets, and, thus, a parallel society.

Hence, rather than play on emotions in a call for grand revolution, many of Han's posts are rational calculations of the costs of the China model of economic development. Like a literary accountant, in blog after blog Han talks about life in China by listing the costs of living in Shanghai: the cost of renting and then buying a home and of food, drink and gasoline as well as other bread-and-butter issues.[35]

Recounting a friend's personal economic (and then social) crisis, Han begins by noting that his pal "didn't really have any big ideals, but he was upbeat about his future." Han then charts this person's struggle with the cost of city living: since "houses in the suburbs of Shanghai are going for at least RMB 500,000 a pop ($78,000), they would have to work for the next 25 years, go without food and drink, and live between bare walls. Then, if they wanted to actually decorate or furnish the house, they would have to starve for yet another five years."[36] Han makes such calculations over and over for different social groups, ranging from migrant workers to the middle class to playboys like himself.

Han's response to the high-speed train crash near Wenzhou (2011), "A Nation Derailed," took this literary accounting to a new level by exploring the cost of human life. Many other commentators directly criticized the party-state for the substandard construction of one of its signature projects and for its arrogant response to the tragedy that killed forty people and injured at least 192 others. However, Han's post satirically explores how officialdom understands the people, rather than the train wreck, as the main problem:

> They [officials] think: we're building you all this stuff, why do you mind a few bumps in the road?... The train from Shanghai to Beijing used to take the whole damn day. Now you're there in five hours— at least when there's no lightning. Why can't you be grateful? What's with all the questions?
>
> Every now and then, there's an accident. The top leaders all show how worried they are. We make someone available to talk to the press. First we say we'll give the victims 170,000 kuai apiece [US$26,000]. Then we say we'll give them 500,000 [US$78,000]. We fire a buddy of ours. We do all that, and you still want to nitpick? How could you all be so narrow-minded? You're not seeing the big picture. Why do you want us to apologize when we haven't done anything wrong? It's the price of development, for crying out loud![37]

This "great leap forward mentality" is reminiscent of the reasoning of He Dongsheng, the high-ranking official in Chan Koonchung's novel *The Golden Age: China 2013* (2010). Han thus is a social critic more than an economic model-builder: for him the China model is a model of injustice and ineptitude.

Han thus hits the party-state where it hurts: Its legitimacy is based on providing the benefits of economic growth, including "big things" (*dashi*) like high-speed trains and consumer items for the everyday life of ordinary Chinese. The leadership thus can hold political reform at bay by warning people that democracy would endanger social stability. However, rather than discuss the macroeconomics of China's GDP growth, Han focuses on the micropolitics of personal finance and personal tragedy. By pointing out the China model's economic and social costs, which include property bubbles, major accidents, inflation, pollution, official corruption, and forced evictions, Han connects with a wide readership that shares these experiences. He reflects the hopes and anxieties of everyone who is struggling to find a job, get a home, start a family—or just take the train from Shanghai to Beijing.[38]

When read together, Han's multiple blogs thus point to the political cost of the party-state's tight control of power. His mocking praise of local party cadre Han Feng after the publication of a diary that documents his laziness, womanizing, and corruption is a case in point. While some called for Han Feng's dismissal, Han Han reasons that "his diary reveals the life of the thriftiest womanizing official in the country. Other officials give their mistresses houses and cars, but his most expensive gifts are mobile phones and MP4 players. By those standards, he is a pretty decent official." Han thus "urges netizens to leave this man and his women alone, and let him retain his position. We may wish to punish them, but they are definitely not typical of the true criminals in the Party." (Perhaps Han is forgiving of Han Feng because he also cultivates the reputation of being a womanizer.) Or more to the point: "If he is dismissed, his successor may be much worse, and may not keep a diary."[39]

In a similar vein, Han criticizes his Chinese compatriots who protest against Japan because "demonstrations against foreigners by people who are not allowed to protest at home are utterly worthless. They are nothing but a group dance."[40] Likewise, in "I'm Only Guessing" Han is pessimistic about China's future, predicting that government control will continue to grow, eventually shutting down the Internet in 2017. While many economists forecast that China will surpass the United States to be the largest economy in the world by 2020, Han forecasts that "the Earth will be destroyed" in 2020, before noting that "the descendants of the Mayans say that a margin of error of plus or minus ten years is normal for such events."[41]

All in all, Han has a singular style that mixes outrage with jokes and formal language with teenage slang, which is as engaging to the post-1980 generation as it is frustrating for people over thirty to fathom.[42] For example, at the start of the Libyan uprising (2011) Han declared that dictators cannot hide behind the legalities of international sovereignty. In a thinly veiled threat to the Chinese leadership, he concluded that "the slaughterer should be invaded and annihilated."[43] But actually Han ends the blog with an additional (and rarely translated) sentence that mixes an astronomical event with a reference to a Japanese cartoon popular in the 1990s: "Yesterday, the moon was the largest it's been for nineteen years, and regardless of who, regardless of why, in the name of the moon I annihilate him."[44] (If you don't get this reference, it means that you're over thirty and should read the footnote for an explanation.)

Some critics dismiss Han's writings as "fast food" that does not measure up either as literature or as political activism.[45] Because Han tells jokes and makes pop culture references, they feel that his popularity represents "the triumph of the mediocre, and the failure of a nation."[46] Han certainly deserves his bad-boy reputation; in the early 2000s he took pleasure in lacerating literati critics with his caustic wit, and he is rightly criticized for his often misogynist opinions.

But during the past few years, Han has changed to become more thoughtful and more responsible. Rather than fire off knee-jerk reactions like most of his blogging brethren, many of Han's posts are sophisticated, extended essays that use evidence to carefully analyze topical issues. He thus weighs different perspectives, including the views of the party-state, before employing his acerbic wit to draw strong and clear conclusions. As Han's "A Nation Derailed" post reasons,

> A friend in government said to me: nothing's ever good enough for you. Forty years ago [during the Cultural Revolution], writers like you would've been shot. So you tell me, have things gotten better, or have they gotten worse?
>
> I said: no, you're the ones for whom nothing's ever good enough. Ninety years ago [at the beginning of the Republic of China], that kind of thinking would have gotten you laughed out of the room. So you tell me: have things gotten better, or have they gotten worse?

Although many Chinese netizens—both hypernationalists and liberals—characteristically appeal to conspiracy theories, Han argues that we must search for "the truth," not just "a truth that meets our needs."[47] Thus, Han is effective because his social commentary is reasonable and moderate—and perhaps moderating of China's "indignant youth."

While Jia and Cai work both inside and outside the system, Han is interesting because he is neither inside the system nor outside it. Although a loner trying to find his own way to "live in truth," Han is not isolated like a dissident; rather, he is omnipresent on the web and television and in magazines and newspapers. Like Jia and Cai, Han is a free agent who picks his own projects. They each focus on the micropolitics of everyday experience at work and with friends and family, showing us how they can build alternative cultures and multiple civil societies. Cai's conclusion thus also applies to Han's work: "through the creative power of individual peasants standing on their own outside the will and actions of the collective, and through the moving stories of individual lives, we can also see the hope of a people pursuing a just, democratic society."[48]

6

The American Dream and Chinese Exceptionalism

ELECTION YEARS TEND to sharpen political rhetoric. President Barack Obama's flippant comments to a British reporter about American exceptionalism helped set the tone for the 2012 presidential election campaign: "I believe in American exceptionalism, just as I suspect that the Brits believe in British exceptionalism and the Greeks believe in Greek exceptionalism." Although Obama went on to robustly endorse America's exceptional values, many Republicans expressed outrage at this statement during the 2012 campaign. Mitt Romney, for example, felt that this statement reflected Obama's view of declining American power and Newt Gingrich even seized the opportunity to write a whole book: *A Nation Like No Other: Why American Exceptionalism Matters.*[1]

It's not just Americans who discuss fundamental values in election years. During his election campaign in 2012, French president François Hollande told a political rally that "the French Dream is confidence in the future, in democracy," where a better life is built on equality, justice and secularism.[2]

As we've seen in this book, "The China Dream" has recently become a hot topic in greater China. Although the People's Republic of China (PRC) doesn't select leaders through democratic elections, the political elite actively campaigned in 2012 to get one of the five empty seats in China's top decision-making body, the Politburo Standing Committee of the Chinese Communist Party (CCP). Since they will rule China for the next decade, and many forecast that China will become the world's largest economy by 2020, it is important to understand the ideas that inspire these new leaders. While Beijing started to crack down on dissidents in 2011 in response to the Arab

Spring, China has also seen an "election campaign" of competing ideas about China's future direction among citizen intellectuals.

How seriously should we take China's unofficial futurologists? Many people think that "dreams" and "exceptionalism" are simply propaganda (in China) or empty political rhetoric (in the United States). In *The Myth of American Exceptionalism*, British journalist Godfrey Hodgson marshals historical facts to "prove" that America is not special at all; to him, American values are simply poor copies of European civilization.[3] Others look to the dark side of American history—slavery and militarism—to tell us that America is exceptionally *bad*.[4]

But these efforts to disprove the American dream miss the point. A myth is not simply a falsehood; as Aristotle told us, a myth is "made up of things to wonder at."[5] The American dream and the China dream thus are not facts to be proven or disproven, but moral dramas that express a community's aspirations and fears. Rather than denouncing or mocking such dreams, we should take them seriously as a way of thinking about a community's values. Recall what American philosopher Richard Rorty said about dream countries: "You have to describe the country in terms of what you passionately want it to become, as well as what you know it to be now. You have to be loyal to a dream country rather than to the one to which you wake up every morning. Unless such loyalty exists, the ideal has no chance of becoming actual."

This chapter will compare American and Chinese dreams and American and Chinese exceptionalisms. As sociologist Richard Madsen explains in *China and the American Dream*, neither culture is fixed or unitary: They are conversations that include many voices in debates about the good life, civilization, and progress.[6] Therefore, the chapter will summarize, first, China's dreams and, then, outline the meaning of the American dream and American exceptionalism and, finally, relate them to China's new exceptionalism. The purpose of comparing American and Chinese dreams is to challenge those who see them as either completely different or completely the same. I also hope to add a dose of humility to expressions of American exceptionalism and Chinese exceptionalism while laying the groundwork for the Chimerican dream scenario offered in the next chapter.

20　China Dreams

China is "a great nation of idealists," according to the narrator in Chan Koonchung's sci-fi novel *The Golden Age, China 2013*.[7] But what are their ideals? At the risk of oversimplification, this brief summary can help us to see the contours of the China dream:

- Former president Hu Jintao dreamt of social harmony in a harmonious world of cooperating civilizations that are equal on the world stage.
- New president Xi Jinping's direction of the Beijing Olympics (2008), the National Day Parade (2009), and the Shanghai Expo (2010) show that he dreams of the rejuvenation of the Chinese nation as a strong and prosperous party-state that has global influence.
- Dissident Liu Xiaobo dreams of a liberal democratic China where people have political, civil, and economic rights and the responsibility to govern themselves.
- Artist-activist Ai Weiwei has nightmares about totalitarian Beijing and dreams of an accountable government.
- Former Chongqing leader Bo Xilai wanted to apply his model of state capitalism and red culture to the PRC as a whole (by getting appointed to the Politburo Standing Committee in 2012); now he is concerned with his own survival.
- Economist Justin Yifu Lin hopes that China will complete its transition to a market economy that is fueled by domestic consumption, with the end goal being Great Harmony—not liberal democracy.
- Economist Hu Angang dreams of China "leaping forward" to overtake the United States by 2020 in a "great reversal" of power in which American hegemony is replaced by a World of Great Harmony controlled by the Global South.
- Political scientist Pan Wei's China model dreams of a World of Great Harmony where the indigenous Chinese ideals of people-centered politics, public/private economy, and the organic village society are taken seriously in a Cold War–type struggle against the "Western" universals of democracy and human rights.
- Political-economist Cui Zhiyuan's Chongqing model dreams of prosperity and social justice in a new style of socialism for the 21st century.
- In *The Golden Age*, novelist Chan Koonchung's characters have conflicting dreams: some just want to remember, others want the freedom to be unhappy, while most are satisfied with 90 percent freedom and 100 percent prosperity.
- Philosopher Zhao Tingyang is uneasy about the liberalization of economic reforms; he thinks that China needs to exploit is own cultural resources to build the Under-Heaven system of unified global

government, which will guarantee peace and harmony for China and the world.

- Senior Colonel Liu Mingfu also thinks that economic reform has gone too far; he wants to rebalance China's power from civil to military so the PRC can sprint to the finish to become the world's number one power; like Chan Koonchung's character He Dongsheng, Liu sees international politics as the struggle between "yellows" and "whites."
- China's fundamentalists dream of a pure race-nation led by a Han race-state in the social Darwinist struggle against whites, blacks, and China's minority groups.
- Scholar-official Kang Youwei dreamt of an egalitarian unified world of Great Harmony that combines yellows and whites, while blacks and browns fade from the Earth.
- Novelist Jiang Rong hopes the wolf-like blood of Mongolians and Westerners will rejuvenate the Chinese race so it can become a "highly evolved world civilization people" that has an "advanced level of liberal democracy."
- Social critic Lung Ying-tai's China dream is for a homeland that is inspired by the "power of civility," which combines some traditional Chinese values with liberal democracy.
- The Shanghai World Expo, which itself was described as China's century-long dream, built a cosmopolitan world of science and technology that combines the best of China and the West in a mixed-race consumer family.
- Jia Zhangke's film *Shanghai Legends* contrasts the Expo's clean and orderly vision of the future with a view of the city that intertwines the past and present in stories haunted by anticipation, uncertainty, and loneliness.
- Artist Cai Guoqiang looks to peasants' experiences to question the social injustices of the China model; the peasants themselves dream of flying away to "escape the gravity of their circumstances."
- Blogger Han Han dreams of a society where there is more freedom for writers like himself, and more social, economic and political justice for his friends, who represent the ordinary people of China.

Of these twenty China dreams, only six are from officials or dissidents. Citizen intellectuals, who (as Chan Koonchung would say) have 90 percent freedom, are a growing force in the PRC. It is a fluid distinction: Ai Weiwei went from being a citizen intellectual to a dissident when he was arrested in 2011, and

Lung Ying-tai migrated from citizen intellectual to an official (again) when she became Taiwan's minister of culture in 2012.

Rather than being clearly pro- or anti-CCP, citizen intellectuals represent a wide spectrum of views ranging from racial fundamentalists and militarists to liberals and cosmopolitans. Although they may not talk directly to each other, citizen intellectuals are involved in a raucous debate over the direction of China's future.

As a new phenomenon, the China dream is still taking shape; as we will see in the next section, it is not as coherent as the American dream, which people have been discussing for the past century. But certain debates and values are emerging to define the mainstream view of the China dream.

One of the major dream debates is about the proper relationship between political and economic goals. While Justin Yifu Lin thinks that the transformation to an economy driven by domestic consumption is the key to the China dream, others see economic factors corrupting China's political values—and its political power. Senior Colonel Liu Mingfu thinks that being an economic superpower is risky; he tells us that Beijing must refocus its energies from civil to military in order to build China's "martial spirit" to fight off the American threat. On the other hand, liberal historian Xu Jilin worries that consumerism and income polarization are corrupting the values of the democratic civilization that he and others are trying to develop in the PRC.

There is also a debate between the values of equality and hierarchy. Arguments for expanding egalitarian values at the global and local level are strong in China (see Hu Jintao, Hu Angang, Justin Yifu Lin, Lung Ying-tai, and Kang Youwei). But a new trend unapologetically supports elitism and social hierarchy: Xi Jinping asserts the right of princelings to rule China, Zhao Tingyang creates a hierarchical Under-Heaven system for the globe, Pan Wei's China model is inspired by the patriarchal family of village society, and so on.

Lastly, we've seen a debate about the meaning of "civilization." Those who see China's future in terms of a traditional hierarchical society tell us that China's strength comes from its "civilization-*wenming*." However, rather than praise China's 5,000 years of cultural history, Lung Ying-tai understands *wenming* as "civility," which she uses to describe the ethics of how people treat each other in everyday life. As we saw in chapter 4, this notion of civility integrates Confucian civilization's values of propriety, justice, honesty, and shame with the universal values of democratic civilization. Rather than focus on the large-scale China dream of global greatness, Lung's "power of civility" emerges in the small-scale dreams of ordinary people working together for democracy. It is similar to Nobel laureate Liu Xiaobo's civic consciousness and civic spirit, and it helps us to understand how civil society can emerge in China through the alternative civilities and small-scale work of citizen intellectuals' many China dreams.

Thus, the China dream, like the American dream, is a debate about values. Social harmony and world harmony are the official values according to government policy, which are expressed in a range of ways by officials and citizen intellectuals. The 12th Five-Year Plan explains how the party's new strategy of "social management" will ensure social vitality, harmony, and stability in China.[8] Hu Angang lists China's main values as unity, stability, and prosperity. Zhao Tingyang's Under-Heaven system values order over freedom, ethics over law, and elite governance over democracy and human rights. The Confucius Peace Prize, which was awarded to Vladimir Putin in 2011 for waging war in Chechnya, promotes unity, stability, and peace through war.

Although there has been much talk about the rise of Confucian cultural nationalism in China, these China dreams show a shift from nationalism to "statism."[9] While Lung Ying-tai is critical of both big government and big business, many other citizen intellectuals see enhancing state power as the key to their final goal: China as a wealthy country with a strong military.

Zhang Wei-wei argues that Chinese people have an overwhelming collective fear of chaos. Hence, the debate in China is not about getting the correct balance of freedom and security (which we saw in American debates about the "War on Terror") but about a stark choice between total Order and total Chaos. *The Golden Age's* He Dongsheng explains that when offered the Hobbesian choice between anarchy's "war of all against all" and the order of absolute dictatorship, the Chinese people always pick the Leviathan. In this Utopian/dystopian novel, economic prosperity depends upon state violence.

"Socialism with Chinese characteristics" here stresses the Leninist value of state power more than Confucian values. The main goal of the China model is to affirm and support Beijing's current system of governance that is dominated by the CCP's control of the nation-*state*. Zhang Wei-wei and others talk about China as a civilization-*state*. Both the Under-Heaven system and the World of Great Harmony require strong world-*state* institutions. For many, the China dream thus involves tight state control of politics, economy, and society to promote the key values of stability, unity, and statism.

Or to put it another way, "inciting subversion of state power" is the party-state's charge-of-choice for incarcerating dissidents like Liu Xiaobo.

Beyond statism, China's key value is difference. Because of its uniquely continuous history of 5,000 years of civilization, we are often told that outsiders cannot understand China. Zhao Tingyang and Pan Wei each reason that China's success can be judged only according to "Chinese characteristics" because it is fundamentally different from the West. Hu Angang agrees, declaring that Western economic theory cannot understand China's unique "national conditions." The goal here is to develop Chinese discursive power, the Chinese perspective, and the Chinese school of social science to fight for the PRC in global ideological battles.

Chinese citizen intellectuals who do not endorse this pure view of China's unique superiority are denounced as "Western slaves." The prominent Maoist website Utopia named them on a "Most Wanted" list complete with red Xs over their pictures, and 2012 was declared the "Year of Eliminating Traitors."[10] Utopia was finally shut down in April 2012, but not because of its violent taunting of Liberals; the party-state closed the website because it had become a rallying point for Bo Xilai supporters after his downfall.

The American Dream and American Exceptionalism

The meaning of the American dream seems very clear. But when you try to nail it down you realize that it has many, often contradictory, meanings. American exceptionalism has the same problem. Yet, rather than try to fix the meaning of these ideas, I think that it is best to treat them the way we have treated the China dream: as part of a vigorous conversation that knits together culture and politics.

Since discussions of the American dream and American exceptionalism overlap—often invoking the same events, documents, and people—it is helpful to consider them together. This section thus will explore the debate by comparing Jim Cullen's *The American Dream: A Short History of an Idea That Shaped a Nation* (2003) with Newt Gingrich's *A Nation Like No Other: Why American Exceptionalism Matters* (2011).[11] Cullen is a pop historian who gives a critically sympathetic account of the American dream. Gingrich wrote his book in sharply partisan terms as part of his 2012 presidential election campaign.

Although everyone traces its roots back to the Pilgrims, the "American Dream" itself is actually a 20th-century idea. According to Cullen, James Truslow Adams coined the phrase in his popular history, *The Epic of America* (1931). The idea quickly became popular in the United States—and around the world—as shorthand for America's national values. An intellectual history of the American dream is important because, as Richard Hofstadter famously stated, "It has been our fate as a nation not to have ideologies, but to be one."[12] The American dream thus is part of the ideology of Americanism, the American creed, which Abraham Lincoln called the "political religion of the nation."

Cullen gives six interrelated examples of the dream—religious freedom, political freedom, upward mobility, equality, home ownership, and fame and fortune—to trace the development of the idea of "America" over four centuries. Starting with the Puritans' search for religious Utopia, Cullen explains that they came to America in search of the freedom to pursue their Calvinist version of the good life. Freedom thus is crucial to the American dream. But this was religious freedom, rather than political or social freedom. From the very beginning the American dream was not just for Americans: The Puritans sought to be an example to the world. John Winthrop's 1630 sermon "A Model of Christian Charity," which was invoked by both John F. Kennedy and Ronald Reagan, preached that America is "a city upon a hill" that would be judged not just by God, but also by the world because "the eyes of all people are upon us." The principles of this American dream are hope and liberty, and they continue to animate the search for the good life in the United States.

Cullen's second American dream looks to the Declaration of Independence as America's "Dream Charter," especially its most famous passage: "We hold these Truths to be self-evident, that all Men are created equal, that they are endowed by their Creator with certain unalienable Rights, that among these are Life, Liberty, and the Pursuit of Happiness." The American dream of the Founding Fathers thus is freedom: the political freedom of self-determination, which is different from the religious freedom of the Puritans.

Like with the China dream, Cullen argues that the American dream mixes aspirations and anxieties: "The flip side to the sense of hope that goes to the core of the Declaration and the Dream is a sense of fear that its promises are on the verge of being, or actually have been, lost." While the China dream is confident that the PRC *should* be number one, here the American dream is haunted by ambiguity and "a sense of dissatisfaction, a belief that the nation we inhabit isn't quite right—but *could* be." According to Cullen, this represents the American dream's "most important legacy."[13]

The Declaration of Independence has become a moral standard used to judge the political health of the nation. Martin Luther King Jr. invoked it in his speech at the Lincoln Memorial in 1963: "I still have a dream. It is a dream deeply rooted in the American dream that one day this nation will rise up and live out the true meaning of its creed—we hold these truths to be self-evident, that all men are created equal."

Cullen's third American dream is the rags-to-riches story of upward mobility. Here, the individual success of "self-made men" enters the moral drama. Alexis de Tocqueville, the French chronicler of *Democracy in America* (1835, 1840) coined the word *individualism* to describe this new secular and materialist sort of striving, which he saw as an alternative to Europe's static class-based society. Cullen cites Benjamin Franklin and Abraham Lincoln as the best examples of the dream of upward mobility, where hard work is rewarded with material success. Franklin's pithy sayings—"Early to bed and early to rise makes a man healthy, wealthy and wise"—satirized Puritan piety; but they also voiced the values of American meritocracy. Lincoln's rise from birth in a log cabin to living in the White House is a classic tale of an individual taking advantage of equal opportunity to work hard for success.

Lincoln's American dream is not just for Americans; he declared that the dream of equal opportunity for upward mobility is for the world because the American dream gives "liberty not alone to the people of this country, but hope to the world for all future time. It was that which gave promise that in due time the weights should be lifted from the shoulders of all men, and that *all* should have an equal chance." Lincoln thus concludes that America is "the last, best hope of earth."[14]

Unfortunately, in the past few years, upward mobility has stalled in the United States, creating a more stagnant class system in America; "old Europe," on the other hand, has overtaken America to be the land of opportunity for self-made men and women.

Cullen's fourth American dream is for equality. While freedom defines the first three American dreams, Cullen points to America's history of slavery, Jim Crow laws, and the civil rights movement to remind us that freedom does not necessarily include equality. In the American dream, freedom is liberty from political or social constraints: the freedom to succeed, to be different. Equality, on the other hand, speaks to a "leveling instinct" where everyone is the same that sometimes is criticized as being "foreign" or "socialist." Lincoln and others squared this circle by arguing that America provides "equality of opportunity" rather than "equality of results."

But Swedish sociologist Gunnar Myrdal's *The American Dilemma: The Negro Problem and Modern Democracy* (1944) pointed out the huge gap between the ideal of equality and the reality of gross inequality for African Americans. Myrdal thus argues that the "American Creed" needs to pursue different and often conflicting values: "liberty, equality, justice, and fair opportunity for everybody." Neither freedom nor equality of opportunity is enough for a democratic society because only the state can promote equality in a meaningful way. Cullen thus tells the optimistic story of Americans working through their government to overcome racism, sexism, and other obstacles in the quest for political, social, and economic equality. While other dreams look to individuals and families, the dream of equality is for community, and it is pursued through the collective institutions of civil society and the state.

Cullen's last two American dreams are the most familiar: home ownership, and fame and fortune. Both are modern twists on earlier ideals. Home ownership is part of upward mobility. It expresses the right to private property, the autonomy of the nuclear family, and the expanding wealth of industrial and now postindustrial society. The religious and political piety of earlier eras is replaced here with reverence for the material goods of consumerism.

The American dream of fame and fortune, Cullen explains, is more quantitative than qualitative: more is better. Success here does not come from hard work: "It's less about accumulating riches than about living off their fruits, and its symbolic location is not the bank but the beach."[15] The American dream here morphs into the "California Dream," where complex experiences of political struggle are replaced by Hollywood's romanticized images fame and fortune.

The American dream thus is like the China dream: It has many versions, and it promotes diverse and often conflicting values. The tension between freedom and equality is indicative of its complexity. The idea has changed over the past four centuries. But certain norms remain meaningful: the Declaration of Independence's rights to "life, liberty and the pursuit of happiness" and Myrdal's American creed of "liberty, equality, justice, and fair opportunity for everybody." Throughout the book, Cullen keeps returning to one of the early themes of the American dream: the tension between the optimism of grand aspirations and the disappointment when individuals—and the country as a whole—fail to measure up.

Can America again fulfill its promise to be the land of opportunity, where new ideas and hard work produce material and spiritual rewards?

The anxiety of America's "looming national decline" defines Newt Gingrich's discussion of American exceptionalism. Gingrich looks to many of the same documents and national heroes for his story: the Declaration of Independence, the Founding Fathers, Lincoln, and even Martin Luther King, Jr. But, not surprisingly, he builds them into a conservative narrative about America's past, present, and future. He opens his book with the story of an American military officer reading the Declaration of Independence to his troops in lower Manhattan on July 9, 1776. This story links tyrannies old and new (British troops and al-Qaeda terrorists) and stresses the role of

Christianity to highlight the righteousness of the American struggle for independence. Americans here are the underdog fighting for freedom against "the greatest transoceanic invasion force in history." The ideals of this struggle, he tells us, were "worth fighting for, suffering for, and dying for. That is what made Americans unique in human history and made America, from its inception, a nation like no other."[16]

America is uniquely superior, Gingrich explains, because the country is founded on ideals rather than on Europe's "blood and soil" nationalism: "The ideals expressed in the Declaration of Independence, and the unique American identity that arose from an American civilization that honored them, form what we call today 'American Exceptionalism.'" To keep America's "singular set of vigorous virtues and habits of liberty" alive, Gingrich feels that people need to practice them in their everyday political, economic, and cultural life.[17]

To explain his American creed, Gingrich highlights the following values: religious liberty, private property and economic opportunity, freedom of assembly, the right to know laws, and national defense as the government's primary role.[18] He thus hits hot-button conservative issues: America as a Christian nation, individual rights and responsibilities, family values, free enterprise, military strength, and a deep suspicion of government. Gingrich celebrates the Puritans at Plymouth Plantation for their religious values and the Jamestown settlement for its capitalist values. While individual rights are the bedrock of the American creed, Gingrich tells us that traditional family values are crucial for spiritual, political, and economic success.

Gingrich's book thus confirms Seymour Martin Lipset's scholarly analysis of American exceptionalism that sees its key values as liberty, egalitarianism, individualism, populism, and laissez-faire. Americans are exceptionally "liberal" in the "classical anti-statist meaning of the term" from the 18th and 19th centuries. But by American exceptionalism, Lipset does not mean exceptionally *good*. Rather, he sees America's political religion as a "double-edged sword" that produces both positive and negative outcomes: "It is the most religious, optimistic, patriotic, rights-oriented, and individualistic. With respect to crime, it still has the highest rates; with respect to incarceration, it has the most people locked up in jail; with respect to litigiousness, it has the most lawyers per capita of any country in the world." The United States is the wealthiest and most productive country, but it is also least egalitarian in terms of income distribution among developed countries. For Lipset, America is exceptional in the sense of being an "outlier," of being qualitatively different from other developed nations.[19]

Gingrich, however, sees America as exceptionally good, the "land of infinite possibility" where people are "free to try, fail, try again, and succeed."[20] America for him is a moral nation: a beacon to the world. Even when the United States goes to war, Gingrich tells us, it fights for peace. To explain "peace through strength" in ways similar to Senior Colonel Liu Mingfu, Gingrich recalls Ronald Reagan speaking on the campaign trail in 1980: "We're not a warlike people. Quite the opposite. We always seek to live in peace. We resort to force infrequently and with great reluctance, and only when we've determined that it's absolutely necessary.... We know only too well that war comes not when the forces of freedom are strong; it is when they are weak that tyrants are tempted."

The American dream of American exceptionalism is available to foreigners too, Gingrich explains, because it "embodies truths that apply beyond America's borders; it is an invitation to all mankind to affirm its unalienable rights and pursue happiness."[21] An interventionist foreign policy that spreads the universal values of the American dream around the world thus is an important part of American exceptionalism. At the same time, it also inspires Christian and white fundamentalist groups like the John Birch Society, which try to guard the racial and ideological purity of American exceptionalism. (The John Birch Society is named after a Christian missionary and American spy who was killed by Chinese communists in 1945.)

While the threat during the Cold War was the Soviet Union's "Evil Empire," Gingrich feels that American exceptionalism is now threatened by a different set of enemies: America's "radical-secularist Left," European socialism, and President Obama. Although the global financial crisis was the result of laissez-faire capitalism run amok, for Gingrich the key problem is the "failed" European model of a big-government welfare state that is biased against religion. Although negative images of China later became prominent in the general election campaign, Gingrich only mentions the PRC in passing. His main audience is Republican Party activists; thus, the main enemies are Democrats.

Like a good futurologist, Gingrich ends his book with a scenario that forecasts how the world will be on January 20, 2021, when he would have fulfilled his own American dream of being a two-term president. Gingrich's dream presidency will "restore American exceptionalism" with a strategic vision that "reverses the damage the Left has done to America." In the "new American century...excellence, hard work and merit will be honored and admired, not punished and scorned." Gingrich concludes that after his time in office, "A richer, freer, and stronger America will be an even more generous and more virtuous America." Hence, in the last paragraph of his book Gingrich declares that the way to save America is to elect him president: "The fight to renew America starts in 2012. I ask you to join us in this effort to restore America as a nation like no other."[22]

Although Gingrich's election campaign eventually failed in 2012, his understanding of American exceptionalism is important because it expresses ideas that are popular among conservatives in the United States.[23] In other words, Obama's victory in 2012 does not mean that American exceptionalism will fade away as a rallying point.

Chinese Exceptionalism

The idea that Chinese civilization is not just uniquely unique but "uniquely superior"—and uniquely threatened—is where the China dream becomes Chinese exceptionalism (*Zhongguo teshulun*). While American exceptionalism grows out of the idea that the United States is the world's first new nation, Chinese exceptionalism looks to 5,000 years of uniquely continuous civilization to see China as the world's first ancient civilization.

While American exceptionalists see the United States as a beacon of freedom and democracy, Chinese exceptionalists see their country as a peaceful and harmonious alternative to Pax Americana. Although historians have provided a nuanced analysis of China's turbulent imperial history,[24] many strategists and public intellectuals still take for granted the exceptionalist argument of China's civilization as "inherently peaceful." But Chinese exceptionalism actually involves more than just trumpeting the country's "peaceful civilization."

Just as in the United States, Chinese exceptionalists assume that their country is exceptionally *good*. Chinese philosopher Kang Xiaoguang explains this in his seminal essay "Chinese exceptionalism": "Chinese people themselves think that their race-nation is the most superior in the world. Even when they are in dire straits, they always feel that they should be the number one in the world."[25]

Kang's fascinating article repeats many of the fundamentalist themes discussed in this book—racial superiority, a unique China model, an elitist government, a paternalistic dictatorship, and radical cultural difference. Like Gordon Gecko proclaiming "greed is good" in *Wall Street*, Kang proudly endorses the "arrogance" of China's new self-confidence.

Although his ultimate goal is a World of Great Harmony (*shijie datong*) based on China's "inherently peaceful" civilization, Kang primarily sees

Chinese exceptionalism as a negative factor—defining not what China is but what it isn't. The short answer is: China is exceptional simply because it is *not* Western or democratic. Since China's experience is different from that of the West, he explains, "Western experience cannot dictate the future of China, and China's future will not simply repeat the past experience of others." Here Kang joins those who question the economic determinism of the Washington Consensus that tells us that liberal markets inevitably lead to liberal democracy.

But he goes further: because China is uniquely unique, the experiences of the Third World, post-socialist states in eastern Europe and Russia, and the "Confucian cultural circle" of East Asian countries (including Japan) are also irrelevant to China's development path. A major theme of Chinese exceptionalism, then, is not just promoting China's road as an alternative to mainstream development theory. To make sense of China as an alternative, Kang needs to go beyond criticizing economic theory to figure his model as the "opposite of Western individualism and a rejection of Western culture."

Here Kang joins others who can paint a rosy picture of the China dream only *after* they have "Occidentalized" the West through negative stereotypes. "Orientalism," according to Edward Said, was not simply a description of "the East" produced by Europe's imperial bureaucrats. Orientalism mixed culture and politics to become European imperialism's "corporate institution for dealing with the Orient—dealing with it by making statements about it, authorizing views of it, describing it, by teaching it, settling it, ruling over it; in short, Orientalism as a Western style for dominating, restructuring, and having authority over the Orient."[26] The motto of London's School of Oriental and African Studies, which was set up to train imperial functionaries, is "Knowledge is Power."

Occidentalism works the same way as Orientalism, except in reverse: China asserts authority over itself and the West by first rejecting the West, and then searching for Chinese values in a negative quest. Criticizing the West is thus a crucial part of producing China's martial spirit (Liu Mingfu, Chan Koonchung, Jiang Rong) and its organic conflict-free society (Zhao Tingyang, Pan Wei, the Shanghai Expo). Recall that Hu Angang points to America's "excessive individualism" to show the value of Chinese harmony; to promote what he calls the "China road," he has to denounce the Washington Consensus as the "evil road."

Prominent strategist Yan Xuetong likewise Occidentalizes the United States in his discussions of geostrategy. In *Ancient Chinese Thought, Modern Chinese Power* (2011), Yan argues that we need to understand global politics in moral terms.²⁷ To make his case, he looks to the ancient distinction between the "Kingly Way" (*wangdao*) and the "Hegemonic Way" (*badao*). But rather than using these concepts for a sophisticated analysis of ethics and international affairs, Yan defines the Kingly Way as unquestionably good and the Hegemonic Way as thoroughly evil. Yan then follows the Occidentalist trend to code China and America: China is the exemplary moral power, while the United States is the hypocritically evil hegemon. Thus, Yan concludes that China's rise will benefit the world simply because it is not "America."

Beijing often says that the PRC will be a moral power, as opposed to a "hegemonic" one like the United States. Yet, when Chinese leaders and citizen intellectuals insist that the PRC will never be hegemonic, they are not saying that China will not dominate; they are merely saying that the PRC will never see itself as immoral, which, as experience shows, few countries do. To be fair, the United States often makes the same arguments—but this suggests that China will not be a different kind of world leader if and when it gains global power.

As we have seen throughout this book, many citizen intellectuals are much clearer about what they do not like—the West and the United States—than they are about China's alternative to it. Their impact thus may be more negative—to delegitimize the current U.S.-guided world order—than positive in the sense of promoting a coherent post-American world order.

This is because China's Occidentalism is not a conclusion drawn from rigorous analysis. Rather, it is the starting point of Chinese exceptionalism: Citizen intellectuals first decide that they don't like the "West," and only then go in search of proper Chinese values (which then are presented as China's eternal moral code). While there is much discussion of Chinese culture's "inherent tolerance," Kang states that the "Chinese public's anti-American sentiment" is provoked by the "resentment of American values and norms."

After reading these books, you could be forgiven for thinking that there are no families in America and no individuals in China, and that the PRC is a peaceful Utopia while the West is a sea of chaos and violence. As many China dreamers conclude, we are in a grand civilizational battle between the Chinese system and the Western system. Pan Wei thus asks, "In the next 30 years; which direction will the Chinese nation take? Will it preserve China's rejuvenation? Or will it have superstitious faith in the Western 'liberal democracy' system, and go down the road of decline and enslavement?"

The East/West logic of this Occidentalism, in which Chinese authors construct an evil and failing West as the opposite of a virtuous and successful

China, inflames Chinese readers' righteous rage and sense of global injustice. While it is laudable to question the economic determinism of the Washington Consensus, it is unfortunate that many Chinese authors replace it with a cultural determinism of "inevitables" and "undeniables" that tell us what Chinese people can—and, more importantly, *cannot*—do.

This stereotypical view of China as a timeless civilization that is on a uniquely superior path is also popular in books written by left- and right-wing authors in the West. Martin Jacques's *China Rules the World* (2009) and Henry Kissinger's *On China* (2011) both use idealized views of the Chinese empire to tell us about the PRC's 21st-century politics.[28] Their negative vision of China's destiny follows Kang's Occidentalist lead: "it is inconceivable that Chinese politics will come to resemble those of the West."[29]

Of course, many different views are found in China. In "Does China Need a Leviathan?" Shanghai historian Xu Jilin provides a biting critique of current trends in Chinese thought. He argues that the shift from nationalism to statism (in the sense of Thomas Hobbes's Leviathan that has complete control over people) is indicative of the "collective right turn" of many of China's intellectuals over the past decade. People who were liberals in the 1980s and nationalists in the 1990s are now statists. Xu's critical discussion of trends among China's top thinkers confirms Chan Koonchung's novelistic description of ideological debates in China where Hobbes's Leviathan is also more prominent than Confucius.

Both Chan and Xu are worried about the possible outcome of the PRC's current ideological debate that feeds on China's exceptional values. Xu explains how Nazi Germany and Imperial Japan had similar statist/exceptionalist debates in the 1930s. One of Chan's subplots in *The Golden Age* describes the rise of a popular fascist movement in Beijing in 2013. Xu thus worries that the PRC's current ideological debate that feeds on China's exceptional values risks becoming the road to fascism, which he concludes would push China "off a cliff."[30]

Conclusion: Comparing Dreams and Exceptionalisms

The discourse of the American dream/exceptionalism shares a common rhetoric with the discourse of the China dream/exceptionalism. Both countries see themselves as uniquely unique and uniquely superior moral communities that have something great to offer the world. Both are characteristically optimistic and pragmatic with a can-do attitude that animates people to work hard for a better future. Like the United States, China expects the world to be both surprised and grateful for its offers of help—and it gets upset when the world is not enthusiastic about its activities.

Yet, Chinese and American citizen intellectuals all worry that their treasured values are at risk. Chinese deal with this existential threat through "patriotic worrying" (see the introduction), while Americans do it through "jeremiads," the bitter political sermons from people such as John Winthrop and Newt Gingrich that criticize the moral corruption of society and lament the nation's imminent decline.[31] The more extreme Chinese voices actually sound like Gingrich: both hate liberals and see their mission as fighting against a conspiracy of evil empires bent on snatching away what is seen as their countries' rightful—and righteous—place in the sun. For American exceptionalists in the Republican Party, Europe and its welfare state are the main threat; for Chinese exceptionalists, America and its democratic political system are the main enemy.

Lastly, both have plans not only for saving their nation from ruin, but also for saving the world. Each country's uniquely superior values, we are told, are so good that they need to be exported to other countries—whether these countries like it or not. American exceptionalism informs the foreign policy of spreading freedom and democracy around the world—often through military intervention. Remember that Abraham Lincoln felt that its universal ideals made America the "last, best hope of earth."

Many Chinese citizen intellectuals have a similar mission for their country. China no longer needs to just save itself; Chinese people, we are told, must accept the demands of the "yellow man's burden" and look to their ancient culture for ideas to save the world—usually from America. Thus, Chinese exceptionalism looks to China's uniquely superior civilization to unite the globe in a World of Great Harmony that promises peace and prosperity. Here harmony risks becoming "harmonizing" and peace "pacifying."

Kang Xiaoguang explains this inevitable—but uneasy—future in characteristically blunt terms: "The West does not like the future of China, and Chinese people do not necessarily like it either. But both foreigners and Chinese must accept reality. We all need to learn to live with a 'different' China." The PRC's official news agency Xinhua has a more optimistic version of China's inevitable destiny: now the "Chinese dream" is for Americans to come to China to pursue fame and fortune.[32] Horace Greeley's advice to "Go west, young man," is transformed into "Go East, young person!"

Such unabashed boosterism should not be surprising. The American dream emerged as a topic of discussion in the 1930s when the United States was struggling through a devastating depression while also rising to global power. The China dream emerged with the rise of China in the 21st century. Rising powers characteristically see themselves as both unique and better than the incumbent world power (the United Kingdom for America, and the United States for China). As American exceptionalism shows, part of the pleasure of being a great power is celebrating the moral value of your new world order.

In *China and the American Dream*, Madsen explains how America's pre-1949 Christian missionary experience in China continues to shape its view of the PRC. "Red China," as is well known, inspired Cold War rivalry abroad and McCarthyism at home for American exceptionalists. Madsen, however, shows how the PRC also inspired liberal American dreamers to convert China to democracy after U.S.-China diplomatic relations were reestablished in 1979. Through his detailed study, Madsen shows how these Americans didn't simply work to reinvigorate science, culture, and democracy in China: "The liberal myth about China helped to reinvigorate American institutions with a new, hopeful justification, seeming to provide a new validating purpose for their practices."[33] The new mission to convert China to democratic modernity thus rejuvenated key institutions of the American dream, namely universities, foundations, and churches.

In recent years, China has revived its own missionary tradition. Certainly, it is common for Chinese citizen intellectuals to contrast the positive factors of China's secular ethical tradition with what they see as the negative factors of American evangelism, especially intolerant missionaries such as John Birch before 1949, and now arrogant democrats who hope to convert China in the 21st century. Chinese voices thus say that China doesn't have a missionary tradition; rather than actively spreading its ideas abroad, its civilization has attracted people to come to China to study its culture and values.

But as we've seen in this book, many Chinese intellectuals have a missionary mentality. The officials and citizen intellectuals discussed in chapter 2 conclude that the PRC has a moral mission to improve the world either as a peace-loving nation or through its martial spirit. Many citizen intellectuals, as noted in chapter 3, feel that the China model will make the PRC a new type of superpower that will spread peace and prosperity around the world. Throughout the book the ancient ideal of a unified world of Great Harmony keeps cropping up as China's final goal. Since 2004, Beijing has opened 691 Confucius Institutes around the world, including 287 in the United States, to spread Chinese language, culture, and values to foreigners. As China's propaganda czar Li Changchun has declared, Confucian Institutes are an "important component of China's grand external propaganda program."[34]

Thus, the soft power of spreading Chinese culture and values around the world is often joined to the hard power of Beijing pursuing its national interests on the world stage. Like "Americanism," Chinese civilization here works as an ideology, the "political religion of the nation": recall that "Chinese" was one of the options on a menu of world faiths offered at the Shanghai Expo. And like Americans and the American creed, Chinese people are increasingly confident about spreading the gospel of Chinese values around the world.

This is also not a new phenomenon either. During the imperial period, Chinese authorities often enforced a strict division between "civilization" and "barbarism" that had serious political consequences.[35] In other words, if China's neighbors did not accept imperial Confucianism, then they risked invasion—and even extermination. Thus, the morality of Chinese exceptionalism exhibits a strong political piety that predates the moralized politics of American exceptionalism by millennia.

While the rhetoric of American and Chinese dreams and exceptionalisms is often quite similar—appealing to fundamentalist notions of civilization and race—their content differs in important ways. The goal of the China dream/exceptionalism generally is national rejuvenation through state power. Both Liu Mingfu's and Hu Angang's China dreams are for the PRC to be the number one country in the world. As mentioned, everyone seems to see the super state of the World of Great Harmony as their ultimate goal. The American dream, however, generally promotes individual freedom and success, and it tends to be suspicious of state power. In his discussion of Chinese exceptionalism, Kang Xiaoguang talks about the problems and achievements of the CCP and the Chinese state rather than those of the Chinese people. He is optimistic because the government—rather than the people—has a "strong learning ability." In the United States, we are often told, it is the job of the people to save themselves—often from government interference. As California businesswoman and U.S. Senate candidate Carly Fiorina put it: "The federal government does not create the American dream, although the federal government can surely destroy the American dream."[36]

Yet, some American dreams are collective: The dream of equality is expressed by many groups in civil society, which aim to use state power to build an egalitarian society at large. Curiously, the dreams of most Chinese citizen intellectuals are turning away from the quest for equality that characterized their 20th-century experience to advocate native Chinese hierarchical visions of social order and world order. The family values of traditional village society and the Confucian values of imperial China are both back in vogue.

Scenario

A CHIMERICAL DREAM

BEYOND UNDERSTANDING HOW Chinese people—especially the PRC's new citizen intellectuals—see their future, one of the book's main goals has been to appreciate the intimate connections between things that we thought were hostile opposites, like East/West and fundamentalism/cosmopolitanism. It is appropriate then to conclude the book by looking beyond scenarios that use hard official data to forecast clear geopolitical futures for "China" and "the United States" as discrete entities. By highlighting the partial overlaps and strange crossovers of a particular Chimerican dream, we can see a different range of possibilities for China's role in the world, which then entails a different set of outcomes for the West.

Perhaps Chimerica is not the most felicitous term for this new dynamic. British historian Niall Ferguson and German economist Moritz Schularik coined it in 2006 to describe America and China's codependent relationship, where the PRC produces and the United States consumes, that defines the global economy, which now is in danger of unraveling.[1] Rather than speak in such epic terms, which tend to encourage a macho style of exceptionalism in the United States and China, this scenario will look to the global implications of the personal politics of one young woman's Chimerican dream. In this way we can complicate the simple forecasts about China's "inevitable" rise to wealth and power, and we can acquire a more nuanced understanding of how it will impact people in the West as well.

Du Lala as China's Everywoman

While it is common to see U.S.-China relations in terms of a battle of stereotypes—Chinese families versus American individuals—the blockbuster film *Du Lala's Promotion Diary* (*Du Lala shengzhi ji*, 2010), which is based on a novel by the same name, tells quite a different tale.[2] Although China's fundamentalists and exceptionalists characteristically see international politics as a grand struggle between China and the United States, this feature film shows how American and Chinese people can work together for mutual benefit.

The film tells the story of a young woman, Du Lala, pursuing her dream job in DB, an American Fortune 500 corporation that is trying to penetrate the Chinese market. Hence, the two national dreams dissolve into the Chimerican dream: the American "China dream" of the PRC as the "last great untapped market on Earth,"[3] and a Chinese woman's "American dream" of upward mobility in the PRC.

The point is to see how this particular Chimerican dream of overlapping interests and shared values has wider implications for ordinary Chinese and Western people. What can Du Lala's rise in the cosmopolitan corporate world tell us about the rise of China in the global community? What are the economic, social, cultural, and political costs and benefits of a Du Lala–like rise for China?

The first half of the film charts Lala's advancement in DB as a metaphor for China shifting from national economic plans to enter the global market economy. Here the corporate world is a new world of endless possibilities and dangers. Even the task of finding a job is relatively novel in China: until the end of the 1990s the party-state assigned jobs to most college graduates. So the details of applying for a job, interviewing, and job training that appear ordinary to Western viewers are still extraordinary to the Chinese audience.

While exotic ideas like "face" and "networks" dominate Western management books about business in China, Lala is presented to us as an ordinary woman. She has no family connections, a B.A. in English from an average university, and is pretty in a girl-next-door kind of way. Lala thus represents the Chinese everywoman from the post-1980 generation: She has to compete for the entry level receptionist job at DB through the normal application process. Lala thus is a self-made woman who climbs the corporate ladder by working hard and taking advantage of opportunities. Like a Chinese Ben Franklin, she declares "I believe hard work can bring success. Laziness never accomplishes anything."

We follow Lala as she is introduced to the exotic experience of working in a foreign multinational corporation in Beijing. The film thus takes us to Lala's orientation meeting where the Human Resources Department (HR) explains that "DB is a global Fortune 500 company. Everything we do is S.O.P. [Standard Operating Procedure]. . . . DB is an American company that values efficiency and innovation." HR gives Lala a handbook full of rules and

FIGURE 7.1 Du Lala at DB
Source: Screenshot from *Du Lala's Promotion Diary*

regulations, but while they are shopping after work Lala's new office friend Helen explains the two most important rules: (1) don't embezzle the company's money, and (2) no office romance. Helen then gives Lala the lay of the land at DB, in a class analysis reminiscent of Mao Zedong's "Report on the Peasant Movement in Hunan" (1927):

- Everyone below management is "small potatoes": they make less than 4000 RMB per month.
- Managers are the middle class: they have their own cars and an annual salary over 200,000 RMB.
- Directors are the upper class: they make over 500,000 RMB a year.
- The Beijing-based CEO makes more than 1 million RMB a year.

While Helen is describing each level, the film cuts to shots of people in DB who exemplify each category. So when she concludes "What does it mean to be rich? That's what it means to be rich," the screen shows Howard the American CEO lounging in the garden outside his huge house in the Beijing suburbs.

Rather than fighting this "American imperialist" to promote the China model as Pan Wei and Liu Mingfu would demand, Lala takes Howard as her role model for career success.

The secret of Lala's success is not radical: find out the rules and exploit them. Her career strategy, which she discusses in an online diary, repeats the "efficiency and innovation" mantra of the orientation meeting: "How to keep your boss appreciating you. Work effectively. You also must show potential. If you don't work hard and don't show your talent then you won't get anywhere."

Lala's career plan seems to employ a naïve mish-mash of self-help slogans. Yet, it's hard to be too critical because she is so fabulously successful. Lala gets a promotion each year, with the film charting her rise with an on-screen personnel file-like accounting that lists her age, new title, and new salary for each new job.

Lala's meteoric rise is also reflected in her wardrobe. Helen not only teaches Lala the unspoken rules of the game, but also gives her advice on how to shop and what to wear. As Lala climbs the corporate ladder she not only gains self-confidence, but also gets more fashionable clothes. To highlight the shared values of global business and the world of fashion, the film's producers recruited the costume designer from "Sex in the City" to be the fashion adviser for *Du Lala*.

Du Lala thus is an instruction manual both for how to succeed in corporate China and for how to be a global consumer. China's 12th Five-Year Plan promises that the country's economy will soon be fueled by domestic consumption. *Du Lala's Promotion Diary* gives an idealized view of how this would work. The movie's establishing shots show Beijing as a capitalist utopia reminiscent of the Shanghai World Expo site: The film cuts between billboards, shiny skylines, moving traffic, clear blue skies, and shopping malls. At one point, Lala explains that there are two ways for women to decompress from hard work: eat chocolate and go shopping. To recover from breaking up with her boyfriend, Lala pushes retail therapy to the limit, spending all of her savings on a sports car, which she buys with a credit card. Although this may not be remarkable to Western viewers, buying your first car and using a credit card are still exotic and exciting experiences for China's new middle class.

Thus, the film and the novel both tell people how to be modern: how to work, live—and succeed—in the ruthless global market economy that knits together Chinese and American individuals, rules, aspirations, and values.

The Du Lala *Industry*

Du Lala's Promotion Diary is hugely influential in China, especially among recent college graduates and white-collar workers. It has become much more than a novel or a film: It is now an industry. The original novel was a bestseller, and its author Li Ke published two sequels that were also very popular. *Du Lala* was made into a movie by actor-director Xu Jinglei, a stage play, and a television series—all of which have been successful. The novels sold millions of legitimate copies and even more pirated copies. In China, knock-offs— different books that parody the successful title—are another mark of success: *The Story of Mao Mao's Promotion*, for example, is a novel about a female cat's "white-collar" life.[4]

Du Lala's Promotion Diary is part of a new genre of "workplace novels" that has taken China by storm. *The New Yorker* correspondent Leslie T. Chang describes their appeal in simple terms: "What do Chinese, some of the hardest-working people on the planet, read in their spare time? Novels about work."[5] Some people read workplace novels for fun as "chick lit" or "fast food fiction." But most see *Du Lala's Promotion Diary* as a "reference book" of strategies for getting ahead in the corporate world. Li Ke, the pseudonym for someone who worked at IBM China, thus shares the riches of her experience in an American multinational with China's up-and-coming middle class.

While many of the China dreams we've examined describe a vague Utopia—Under-Heaven, Great Harmony, the Kingly Way, organic village society—with little sense of how each could be put into practice, Li Ke's novel provides a detailed roadmap of instructions for the path to success: find a good industry, a good company in that industry, the strongest sector in that company, a strong and supportive boss, and so on.[6] The book's preface declares that Lala's story of working in a foreign company is even more "valuable than Bill Gates."[7]

Du Lala is a very different kind of intervention from Chan Koonchung's sci-fi novel *The Golden Age,* which offers a detailed description of the China model and its political costs. *Du Lala*, both as a novel and as a film, is like Lala as a character: It is about how to succeed in the office politics of global capitalism. While others worry about surviving the hazards of everyday life in China (see Box 7.1), *Du Lala* celebrates the fruits of corporate struggle.

Rather than being a story of life-or-death struggles in the corporate world, *Du Lala's Promotion Diary* is more like Dale Carnegie's *How to Win Friends*

We Survived a Day in China!

Man: I'm so glad you weren't poisoned (to death) by gutter oil, Sudan red, lean meat essence, or toxic buns!

Your house didn't catch on fire!

The bridge in front of your house didn't collapse, right?

You're so lucky that the escalator didn't malfunction when you went to work!

It's wonderful! We survived another day!

Woman: I was so worried you'd get run over by someone supposedly going 70 kph on your way to work!

Or get stabbed eight times in a row!

My gravest fear was that you would be accidentally injured by security guards who were beating up someone else!

I was also worried you would need to ride the high speed train!

> But I didn't dare to call you, because I was afraid your cell phone would explode!
>
> [These worries each refer to actual incidents and scandals that have rocked China over the past few years.]
>
> *Source*: Danwei.org[8]

and Influence People (the Chinese translation of which is very popular in the PRC). Lala's career strategy employs Lung Ying-tai's "power of civility" for success in China's corporate world. It shows how an ordinary woman—"a good girl"—can succeed in business through hard work and talent rather than through scheming and back-stabbing.

Du Lala's uncritical view of the China dream and the China model is wildly popular, especially among young women. The *Du Lala* industry has generated fan-books: *We All Could Be Lala* highlights how the Du Lala character itself has become a role model.[9] As one young woman explains: "I don't feel alone anymore. There are thousands of Du Lalas who try to make it on their own and live better lives, like me. It's a very practical book for active young women."[10]

Even those with relatively stable university jobs, like Ms. Wang Baixue, feel that Du Lala's experience of a successful career that does not rely on family connections "rings true, it's our own story." Lala "represents the post-1980 generation's way of thinking," Wang explained. "She's a good girl, who respects her parents, but doesn't necessarily do what they say. She listens to them, and then does what she wants."[11] *Du Lala* thus shows young women how they can live life on their own terms.

While young men are attracted to Han Han's adventures, many young women look not only to Du Lala as a role model, but also to actor-director Xu Jinglei. Xu's attributes actually reflect many of Lala's. Xu comes from an ordinary family, and she took advantage of China's expanding educational opportunities to attend the elite Beijing Film Academy. She started acting in a TV drama while still a student, and she has steadily built her career over the past fifteen years. In addition to acting and directing, she publishes *Kaila,* an e-magazine for yuppie women like Lala. Soon after she started her "Lao Xu" blog in 2005, it rose to become the most popular blog in the world—until it was unseated by Han Han's TwoCold blog in 2008.

Even with all of these ventures, Xu is single-minded in her focus on making interesting films: She uses the blog primarily to promote her films and uses the e-mag to court advertisers to fund them. Thus, she convinced Lenovo, China's top computer corporation, to fund *Du Lala* through product placements—which are not hard to miss since Lenovo computers are on every desk as well as on many billboards in exterior shots. (The irony here is that Li Ke used to work at IBM China, and Lenovo bought IBM's PC division in 2005).

Thus this film about how to succeed in business is itself a business venture: although Xu Jinglei is better known for directing award-winning art house films like *My Father and I* (2004), *Du Lala* is an unashamedly commercial film. While it probably isn't Xu's best film aesthetically, it was very successful at the box office. Xu thus has both creative abilities and skills as a deal maker. She shows young women how to take control of their own lives: "I won't do things because of the expectations of others," Xu explains. "I do things because I want to do them. That's the only reason I can do things well."[12] Thus, in addition to winning film awards, Xu is the most commercially successful female director in China.

In this way, Li Ke and Xu Jinglei represent a different kind of citizen intellectual: like Lala, they are career women who play with the system's rules to gain the material success of fame and fortune.

Mixed Feelings

If the first half of the movie is a guidebook about how to be a modern business-woman—and how to be a global consumer—then the second half shows the costs of following the rules. Lala is known in her office for her single-minded pursuit of corporate success. The best comparison here is not *Sex in the City*, but *The Good Wife*, which focuses on the trials and tribulations of a woman pursuing a career—rather than taking care of a husband.

Lala's promotion diary thus is a story of women, by women, and for women. She is surrounded by the problems of modern life in which women constantly have to choose between career and family in a system dominated by men. She left her previous job because her old boss was sexually harassing her. At DB the secretaries are all women, whose career objective is to join the middle class by marrying a manager. DB's rule against office romance is also weighted against women: when Helen's affair with a manager is discovered, she's forced to quit because secretaries are expendable. (Helen reappears later in the film as a happy manager's wife, so she "wins" in the end.)

Lala feels these social pressures too. After a one night stand with Wang Wei (a.k.a David), DB's high-flying sales director, she ponders the risks and rewards of dating him. Lala's younger brother Man Yi thinks David is "a good catch." But Lala hesitates: "I think I should focus on my career. I think I have a future there. According to the company rules, I would lose my job" if the affair were discovered. Man Yi replies: "At your age you should concentrate on finding Mr. Right and settling down."

Here Lala faces the double risk of losing her job if she dates David or ending up an "old" unmarried career woman—a "leftover woman" (*shengnü*), according to Chinese slang—if she doesn't. Lala squares this circle in a typically ambitious way: She decides to secretly date David.

But by trying to have it all, Lala's Chimerican dream of corporate success and true love starts to unravel. She wonders whether pursuing her dream job ultimately will lead her to the good life. Rose, Lala's sometime boss and rival, expresses the mixed feelings she had when finally promoted to the upper class of DB's directors: "I used to care so much about promotions. I thought only a promotion could prove my value. Different title now, but so what? I'm not happy at all. Whatever." *Du Lala's Promotion Diary* thus counts the costs of the China model, much like we saw in chapters 4 and 5.

The novel explores the uneasy relationship between work and values in its penultimate chapter, "The Free and Easy Life" (*Ziyou zizai dihuo*), which the preface tells us is the "essence" of Du Lala's story. Discussing life goals with a stranger on a plane, Lala decides that getting her dream job is not as important as pursuing the "free and easy dream," which is better understood as the dream of being free to live life on your own terms. As Lala explains:

> Considering the characteristics of the middle class, it is the most tired class. Having no special family background, they struggle for success as individuals, completing their tasks and obeying the law to honestly pass the days. But what does enduring all of this have to do with "being free to live life on your own terms"?[13]

The goal, Lala decides, is not to work hard at building something important like the nation, the company, or the brand. The best life objective is to earn enough money to retire early and be your own boss. Thus, financial freedom is necessary to pursue the good life.

In the film, David does just that. He quits DB and opens up a guest house in Pattaya, Thailand. The film ends when Lala returns to Pattaya to reminisce about their first romantic encounter. She meets him by chance and, thus, is able to fulfill her dream of being with him again—if only for a short time.

Chimerican Values

Du Lala's Chimerican dream offers an interesting cocktail of values that lead to different versions of the good life. Like the American dream, *Du Lala's Promotion Diary* is a story of upward mobility. When provided with equal opportunity Lala succeeds as an individual, a self-made woman, based on her own hard work and talent. As the novel's preface explains, you must identify opportunities, create opportunities, and seize opportunities. We also see the flipside of this dream: anxieties over the high probability of failure. As he's about to be fired, David admits that "anyone can be replaced."

Workplace novels also pursue the American dreams of home ownership and fame and fortune. As we saw in the film's class analysis, the ultimate goal is a house in the leafy suburbs. *Du Lala* also teaches young Chinese how to consume luxury goods.

Here Lala's Chimerican dream goes against some of the China dreamers examined in this book. While socialism still needs to be taken seriously in assessments of Beijing's geostrategy and China's economic plans, building socialism is, to say the least, not a priority in *Du Lala's Promotion Diary*. Yet *Du Lala* can inform the China model in a different way if we think of DB as a microcosm of the PRC. Here China is neither a nation-state nor a civilization-state; rather, it is an "enterprise-state," as the Naisbitts put it in *China's Megatrends*. In the enterprise-state, as in corporations, people don't have rights, they have tasks; the company is not a commonwealth organized for the good of its members—its purpose is profit. As the Naisbitts explain, "Survival of the company has to take priority over individuals' interests and benefits. Those who would prefer to fight against the company's culture and goals would have to choose: leave or adjust."[14] Since this enterprise-state is a country, I suppose resigning means you leave China, while being fired means you end up in jail.

In this sense, Lala's ambitious goals inspire unease for many of China's citizen intellectuals: she is the epitome of an individual consumer who lacks Chinese values (for Zhao Tingyang), socialist values (for Pan Wei and Cui Zhiyuan), the martial spirit (for Liu Mingfu), and democratic values (for Lung Ying-tai and Xu Jilin). For different reasons, they all would think that Lala's "money-worship" lifestyle in China's enterprise-state offers a ruinous scenario for the PRC's future.

On the other hand, Lala's career as a domestic consumer would help rebalance the global economy, which is a goal shared by Beijing and Washington. But this consumer lifestyle would have a huge impact on the environment in China—and the global environment as well. In an alternative Chimerican venture, Peggy Liu heads a bilateral NGO that aims to reshape the China dream. This Chinese-American activist, who is known as "China's Green Goddess," is working to "decouple the rise in living standards from a rise in consumption." She hopes that this new lifestyle will result in a progressive shift from the American dream of unlimited consumption to a sustainably green "China dream."[15]

Du Lala author Li Ke would actually support Peggy Liu's new China dream, thinking that "The happiest thing is to have health and free time. My dream is to have good air, no traffic and quality education."[16]

While resolutely individualist, "Du Lala" is also quite cosmopolitan. The novel and the film mix in English words and phrases: S.O.P., "sexual harassment," EQ, "fight back," frustrate, "You deserve it," SMART, Nike, "I totally agree with you," and "Whatever!" The name of Lala's company, "DB," is always written in English; we never find out what it stands for or even what it sells. Using English is useful for explaining management-speak to readers who treat the novel as a guidebook for success in foreign corporations. Rather than branding people as "slaves to foreigners," English here is a sign of worldliness and prestige.

The film is also cosmopolitan in the Chinese sense of including famous actors from around greater China: David is played by Stanley Huang, Taiwan's top singer and actor; Rose is played by Karen Kok, a famous Hong Kong singer and actress; and Helen is played by Pace Wu, a model, singer, and actress from Taiwan. Lala's immediate boss is a mixed-race man who has a blonde wife; DB's Beijing-based CEO is an American who speaks fluent Chinese; and David's mother lives in the United States. The film's star and director, Xu Jinglei, is known as a citizen of the world: She went on a goodwill tour of South Africa as a citizen ambassador in 2008.[17]

The film is cosmopolitan in another way: rather than promote China's (or America's) national culture, people at DB promote the transnational corporate culture of global capitalism. To reward staff for a successful year, DB sponsored a company trip to the seaside resort of Pattaya, Thailand. While Beijing's aggressive foreign policy has alienated countries in East Asia and the West, Du Lala's cosmopolitan world happily mixes people from greater China, Southeast Asia, and the West. Of course, there are limits to her cosmopolitan utopia: Lala herself rarely speaks English and no one calls her by an English name.

Is this global corporate cosmopolitanism the preferred future for China in the world? It fits into Washington's view of China as a responsible power that rises within the current global system (that is dominated by America). Many of China's citizen intellectuals, however, would reject this model in favor of a world order designed by and for the PRC.

Yang Qianru, a young historian who is part of the Du Lala generation, is one of the few Chinese voices to question Beijing's quest for global leadership. She argues that China's "problem—both now and into the future—is to guarantee our own survival, development, and security, not to lead the world." While Zhao Tingyang quotes the Daoist classic the *Daode jing* (6th century BC) to argue that Beijing should set up the Under-Heaven system, Yang quotes the same book to explain how such leadership ambitions are doomed to failure: "I have seen that it is not possible to acquire Under-Heaven by striving.... To try to run it ends in failure; to try to grasp it leads to losing it."[18] Rather than striving for world leadership, Beijing should concentrate on building prosperity and values at home for the benefit of ordinary Chinese people.

But is it okay for China to be number two?

Lala's last dream of the good life—being free to live life on her own terms—recalls earlier American dreams inspired by the Declaration of Independence: the unalienable rights to life, liberty, and the pursuit of happiness. Even in Chinese, the phrase *ziyou zizai* entails a freedom from constraint: *ziyou* means liberty and *zizai* means unrestrained. Like artist Cai Guoqiang's Peasant da Vincis, Du Lala wants the freedom to escape the system to follow her dreams.

The strangest thing about the film is that this freedom is elsewhere: David and Lala find happiness abroad in Thailand. Chinese people thus have to leave the PRC to realize the Chimerican dream of "being free to live life on their own terms." (Perhaps this explains the recent trend of China's super-rich settling abroad.)

Certainly, we can't take for granted that Lala's mixture of values that highlights a lifestyle of careerism and consumption is ideal for China or the United States. The point of outlining this Chimerican dream, however, is not to provide a ready-made template for an alternative world order, which is the goal of the more fundamentalist China dreams considered in this book. Rather, it shows how the post-American order will not necessarily exclude the United States (or exclude the West from a post-liberal order), but that the new world order can include America in new and interesting ways. This Chimerican dream's goal, then, is to show the complexities of human experience, and highlight how positive and negative values are intertwined in our pessopti-mistic world.[19]

Du Lala's Promotion Diary, however, does not directly draw such political conclusions. If anything the novel and the film are intentionally apolitical. Both celebrate the China model and the China dream with few reservations. But like the work of many citizen intellectuals—Jia Zhangke's films and Cai Guoqiang's art come to mind—this deliberately apolitical approach is in itself quite political. It hints at other dreams, including alternative political possi-bilities. While Zhao Tingyang, Liu Mingfu, Hu Angang, and Pan Wei insist that we judge China on its own terms, Lala shows us how to question the Chimerican system to live life on our own terms.

Lala tells us that we need financial freedom to gain this social freedom. Is it too much of a stretch to think that Lala—who, as we are told, represents China's youth—could and would grow into Lung Ying-tai's China dream of political freedom and social responsibility?

Does *Du Lala* thus provide us with an alternative scenario for a China that works with the United States and its Asian neighbors not just for shared interests, but also for shared values?

Stay tuned. As the Chimerican dream portrayed in *Du Lala* shows, noth-ing is inevitable and the possibilities are endless.

Notes

INTRODUCTION

1. "China's Leap in Supercomputer Rankings," *Bloomberg Businessweek Online*, October 5, 2010; Sam Dillon, "Top Test Scores from Shanghai Stun Educators," *New York Times*, December 7, 2010.

2. Chan in Jeremy Godkin, "2013: Interview with Chan Koonchung," Danwei.org, June 25, 2010; also see Jaivin, "Yawning Heights."

3. "Xi Jinping: Kongtan wuguo shigan xingbang" [Xi Jinping: Talking about rejuvenating the country through hard work], Caixin wang, November, 30, 2012, http://china.caixin.com/2012-11-30/100466950.html.

4. Ai Weiwei in Obrist, *Ai Weiwei Speaks*, 69.

5. Rorty, *Achieving Our Country*, 101.

6. David Pilling, "Lunch with the FT: Han Han," *Financial Times*, April 21, 2012.

7. Jacques, *When China Rules the World*.

8. Kissinger, *On China*; Yan, *Ancient Chinese Thought*.

9. Howard W. French, "In Case You Missed Them: Books by Martin Jacques and Yasheng Huang," The China Beat, February 1, 2010; also see Anderson, "Sinomania."

10. See "Hawaii Research Center for Futures Studies," http://www.futures.hawaii.edu/.

11. Jin, *Zhongguo de weilai*; Hu and Yan, *Zhongguo*; Hu, *China in 2020*; Xiang, *2025: Zhongguo meng*; Hu, Yan, and Wei, *2030 Zhongguo*; Wu, Yu, and Fogel, *Zhongguo weilai 30 nian*; Bai, *2049*; Zhang, *Zhongguo zhenhan*.

12. See Andersson, "The Future Landscape," 17.

13. Naisbitt, *China's Megatrends*, xii.

14. See Callahan, *China: The Pessoptimist Nation*, 31–59.

15. Fong, "Filial Nationalism," 631.

16. Waldron, "The Rise of China," 728.

17. Studwell, *The China Dream*; Mann, *The China Fantasy*.

18. Woodside, "The Asia-Pacific Idea as a Mobilization Myth," 41–42.

19. Naisbitt, *China's Megatrends*, x.

20. Yang, "Weilai xuejia jiang 'Zhongguo gushi,'" 110.
21. See Liu, *Zhongguo meng*; Pan, *Zhongguo moshi*; Qin, "Guoji guanxi lilun Zhongguo pai."
22. Liu, *Zhongguo meng*, 88, 292; Pan, "Zhongguo weilai 30 nian," 62–64.
23. See Callahan and Barabantseva, *China Orders the World*.
24. "Qianyan" in Wu, *Zhongguo weilai 30 nian*, 1.
25. Bai, *2049*, 282.
26. Ferguson and Schularick, "Chimerica and the Global Asset Market Boom."
27. See Bandurski, "Zhang vs. Yang."
28. Hu and Yan, *Zhongguo*, 1; "A Plan Is Born," *Beijing Review*, September 13, 2010.
29. These two terms come from Andersson, "The Future Landscape," 17.
30. Hu and Yan, *Zhongguo*, 2.
31. "Zhe shi ganyu mengxiang de ni" [This is what you dare to dream], *Nanfang zhoumou*, August 12, 2010, p. 21.
32. Chan, *Shengshi*; Chan, *The Fat Years*. For a sense of the controversy in China see Paul Mooney, "2013: Them and Us," *South China Morning Post*, February 7, 2010; Lovell, "Preface."
33. See Liu, *Zhongguo meng*.
34. See Davies, *Worrying about China*.
35. See Chang, *The Coming Collapse of China*; Chang, "The Coming Collapse of China: 2012 Edition."
36. Liu, *Zhongguo meng*, 288, 290.
37. Callahan, *China: The Pessoptimist Nation*.
38. Liu, *Zhongguo meng*, 9. Also see Hu and Yan, *Zhongguo*, 1; Pan, "Zhongguo weilai 30 nian," 58.

CHAPTER 1

1. Yu, *Zhongguo yingdi*. Yu was forced into exile in 2011.
2. American Embassy Beijing, "Portrait of Vice President Xi Jinping"; Wu, *Zhongguo xin lingxiu*. For analysis that relies on more solid evidence, see the Hoover Institution's *China Leadership Monitor*, edited by Alice Miller; Lawrence, *China's Vice President Xi Jinping*.
3. "Xi Jinping: Kongtan wuguo shigan xingbang" [Xi Jinping: Talking about rejuvenating the country through hard work], Caixin wang, November 30, 2012, http://china.caixin.com/2012-11-30/100466950.html.
4. See Jane Perlez, "Dispute Flares Over Energy in South China Sea," *New York Times*, December 4, 2012.
5. Fewsmith, "Bo Xilai Takes On Organized Crime," 3.
6. Su, Yang and Liu, *Chongqing moshi*.
7. Associated Press, "Red Songs Fuels Chinese Politician's Ambitions," March 3, 2011.

8. Chris Buckley, "Briton Killed after Threat to Expose Chinese Leader's Wife," Reuters, April 16, 2012.

9. Cited in Wishik, "The Bo Xilai Crisis."

10. Cited in Geoff Dyer, "Who Will Be China's Next Leaders?" *Financial Times*, March 4, 2011.

11. Liu, "Charter 08" in *No Enemies, No Hatred*, 301.

12. Lovell, *The Politics of Cultural Capital*; Julia Lovell, "Beijing Values the Nobels: That's Why This Hurts," *The Independent* (London), October 9, 2010.

13. Alison Flood, "Nobel Winner Mo Yan Speaks Up for Jailed 'Subversive' Liu Xiaobo," *Guardian*, October 12, 2012.

14. Cited in Barmé, "Confession, Redemption, and Death."

15. Barmé, "Confession, Redemption, and Death."

16. Liu, Zhou, Hou, and Gao, "June Second Hunger Strike Declaration," in Liu, *No Enemies, No Hatred*, 278.

17. Zha, *Tide Players*, 210.

18. Liu, "I Have No Enemies," in Liu, *No Enemies, No Hatred*, 325.

19. Liu, "I Have No Enemies," 325.

20. Bei Ling, "Grin and Bare It," *South China Morning Post Magazine*, August 28, 2011.

21. For samples of Ai's blog, see Ai, *Cishi cidi*; Ai, *Ai Weiwei's Blog*.

22. Li and Chang, "Ai Weiwei shi yige you chuangzaoxing de yishujia."

23. Osnos, "It's Not Beautiful."

24. "Law Will Not Concede before Maverick," *Global Times*, April 6, 2011.

25. Ai Weiwei, "The City: Beijing," *Newsweek*, August 28, 2011.

26. Havel, *Living in Truth*, 80, 86, 101–103, 108.

27. Barmé, *In the Red*, 179–200.

28. Osnos, "The Long Shot," 95.

29. Weller, *Alternative Civilities*.

30. "China's Development 'Not a Model': Premier Wen," Xinhua, March 14, 2011.

31. Zhang, "Liu Xiaobo hu nuojiang." For a partial translation, see China Digital Times, http://chinadigitaltimes.net/2010/10/zhang-minchang-liu-xiaobo-wins-the-nobel-peace-prize-a-victory-for-universal-values/; also see the *Global Times* cited in "State Media Say Dissident Nobel Shows West's Fear," Reuters, October 11, 2010.

32. Zhang, "Yige qijo de pouxi." For a partial translation, see David Bandurski, "Zhang vs. Yang on the China Model," *China Media Project*, March 29, 2011.

33. Pan, "Dangdai Zhonghua tizhi"; Zhang, *Zhongguo zhenhan*. In 2012, Zhang's book was revised and translated into English as *The China Wave*.

34. Pan, *Nongmin yu shichang*.

35. Zhang, *Ideology and Economic Reform under Deng Xiaoping*; Zhang, *Transforming China*.

36. Zhang, "Liu Xiaobo hu nuojiang."

37. Cited in John Garnaut, "Profound Shift as China Marches Back to Mao," *Sydney Morning Herald*, October 9, 2011; Mark MacKinnon, "Political Rivalry Reflects a Split within China's Communist Party," *Globe and Mail* (Toronto), October 8, 2011.

38. Han Han, "Yao ziyou" [Wanting freedom], TwoCold blog, December 26, 2012, http://blog.sina.com.cn/twocold. For a translation see "Han Han On Wanting Freedom," EastWestNorthSouth blog, December 27, 2012, http://zonaeuropa.com/201112a.brief.htm#009.

39. Johnston, *Social States*.

40. Foot and Walter, *China, the United States, and Global Order*.

41. See Nordin, "Space for the Future."

42. Yan, *Ancient Chinese Thought*.

43. Zhang, *Lun Zhongguo haiquan*.

44. Chan Koonchung, *The Fat Years* (London: Doubleday, 2011), 267–278; Joshua Kurlantzick, *Charm Offensive: How China's Soft Power Is Transforming the World* (New Haven, CT: Yale University Press, 2007), 11; Hughes, "Reclassifying Chinese Nationalism."

45. "Don't Take Peaceful Approach for Granted," *Global Times*, October 25, 2011.

CHAPTER 2

1. Hu, "Nuli jianshe tejiu heping, gongtong fanrong de hexie shijie," 1.

2. Zhao, *Tianxia tixi*; Liu, *Zhongguo meng*.

3. Pieke, *The Good Communist*.

4. Shi, *Quanqiuxing de tiaozhan yu Zhongguo*.

5. Carlson, "Moving Beyond Sovereignty?" 98; also see Saunders, "Will China's Dream."

6. State Council, "China's Peaceful Development Road"; Hu Jintao, "Hold High the Great Banner of Socialism with Chinese Characteristics."

7. See Wang, *Harmony and War*; Reid and Zheng, *Negotiating Asymmetry*.

8. Fu, *Zhongguo lidai zhanzheng nianbiao*, cited in Wang, "The Chinese World Order."

9. State Council, "China's Peaceful Development."

10. Qin Xiaoying, "Harmonious Society to Be Model for the World," *China Daily*, October 13, 2006.

11. "Wen Wei Po Reports 17th Party Congress Report to Include "Harmonious World" Concept," *Wen Wei Po* (Hong Kong), October 15, 2010, translated in Open Source Center (OSC): 20071015710009.

12. Beijing's recent White Papers continue this trend (State Council, "China's Peaceful Development").

13. Jin, "Guang yu ying hexie shijie."

14. "PRC Academics Advocate Building More Harmonious World, Society," *Renmin wang*, November 9, 2005, translated in OSC: 200511091477. Wang has since moved to Peking University.

15. This section builds on analysis done in Callahan, *The Pessoptimist Nation*, 208–209.

16. Zhao, "All Under Heaven," 15.

17. Zhao, *Tianxia tixi*, rev ed.

18. Zhao, *Tianxia tixi*, 1.

19. Zhao, "Guanyu hexie shijie de sekao," 1.

20. Zhao, *Tianxia tixi*, 108, 40.

21. Yan, *Wangba tianxia sixiang ji qiyou*, 271.

22. Zhao, *Tianxia tixi*, 33.

23. For this idealized view of the tributary system and East Asian regional order, see Kang, *East Asia before the West*; Kang, *China Rising*; Zhang, "Chinese Exceptionalism."

24. Zhao, *Huai shijie yanjiu*, 119–120.

25. Interviews in Thailand with a military officer, a Chinese politics specialist, a philosopher, and a political theorist; in Singapore with social scientists (January 2011).

26. Zhao, "Rethinking Empire," 29, 38.

27. See for example, Qin, "Guoji guanxi lilun;" "Zhongguo zhexuejia yi 'Tianxia' linian qiujie hexie shijie" [Chinese philosopher uses the 'Tianxia' concept to explain harmonious world], Xinhua Wang [Xinhua net] (Beijing), March 17, 2007.

28. Zhang, "Tianxia lilun he shijie zhidu."

29. Zhao, *Tianxia tixi*, 10–11.

30. Yu Keping, "We Must Work to Create a Harmonious World," *China Daily*, May 10, 2007.

31. Yan, "Xun zi's Thoughts," 148, 159; Yan, "The Rise of China," 13.

32. Nyiri, "The Yellow Man's Burden," 106.

33. Liu, *Zhongguo meng*, 255, 244.

34. Liu, *Zhongguo meng*, 263, 25.

35. Cited in Buckley, "China PLA Officer Urges Challenging U.S. Dominance."

36. Saunders, "Will China's Dream."

37. "Benqi huati: Zhongguo ying zhuaqiu diyi junshi qiangguo diwei ma?" [Current topic: Should China pursue the status of top military power?], Huanqiu Debate website, http://debate.huanqiu.com/2010-03/730727.html.

38. Cheng Gang, "Jiefang jun daxiao Liu Mingfu zhuzhang Zhongguo zhengzuo shijie di yi junshi qiangguo" [Liu Mingfu of the PLA emphasizes that China will become the world's number one superpower], In Wuyouzhixiang [Utopia], March 3, 2010. http://www.wyzxsx.com/Article/Class22/201003/134608.html.

39. Kissinger, *On China*, 504–507, 521.

40. "China's Aim of Being Top Military Superpower May Be a Dream," *Global Times*, March 3, 2010. Also see Zhang, *Lun Zhongguo haiquan*; Major General Luo Yuan,

"Zhongguo yao cheng yiliu qiangguo buxu you shangwu jingshen" [To become first class power China must have martial spirit], *Huanqiu shibao*, December 12, 2010.

41. See Rozman, *Chinese Strategic Thought*.

42. Liu, *Zhongguo meng*, 9–13.

43. Yang, *Tombstone*.

44. Liu, *Zhongguo meng*, 11.

45. Liu, *Zhongguo meng*, 298–302.

46. Liu, *Zhongguo meng*, 283.

47. Liu, *Zhongguo meng*, 184, 245.

48. Liu, *Jiefang jun weishenme neng yi*.

49. Liu, *Zhongguo meng*, 22.

50. "Chi Haotian huo lianheguo shijie hexie renwu jiang" [Chi Haotian wins UN's world peace prize], Beijing: Xinhua, October 28, 2010; also see <http://www.whf-foundation.org>.

51. Quoted in Edward Wong, "For Putin, a Peace Prize for a Decision to Go to War," *New York Times*, November 15, 2011.

CHAPTER 3

1. Geoff Dyer and Jamil Anderlini, "China's Lending Hits New Heights," *Financial Times*, January 17, 2011.

2. Ramo, "The Beijing Consensus"; Jacques, *When China Rules the World*.

3. See de Bary, *Sources of Chinese Tradition*, 218–223.

4. See Schwartz, *In Search of Wealth and Power*, 17–19.

5. Pan, "Dangdai Zhonghua tizhi," 6.

6. Maddison, *Contours of the World Economy 1–2030 AD*.

7. *Zhonghua Renmin Gongheguo guomin jingji he shehui fazhan di shier ge wunian guihua gangyao* [Outline 12th Five-Year Programme for National Economic Social Development of the People's Republic of China], Beijing: Renmin chubanshe, March 2011, Chapter 1.

8. Ash, Porter, and Summers, *China, The EU and China's Twelfth Five-Year Programme*, 24.

9. Hu and Yan, *Zhongguo*.

10. See Barabantseva, *Overseas Chinese, Ethnic Minorities and Nationalism*.

11. Barry Naughton in Perry, "Explaining the Rise of China: A Challenge to Western Social Science Theories?"

12. Since Mo Yan won the Nobel prize for literature in 2012, there is less pressure on Lin to win the economics prize.

13. Osnos, "Boom Doctor," 42; Osnos, "Crossing the Water."

14. Lin, Fang, and Zhou, *The China Miracle*.

15. Lin, *Economic Development*, 5–6.

16. Lin, *Economic Development*, 53.
17. Breslin, "The 'China Model' and the Global Crisis," 1338.
18. See the 1980 letter in Osnos, "Crossing the Water."
19. Chen Weihua, "Time for US to Make Plans for the Future," *China Daily*, November 18, 2011.
20. "Tinker, Taylor," *The Economist*, October 1, 2011.
21. Lin, *Demystifying the Chinese Economy*.
22. Lin, *Demystifying the Chinese Economy*, 287–298.
23. Thornton, "Foreword," in Hu, *China in 2020*, vii.
24. Hu, *2020 Zhongguo*; Hu and Yan, *Zhongguo*; Hu, Yan and Wei, *2030 Zhongguo*.
25. Hu, *China in 2020*, 162.
26. Hu, *China in 2020*, 150.
27. Hu, *China in 2020*, 12.
28. Hu, *China in 2020*, 23–24.
29. For background information that puts Hu's work into context, see Li, "Introduction," in Hu, *China in 2020*, xv–xl.
30. Hu, *China in 2020*, 28, 18–19, 35.
31. For an explanation of the Cultural Revolution's economic benefits, see Kraus, *The Cultural Revolution*, 63–83.
32. "Hu Angang zouke wenhua sushi jiaoyu zhuangchang xulun 'Zhongguo zhi lu'" [Hu Angang lectures on the cultural quality of education on the 'China Road'], Tsinghua University, November 22, 2011.
33. Hu, *China in 2020*, 19, 45, 32.
34. "Hu Angang zouke wenhua."
35. Hu, *China in 2020*, 161.
36. Hu, Yan and Wei, *2030 Zhongguo*, 210.
37. Hu, *China in 2020*, 17, 142.
38. Hu, *China in 2020*, 25, 30.
39. Hu, Yan and Wei, *2030 Zhongguo*, 188.
40. Pan, "Dangdai Zhonghua tizhi," 6.
41. Pan, "Dangdai Zhonghua tizhi," 5, 12, 29, 30.
42. Pan, "Dangdai Zhonghua tizhi," 18, 29
43. Pan, "Dangdai Zhonghua tizhi," 58, 83, 82, 22, 56.
44. Hu, Yan and Wei, *2030 Zhongguo*, 210.
45. Pan, "Dangdai Zhonghua tizhi," 6.
46. Cui, "Chongqing," 5.
47. Su, Yang and Liu, *Chongqing moshi*, 117–144.
48. Cui cited in Emilie Frankiel, "From Scholar to Official: Cui Zhiyuan and Chongqing City's Local Experiment Policy," (December 6, 2010), http://www.booksandideas.net/IMG/pdf/20101206_Cui_Zhiyuan_EN.pdf. Also see Cui, "Partial Imitations of the Coming Whole," 652.
49. Cui, "Partial Imitations of the Coming Whole," 654.

50. Cui, "Chongqing," 9–10, 5; Cui quoted in Frankiel, "From Scholar to Official."

51. Cui, "Partial Imitations of the Coming Whole," 647.

52. Cui quoted in Frankiel, "From Scholar to Official."

53. Cui, "Chongqing," 9.

54. Cui, quoted in Frankiel, "From Scholar to Official."

55. Su, *Chongqing moshi*, 61–90, 23–59.

56. Cui, "Chongqing," 9–10; Cui briefly discusses the ideological campaigns in his English-language article, Cui, "Partial Imitations of the Coming Whole," 657, 658.

57. See Cui, "Chongqing;" Wang Lei and Tang Yaoguo, "Bieyang Chongqing" [A different Chongqing] *Liaowang* no. 16 (April 22, 2010): 22–23, and Huang, "Chongqing—China's New Experiment."

58. "Bo Ouster Undermines Model to Bridge China's Wealth Gap," Bloomberg News, April 20, 2012; "Chinese Infighting: Secrets of a Succession War," *Financial Times*, March 4, 2012.

59. John Garnaut, "Show Them the Money, Old China," *Sydney Morning Herald*, March 26, 2011. For a detailed discussion of Bo and his mafia-style rule of Chongqing see Garnaut, *The Rise and Fall of the House of Bo*.

60. Didi Kirsten Tatlow, "After Scandal, China Takes a Moral Inventory," *New York Times*, April 18, 2012.

61. Yang, "The End of the Beijing Consensus."

62. Qin, "Zhongguo jingji fazhan de di renquan youshi."

63. Yao Liwen and Liu Jianping, "Dayuejin shi fazhan weishenme 'yaoming'" [Why Is Great Leap Forward-Style Development "Deadly"], *Nanfang zhoumo*, September 29, 2011.

64. Xu, "Pushi wenming, haishi Zhongguo jiazhi?"

65. Cited in Annie Maccoby Berglof, "Economic Confucian," *Financial Times*, November 18, 2011.

66. Huang, "Chongqing—Equitable Development Driven by a 'Third Hand'?" 607.

67. Cui, "Partial Imitations of the Coming Whole," 658.

68. For a more sophisticated analysis of these issues see the blogs of Patrick Chovanec and Michael Pettis, http://www.economonitor.com/blog/author/pchovanec/ and http://www.mpettis.com/. To understand how the economic model impacts ordinary Chinese, see David Barboza, "As Its Economy Sprints Ahead, China's People Are Left Behind," *New York Times*, October 9, 2011.

69. "It Isn't Working for Anyone Else," *New York Times*, January 20, 2010.

70. World Bank, *China 2030*; Lin, "The Future of China's Growth," Project Syndicate, March 15, 2012, http://www.project-syndicate.org/commentary/the-future-of-china-s-growth.

71. Chan, *Shengshi*; Chan, *The Fat Years*. Also see Zhansui Yu, "Questioning the Chinese Model of Development: A Critical Reading of *Shengshi: Zhongguo 2013*," TheChinaBeat.org, July 28, 2010.

72. Paul Mooney, "2013: Them and Us," *South China Morning Post*, February 7, 2010; Jeremy Godkin, "2013: Interview with Chan Koonchung," Danwei.org, June 25, 2010.

73. Chan, *The Fat Years*, 33. I have checked *The Fat Years* translations with Chan, *Shengshi*.

74. *Pieke*, "The Communist Party and Social Management in China."

75. Chan, *The Fat Years*, 253.

76. Chan, *The Fat Years*, 254–255. Modified translation.

77. Chan, *The Fat Years*, 256–257.

78. Chan, *The Fat Years*, 259.

79. Chan, *The Fat Years*, 248, 241.

80. Chan, *The Fat Years*, 248.

81. Chan, *The Fat Years*, 251.

CHAPTER 4

1. Liu, *Zhongguo meng*, 75ff.

2. Liu, *Zhongguo meng*, 22. For a critical analysis of this phenomenon, see Nyiri, "The Yellow Man's Burden."

3. Chan, *Shengshi*; Chan, *The Fat Years*, 273.

4. Allen Yu, "Are Chinese Racist or Simply Politically Incorrect?" October 14, 2008, http://blog.foolsmountain.com/2008/10/14/are-chinese-racist-or-simply-politically-incorrect/.

5. U.S. Senate Resolution 201, 112th Congress, October 12, 2011.

6. For a sample of Internet comments and Lou's statement, see Fauna, "Shanghai 'Black Girl' Lou Jing Abused by Racist Netizens," ChinaSMACK, September 1, 2009, http://www.chinasmack.com/2009/stories/shanghai-black-girl-lou-jing-racist-chinese-netizens.html.

7. Dikötter, *Discourse of Race in Modern China*. Also see Dikötter, *The Construction of Racial Identities in China and Japan*.

8. Gilroy, *Against Race*, 14, 15.

9. Jia, "Disrespect and Distrust," 17.

10. See Pieke and Barabantseva, "Old and New Diversities."

11. Sun, *San Min Chu I*, 6, 9, 12. This translation was checked against Sun, *Sanmin zhuyi*, 6, 7–8, 9.

12. Schwartz, *In Search of Wealth and Power*, 19.

13. "Taiwan Leader Pay Tributes to Yellow Emperor," Xinhua, April 4, 2009.

14. Matten, "The Yellow Emperor as Icon of National Identity," 23.

15. Joe Hung, "President Ma Pays Homage in Person to the Yellow Emperor," *The China Post*, April 4, 2009.

16. Su, "River Elegy," 9.

17. Dikötter, "Racial Discourse in China," 32–33.

18. Sautman, "Peking Man," 109.

19. Leibold, *Reconfiguring Chinese Nationalism*, 3.

20. See Callahan, *China: The Pessoptimist Nation*.

21. Schwartz, *In Search of Wealth and Power*, 17–19.

22. Dikötter, "Racial Discourse in China," 16.

23. Xi, *Kexue yu aiguo*.

24. Leibold, "More Than a Category," 556.

25. Cited in Jim Yardley, "Racial 'Handicaps' and a Great Sprint Forward," *New York Times*, September 8, 2004.

26. "Huangzhongren ye neng pao qian heiren" [Yellow race also able to beat blacks in a race], Xinhua net, August 29, 2004.

27. Zha, *Tide Players*, 213.

28. See de Bary, *Sources of Chinese Tradition*, 176.

29. Guo, "Makese jin wenmiao."

30. See Thompson, "Biographical Sketch of K'ang Yu-wei," 11–25.

31. Kang, *Ta T'ung Shu*, 143. These translations are based on Thompson's rendering, which is compared with the Chinese version: Kang, *Datongshu*.

32. Kang, *Ta T'ung Shu*, 141, 142. This paragraph is missing from the 2005 edition, Kang, *Datong shu*.

33. Kang, *Ta T'ung Shu*, 141, 148, 146, 148.

34. Kang, *Ta T'ung Shu*, 85, 161.

35. Jiang Rong, *Lang tuteng*. This section builds on analysis done in Callahan, *The Pessoptimist Nation*, 155–159.

36. Jiang Rong, *Wolf Totem*; "2007 Man Asian Literary Prize Winner Announced," November 10, 2007, http://www.manasianliteraryprize.org/2008/2007winner. php (viewed on November 17, 2008).

37. Howard W. French, "A Novel, by Someone, Takes China by Storm," *New York Times*, November 3, 2005.

38. Jiang, *Lang tuteng*, 364–408.

39. Jiang, *Lang tuteng*, 298.

40. Leibold, "More Than a Category," 545.

41. Liu, *The China Dream*, 255.

42. Jiang, *Wolf Totem*, 217–218.

43. Jiang, *Lang tuteng*, 401, 402.

44. Lung, "Wenming de liliang."

45. Lung, "Qingyong wenming lai shuofu wo"; translated at EastWestNorthSouth, http://www.zonaeuropa.com/20060127_1.htm; Lung, *Dajiang dahai 1949*.

46. Isabella Steger, "Lung Ying-tai: 1911 Anniversary 'Awkward' for China," *Wall Street Journal*, China Real Time blog, October 10, 2011, http://blogs.wsj.com/chinarealtime/2011/10/10/lung-ying-tai-1911-anniversary-awkward-for-china/.

47. Steger, "Lung Ying-tai."

48. Andrew Jacobs, "Taiwan Election Stirs Hopes among Chinese for Democracy," *The New York Times*, January 16, 2012.

49. Lee, "Review of Lung Yingtai."

CHAPTER 5

1. He, *China Modernization Report*, 3–12.

2. The "Olympics for Culture, Economy and Technology" phrase comes from Siemens AG, "A Good Partner for a Better Life," Beijing: Siemens China, 2009.

3. For a discussion of the global significance of world expos, see Maura Elizabeth Cunningham and Jeffrey N. Wasserstrom, "China Discovers World Expo Is No Olympics," *YaleGlobal*, August 17, 2010.

4. See Hu, *Shibo yu guojia xinxiang*.

5. This section is based on three visits to the World Expo site: May 7, 2010, October 8, 2010, and April 1, 2011, when I visited the China Pavilion. Other sources include Shanghai World Expo Organizing Committee, *Chengshi fazhan zhong de Zhonghua zhihui*; and the video "Zhongguo guan yinxiang."

6. Siemens AG, "Expo 2010: Fully Networked and Climate-Friendly Life," http://www.siemens.com/innovation/en/highlights/energy/update_03/expo-2010.htm.

7. Hu, "Nuli jianshe tejiu heping, gongtong fanrong de hexie shijie," 1.

8. Cited in Lee and Koo, "Novelist Han Han."

9. Xu, "Shanghai Culture Lost."

10. Jeffrey N. Wasserstrom, e-mail message, April 3, 2012.

11. Siemens AG, "Expo Opens in Shanghai—Tough Test for Infrastructure Begins," Munich, Germany, April 29, 2010, http://www.siemens.com/press/en/pressrelease/?press=/en/pressrelease/2010/corporate_communication/axx20100459.htm.

12. "Jia Zhangke Focuses on Shanghai Legend," *Beijing Review*, February 16, 2009, http://www.bjreview.com.cn/movies/txt/2009–02/16/content_178260.htm; Jia, "Haishang chuanqui.".

13. See Jia, *Jia xiang*.

14. Translated by Evan Osnos in his blog "Jia Zhangke and Rebiya Kadeer," *The New Yorker*, July 24, 2009, http://www.newyorker.com/online/blogs/evanosnos/2009/07/jia-zhangke-rebiya-kadeer.html.

15. Han Han, "Come Quickly, Leave Quickly," TwoCold blog, April 21, 2010; translated in C. Custer, "Han Han: Answering Questions About the Shanghai World Expo," ChinaSmack blog, April 22, 2010, http://www.chinasmack.com/2010/bloggers/han-han-answers-questions-about-2010-shanghai-world-expo.html.

16. See Lung, *Dajiang dahai 1949*.

17. Cai, *Nongmin*, 21.

18. This is not the first time that Cai has addressed a rural theme; he has commented that he sees Peasant da Vincis as an extention of his earlier work, The Rent

Collection Courtyard, which explores the meaning Mao's "mass line" strategy (Cai, *Nongmin*, 21).

19. Cai, *Nongmin*, 21.
20. Interview with Liu Yingjiu, Rockbund Art Museum Curator, Shanghai, October 12, 2010.
21. Cai, *Nongmin*, 25.
22. Cited in Cai, *Nongmin*, 132.
23. Cited in Cai, *Nongmin*, 146.
24. Cai, *Nongmin*, 186.
25. Cited in Cai, *Nongmin*, 98.
26. Cai, *Nongmin*, 108.
27. Cai, *Nongmin*, 22.
28. Zhang, "'Anti-gravity,'" 36.
29. Han, *Duchang tuan*.
30. For a profile of Han, see Osnos, "The Han Dynasty."
31. Han, "Baozhu feifa zifu" [Protect illegal content], TwoCold blog, September 13, 2010.
32. See Han, "Liuxing de yiyi" [The meaning of demonstrations], TwoCold blog, September 13, 2010. This blog was "harmonized," and it is available at Han Han digest: http://www.hanhandigest.com/?p=206.
33. Han Han, "Tan geming" [Talking about revolution], TwoCold blog, December 23, 2012; Han Han, "Shuo minzhu" [Saying democracy], TwoCold blog, December 24, 2012; Han Han, "Yao ziyou" [Wanting freedom], TwoCold blog, December 26, 2012; For translations see EastWestNorthSouth blog, December 31, 2012, http://zonaeuropa.com/201112a.brief.htm#009.
34. For these and other comments see John Kennedy, "Only Talking about a Revolution," Global Voices, December 26, 2011, http://globalvoicesonline.org/2011/12/26/china-only-talking-about-a-revolution/.
35. Han, "Mashang huidie, diepo yiqian" [Prices will drop below 1000 any moment now], TwoCold Blog, February 22, 2011.
36. Han, "Qingchun" [The bloom of youth], TwoCold Blog, May 28, 2010.
37. Han Han, "Tuojie de guodu" [A nation derailed], TwoCold Blog, July 29, 2011. This blog was quickly "harmonized." A translation, with links to the original Chinese, is available at Han Han Digest, http://www.hanhandigest.com/?p=454.
38. For such political accounting, also see Han, "Gei Li Yanwang xiansheng de yifeng xin" [A letter to Robin Li], TwoCold blog, March 26, 2011; "Houhui youqi" [See you again later], TwoCold blog, December 28, 2010.
39. Han, "Han Feng shi ge hao ganbu" [Han Feng is a good cadre], TwoCold blog, March 4, 2010.
40. Han, "Liuxing de yiyi."
41. Han, "Wo zhi shi zai caixiang" [I'm only guessing], TwoCold blog, January 17, 2010.
42. Official criticisms of Han started early; after the success of his first novel *Triple Door* (*Sanchong men*, 1999), a television panel show "Dialogue," for example, had

a group of old fusty teachers criticize Han as a bad role model for China's youth because he dropped out of high school. See http://www.tudou.com/programs/view/sMyxz5it84M.

43. Han, "Ducaizhe meiyou neizheng" [Dictators don't have internal affairs], TwoCold blog, March 21, 2011.

44. The pop reference is to Sailor Moon (Meishao nü zhanshi), a Japanese manga and anime character well-known to the post-1980 generation, who declares "I represent the moon to annihilate you" as she slays her evil enemies. Thanks to Zhu Wei for pointing this out.

45. See Andy Yee, "Criticizing Han Han," Chinageeks, April 22, 2010, http://chinageeks.org/2010/04/criticizing-han-han/.

46. Xu Zhiyuan, "Yongzhong de shengli" [The triumph of mediocrity], *Fenghuang zhoukan*, May 11, 2010.

47. Han, "Xuyao zhenxiang, haishi xuyao fuhe xuyao de zhenxiang" [The truth, or a truth that meets our needs], TwoCold blog, January 14, 2011.

48. Cai, *Nongmin*, 25.

CHAPTER 6

1. Romney, *No Apology*, p. 43; Gingrich, *A Nation Like No Other*.
2. Steven Erlanger, "Hollande Opens Drive for 'Change,'" *International Herald Tribune*, January 23, 2012, p. 3.
3. Hodgson, *The Myth of American Exceptionalism*.
4. Bacevich, *The Limits of Power*.
5. Madsen, *China and the American Dream*, 227.
6. Madsen, *China and the American Dream*, 209–210.
7. Chan, *Shengshi*, 213.
8. Pieke, "The Communist Party and Social Management in China."
9. Xu, "Zhongguo xuyao liweidan?"
10. "Youpai wangzhang faqi 'shi da hanjian' piaoxuan yanmao zuixing" [Left-wing website launches "Top 10 Traitors" poll], Radio Free Asia, December 30, 2011, http://www.rfa.org/mandarin/yataibaodao/sy2-12302011085147.html.
11. Cullen, *The American Dream*; Gingrich, *A Nation Like No Other*.
12. Quoted in Lipset, *American Exceptionalism*, 18.
13. Cullen, *The American Dream*, 40.
14. Quoted in Cullen, *The American Dream*, 94, 96.
15. Cullen, *The American Dream*, 160.
16. Gingrich, *A Nation Like No Other*, 2.
17. Gingrich, *A Nation Like No Other*, 6.
18. Gingrich, *A Nation Like No Other*, 20.
19. Lipset, *American Exceptionalism*, 31, 32, 26.
20. Gingrich, *A Nation Like No Other*, 230.

21. Gingrich, *A Nation Like No Other*, 168, 229.

22. Gingrich, *A Nation Like No Other*, 230, 231.

23. See Romney, *No Apology*.

24. Wang, *Harmony and War*; Reid and Zheng, *Negotiating Asymmetry*; Perdue, *China Marches West*; Teng, *Taiwan's Imagined Geography*.

25. Kang, "Zhongguo teshulun."

26. Said, *Orientalism*, 3.

27. Yan, *Ancient Chinese Thought*; Cunningham-Cross and Callahan, "Ancient Chinese Power."

28. Jacques, *When China Rules the World*; Kissinger, *On China*.

29. Jacques, *When China Rules the World*, 395.

30. Xu, "Zhongguo xuyao liweidan?"

31. See Bercovitch, *The American Jeremiad*.

32. "Chinese dream," Xinhua, April 4, 2011.

33. Madsen, *China and the American Dream*, xvii.

34. "Li Changchun yaoqiu dali fazhan wangluo Kongzi xueyyuan yongyang Zhonghua wenming" [Li Changchun Requesting Greatly Develop Confucius Institutes to Spread Chinese Culture], Xinhua, April 25, 2007.

35. See Callahan, *China: The Pessoptimist Nation*, 19–28.

36. Frank Bruni, "Carly Fiorina Means Business," *New York Times Magazine*, May 31, 2010, p. 15.

CHAPTER 7

1. Ferguson and Schularick, "Chimerica and the Global Asset Market Boom."

2. Xu, "Du Lala shengzhi ji"; Li, *Du Lala shengzhi ji*.

3. Studwell, *The China Dream*.

4. Mao, *Mao Mao de bailing shenghuo III*.

5. Chang, "Working Titles," 30.

6. Li, "Zixu," v.

7. Hao, "Guanyu 'Du Lala shengzhiji,'" i.

8. "We survived a day in China," translated by Victor H. Mair, August 19, 2011, http://www.danwei.com/we-survived-a-day-in-china/. Although this cartoon was very popular on the web in China, Danwei was unable to trace its origin or author.

9. Cai, *Women de Du Lala*.

10. François Bougon, "Du Lala's World," AFP, January 12, 2010.

11. Pseudonym for an anonymous interview in Beijing, April 28, 2011.

12. Li Yuan, "Xu Jinglei, China's Creative Pragmatist," *Wall Street Journal*, June 6, 2010.

13. Li, *Du Lala*, 255.

14. Naisbitt, *China's Megatrends*, 30.

15. "Bridging East and West to Combat Climate Change," *Huffington Post*, January 28, 2011.

16. Wang Shen, "*Du Lala* yuan zouzhe Li Ke: Geng xinshang Li Guanghuo ban Wang Wei" [*Du Lala* author Li Ke: I would enjoy seeing Li Guanghuo as Wang Wei] *Zhejiang wanbao*, May 7, 2010.

17. Xu, *Gongkai!*

18. Yang, "An Examination of the Research Theory of Pre-Qin Interstate Political Philosophy," 155, 156.

19. See Callahan, *China: The Pessoptimist Nation*, 1–20.

Bibliography

Ai Weiwei. *Ai Weiwei's Blog: Writings, Interviews, and Digital Rants, 2006–2009.* Cambridge, MA: MIT Press, 2011.

Ai Weiwei. *Cishi cidi* [Time and place]. Guilin: Guangxi shifan daxue chubanshe, 2010.

American Embassy Beijing. "Portrait of Vice President Xi Jinping: 'Ambitious Survivor' of the Cultural Revolution." 09BEIJING3128. http://wikileaks.ch/cable/2009/11/09BEIJING3128.html.

Anderson, Perry. "Sinomania." *London Review of Books* 32:2 (January 28, 2010): 3–6.

Andersson, Jenny. "The Future Landscape." Working Paper No. 5. Stockholm: Institute for Futures Studies, 2008.

Ash, Robert, Robin Porter, and Tim Summers. *China, the EU and China's Twelfth Five-Year Programme.* London: Europe China Research and Advice Network, 2012.

Bacevich, Andrew J. *The Limits of Power: The End of American Exceptionalism.* New York: Holt Paperbacks, 2009.

Bai Haijun. *2049: Xiangxin Zhongguo* [2049: Believe in China]. Beijing: Dang'an chubanshe, 2006.

Bandurski, David. "Zhang vs. Yang on the China Model." *China Media Project.* (March 29, 2011) http://cmp.hku.hk/2011/03/29/11205/.

Barabantseva, Elena. *Overseas Chinese, Ethnic Minorities and Nationalism: De-centering China.* London: Routledge, 2010.

Barmé, Geremie R. *In the Red: On Contemporary Chinese Culture.* New York: Columbia University Press, 1999.

Barmé, Geremie. "Confession, Redemption, and Death: Liu Xiaobo and the Protest Movement of 1989." In *The Broken Mirror: China after Tiananmen*, ed. George Hicks, 52–99. London: Longmans, 1990.

Bercovitch, Sacvan. *The American Jeremiad.* Madison: University of Wisconsin Press, 1978.

Breslin, Shaun. "The 'China Model' and the Global Crisis: From Friedrich List to a Chinese Mode of Governance?" *International Affairs* 87:6 (2011): 1323–1343.

Cai Guoqiang. *Nongmin dafenqi* [Peasant da Vincis]. Guilin: Guangxi shifan daxue chubanshe, 2010.

Cai Mingfei, ed. *Women de Du Lala* [We all could be Lala]. Xian: Shaanxi shifan daxue chubanshe, 2009.

Callahan, William A. *China: The Pessoptimist Nation*. Oxford: Oxford University Press, 2010.

Callahan, William A., and Elena Barabantseva, eds. *China Orders the World: Normative Soft Power and Foreign Policy*. Washington, DC: Woodrow Wilson Center Press, 2011.

Carlson, Allen. "Moving beyond Sovereignty? A Brief Consideration of Recent Changes in China's Approach to International Order and the Emergence of the Tianxia Concept." *Journal of Contemporary China* 20:68 (January 2011): 89–102.

Chan Koonchung [Chen Guanzhong]. *Shengshi: Zhongguo, 2013 nian* [The golden era, China 2013]. Hong Kong: Oxford University Press, 2009.

Chan Koonchung. *The Fat Years,* trans. Michael S. Duke. London: Doubleday, 2011.

Chang, Gordon G. "The Coming Collapse of China: 2012 Edition." Foreign Policy. com (December 29, 2011).

Chang, Gordon G. *The Coming Collapse of China*. New York: Random House, 2001.

Chang, Leslie T. "Working Titles." *The New Yorker,* February 6, 2012, 30–34.

Cui Zhiyuan. "Chongqing 'Shi da minsheng gongcheng' de zhengzhi jingji xue" [The Political Economy of Chongqing's "10 people's livelihood project"]. *Zhongyang dangxiao xuebao* 14:5 (October 2010): 5–10.

Cui, Zhiyuan. "Partial Imitations of the Coming Whole: The Chongqing Experiment in Light of the Theories of Henry George, James Meade, and Antonio Gramsci." *Modern China* 37:5 (2011): 646–660.

Cullen, Jim. *The American Dream: A Short History of an Idea That Shaped a Nation*. New York: Oxford University Press, 2003.

Cunningham-Cross, Linsay, and William A. Callahan. "Ancient Chinese Power, Modern Chinese Thought." *Chinese Journal of International Politics* 4:4 (2011): 349–374.

Davies, Gloria. *Worrying about China: The Language of Chinese Critical Inquiry*. Cambridge, MA: Harvard University Press, 2007.

de Bary, Wm. Theodore, et al., eds. *Sources of Chinese Tradition*. Vol. 1. New York: Columbia University Press, 1960.

Dikötter, Frank. *Discourse of Race in Modern China*. Stanford, CA: Stanford University Press, 1992.

Dikötter, Frank. "Racial Discourse in China." In *Construction of Racial Identities*, ed. Frank Dikötter, 12–33. Honolulu: University of Hawaii Press, 1997.

Dikötter, Frank, ed. *The Construction of Racial Identities in China and Japan*. Honolulu: University of Hawaii Press, 1997.

Ferguson, Niall, and Moritz Schularick. "Chimerica and the Global Asset Market Boom." *International Finance* 10:3 (2007): 215–239.

Fewsmith, Joseph. "Bo Xilai Takes on Organized Crime." *China Leadership Monitor,* no. 32 (May 2010): 1–8.

Fong, Vanessa. "Filial Nationalism among Chinese Teenagers with Global Identities." *American Ethnologist* 31:4 (2004): 631–648.

Foot, Rosemary, and Andrew Walter. *China, the United States, and Global Order.* New York: Cambridge University Press, 2011.

Fu Zhongxia, et al., eds. *Zhongguo lidai zhanzheng nianbiao* [Historical chronology of warfare in China]. Beijing: Jiefangjun chubanshe, 2002.

Garnaut, John. *The Rise and Fall of the House of Bo: How A Murder Exposed the Cracks in China's Leadership.* London: Penguin, 2012.

Gilroy, Paul. *Against Race: Imagining Political Culture beyond the Color Line.* Cambridge, MA: Harvard University Press, 2000.

Gingrich, Newt, with Vince Haley. *A Nation Like No Other: Why American Exceptionalism Matters.* Washington, DC: Regnery Publishing, 2011.

Guo Moruo. "Makese jin wenmiao" [Marx enters the Confucian temple]. In *Guo Moruo zuopin jingdian.* Vol. 3 [Guo Moruo's classic works, vol. 3], 394–402. Beijing: Zhongguo huaqiao chubanshe, 1997.

Han Han, ed. *Duchang tuan* [A chorus of solos], no. 1 (July 2010).

Hao Jian. "Guanyu 'Du Lala shengzhiji'" [About "Du Lala's promotion diary"]. In *Du Lala shengzhi ji* [Du Lala's promotion diary], by Li Ke, i–iv. Xian, China: Xian: Shaanxi shifan daxue chubanshe, 2007.

Havel, Vaclav. *Living in Truth.* New York: Faber & Faber, 1987.

He Chuanqi. *China Modernization Report Outlook (2001–2010).* Beijing: Peking University Press, 2010.

Hodgson, Godfrey. *The Myth of American Exceptionalism.* New Haven, CT: Yale University Press, 2009.

Hu Angang. *2020 Zhongguo: Quanmian jianshe xiaokang shehui* [2020 China: Building a Comprehensive Well-Off Society]. Beijing: Qinghua daxue chubanshe, 2007.

Hu Angang. *China in 2020: A New Kind of Superpower.* Washington, DC: Brookings Institution Press, 2011.

Hu Angang, and Yan Yilong. *Zhongguo: Zouxiang 2015* [China: Moving toward 2015]. Hangzhou: Zhejiang renmin chubanshe, 2010.

Hu Angang, Yan Yilong, and Wei Xing. *2030 Zhongguo: Maixiang gongtong fuse* [2030 China: Toward Common Prosperity]. Beijing: Zhongguo renmin daxue chubanshe, 2011.

Hu Bin. *Shibo yu guojia xinxiang* [Expo and national image]. Shanghai: Shanghai jiaoyu chubanshe, 2010.

Hu Jintao. "Hold High the Great Banner of Socialism with Chinese Characteristics and Strive for New Victories in Building a Moderately Prosperous Society in All Respects: Report to the Seventeenth National Congress of the Communist Party of China on Oct. 15, 2007." <http://www.china.org.cn/english/congress/229611.htm>.

Hu Jintao. "Nuli jianshe tejiu heping, gongtong fanrong de hexie shijie—zai Lianheguo chenglie 60 zhounian shounaohuiyi shang de jianghua" [Making an effort to build a sustainable, peaceful, and united prosperous harmonious world—speech at the summit for the 60th anniversary of the United Nations], *Renmin ribao* (September 16, 2005), 1.

Huang, Philip C. C. "Chongqing—China's New Experiment: Editor's Foreword." *Modern China* 37:5 (2011): 567–568.

Huang, Philip C. C. "Chongqing—Equitable Development Driven by a 'Third Hand?'" *Modern China* 37:5 (2011): 569–622.

Hughes, Christopher R. "Reclassifying Chinese Nationalism: The *Geopolitik* Turn." *Journal of Contemporary China* 20:71 (2011): 601–620.

Jacques, Martin. *When China Rules the World: The End of the Western World and the Birth of a New Global Order.* New York: Allen Lane, 2009.

Jaivin, Linda. "Yawning Heights: Chan Koon-chung's Harmonious China." *China Heritage Quarterly,* no. 22 (June 2010).

Jia Qingguo. "Disrespect and Distrust: The External Origins of Contemporary Chinese Nationalism." *Journal of Contemporary China* 14:42 (2005): 11–21.

Jia Zhangke, dir. "Haishang chuanqi" [Shanghai Legends; or I Wish I Knew] (2010).

Jia Zhangke. *Jia xiang: 1996–2008* [Jia thinks: 1996–2008]. Beijing: Peking University Press, 2009.

Jiang Rong. *Lang tuteng* [Wolf totem]. Wuhan: Changjiang wenyi chubanshe, 2004.

Jiang Rong. *Wolf Totem,* trans. Howard Goldblatt. New York: Penguin, 2008.

Jin Canrong. *Zhongguo de weilai* [China's future]. Beijing: Zhongguo renmin daxue chubanshe, 2011.

Jin Shu. "Guangyu ying hexie shijie" [Light and shadow in a harmonious world]. *Beijing fangdi chan,* no. 7 (July 2003): 108–109.

Johnston, Alastair Iain. *Social States: China in International Institutions, 1980–2000.* Princeton, NJ: Princeton University Press, 2008.

Kang Xiaoguang. "Zhongguo teshulun—dui Zhongguo dalu 25nian gaige jingyan de fanse" [Chinese exceptionalism: Reflections on 25 years of reform in mainland China]. Confucius 2000 website (June 2004). www.confucius2000.com/poetry/zgtsldzgdl25nggjydfs.htm.

Kang Youwei. *Ta T'ung Shu: The One-World Philosophy of K'ang Yu-wei.* Trans. Laurence G. Thompson. London: George Allen & Unwin, 1958.

Kang Youwei. *Datongshu* [The book of great harmony]. Shanghai: Shanghai guji chubanshe, 2005.

Kang, David C. *China Rising: Peace, Power and Order in East Asia.* New York: Columbia University Press, 2007.

Kang, David C. *East Asia before the West: Five Centuries of Trade and Tribute.* New York: Columbia University Press, 2010.

Kissinger, Henry. *On China.* New York: Allen Lane, 2011.

Kraus, Richard Curt. *The Cultural Revolution: A Very Short Introduction.* New York: Oxford University Press, 2012.

Krens, Thomas, and Alexandra Munro, eds. *Cai Guo-Qiang: I Want to Believe*. New York: Guggenheim Museum, 2008.

Kurlantzick, Joshua. *Charm Offensive: How China's Soft Power Is Transforming the World*. New Haven, CT: Yale University Press, 2007.

Lawrence, Susan V. *China's Vice President Xi Jinping Visits the United States: What Is at Stake?* Washington, DC: Congressional Research Service, February 6, 2012.

Lee, Leo Ou-Fan. "Review of Lung Yingtai, *Da jiang da hui—1949* (Big River, big sea: Untold stories of 1949) and Chi pang-yuan, *Ju liu he* (The river of big torrents)." *Muse Magazine* 35 (December 2009).

Lee, Sherry, and Shu-ren Koo. "Novelist Han Han: A City Built on a Heap of Money Won't Shine." *CommonWealth Magazine,* no. 443 (April 1, 2010).

Leibold, James. "More Than a Category: Han Supremacism on the Chinese Internet." *China Quarterly,* no. 203 (2010): 539–559.

Leibold, James. *Reconfiguring Chinese Nationalism: How the Qing Frontier and Its Indigenes Became Chinese*. New York: Palgrave MacMillan, 2007.

Li, Cheng. "Introduction: A Champion for Chinese Optimism and Exceptionalism." In *China in 2020: A New Kind of Superpower*, by Hu Angang, xv–xl. Washington, DC: Brookings Institution Press, 2011.

Li Ke, *Du Lala shengzhi ji* [Du Lala's promotion diary]. Xian: Shaanxi shifan daxue chubanshe, 2007.

Li Ke. "Zixu" [Preface]. In *Du Lala shengzhi ji* [Du Lala's promotion diary] by Li Ke, v–vi. Xian: Shaanxi shifan daxue chubanshe, 2007.

Li Xianting, and Chang Yihe. "Ai Weiwei shi yige you chuangzaoxing de yishujia" [Ai Weiwei is a Creative Artist]. *Xin shiji* (May 11, 2011).

Lin, Justin Yifu. *Economic Development and Transition: Thought, Strategy and Viability*. Cambridge, UK: Cambridge University Press, 2009.

Lin, Justin Yifu. *Demystifying the Chinese Economy*. Cambridge, UK: Cambridge University Press, 2011.

Lin, Justin Yifu, Fang Cai, and Zhou Li. *The China Miracle: Development Strategy and Economic Reform*. Rev. ed. Hong Kong: Chinese University Press, 2003.

Lipset, Seymour Martin. *American Exceptionalism: A Double Edged Sword*. New York: W.W. Norton, 1996.

Liu Mingfu. *Zhongguo meng: hou meiguo shidai de daguo siwei zhanlue dingwei* [The China dream: The great power thinking and strategic positioning of China in the post-American era]. Beijing: Zhongguo youyi chuban gongsi, 2010.

Liu Mingfu. *Jiefang jun weishenme neng yi* [Why the Liberation Army Can Win]. Beijing: Wujing chubanshe, 2012.

Liu Xiaobo. *No Enemies, No Hatred: Selected Essays and Poems*, ed. Perry Link, Tianchi Martin-Liao and Liu Xia. Cambridge, MA: Harvard University Press, 2012.

Lovell, Julia. *The Politics of Cultural Capital: China's Quest for a Nobel Prize in Literature*. Honolulu: University of Hawaii Press, 2006.

Lovell, Julia. "Preface." In *The Fat Years,* by Chan Koonchung, 9–21. London: Doubleday, 2011.

Lung Ying-tai. "Qingyong wenming lai shuofu wo: gei Hu Jintao xiansheng de gongkai xin" [Please use civility to convince us—An open letter to Mr. Hu Jintao]. January 27, 2006, http://www.zonaeuropa.com/20060127_2.htm, translated at EastWestNorthSouth, http://www.zonaeuropa.com/20060127_1.htm.

Lung Ying-tai. "Wenming de liliang: Cong 'Xiangchou' dao 'Meilidao'" [The power of civility: From 'Homesickness' to 'Formosa']. Speech given at Peking University, August 1, 2010, http://blog.caijing.com.cn/expert_article-151497-9753.shtml.

Lung Ying-tai. *Dajiang dahai 1949* [Wide river, great sea: 1949]. Taipei: Tianxia zazhi, 2009.

Maddison, Angus. *Contours of the World Economy 1–2030 AD.* New York: Oxford University Press, 2007.

Madsen, Richard. *China and the American Dream: A Moral Inquiry.* Berkeley: University of California Press, 1995.

Mann, James. *The China Fantasy: Why Capitalism Will Not Bring Democracy to China.* New York: Penguin, 2007.

Mao Mao. *Mao Mao de bailing shenghuo III* [Mao Mao's white collar life III]. Xian: Shaanxi shifan daxue chubanshe, 2008.

Matten, Marc. "The Yellow Emperor as Icon of National Identity: An Invented Tradition?" Presented at "Qing Dynasty Politics and National Identity" conference, Renmin University of China (August 2010).

Naisbitt, John, and Doris Naisbitt. *China's Megatrends: The 8 Pillars of a New Society.* New York: Harper Business, 2010.

Nordin, Astrid. "Space for the Future: Exhibiting China in the World at Expo 2010." *China Information* 26:2 (2012): 235–249.

Nyiri, Pal. "The Yellow Man's Burden: Chinese Immigrants on a Civilizing Mission." *The China Journal* 56 (July 2006): 83–106.

Obrist, Hans Ulrich, ed. *Ai Weiwei Speaks.* London: Penguin Books, 2011.

Osnos, Evan. "The Long Shot." *The New Yorker* (May 11, 2009): 88–95.

Osnos, Evan. "It's Not Beautiful: An Artist Takes on the System." *The New Yorker* (May 24, 2010): 54–63.

Osnos, Evan. "Crossing the Water." *New Yorker* blog (October 4, 2010).

Osnos, Evan. "Boom Doctor." *The New Yorker* (October 11, 2010): 42–51.

Osnos, Evan. "The Han Dynasty." *The New Yorker* (July 4, 2011): 50–59.

Pan Wei. "Dangdai Zhonghua tizhi: Zhongguo moshi de jingji, zhengzhi, shehui jiexi" [Modern Chinese system: Analysis of the China model of economics, politics, and society]. In *Zhongguo moshi jiedu renmin gongheguo de 60 nian* [The China model: Reading 60 years of the People's Republic], ed. Pan Wei, 3–85. Beijing: Zhongyang bianshi chubanshe, 2009.

Pan Wei. "Zhongguo weilai 30 nian: Yuanjing yu xianjing" [China 30 years in the future: Vision and booby-trap]. In *Zhongguo weilai 30 nian* [China: 30 years in the future], ed. Wu Jinglian, Yu Keping and Robert Fogel, 52–64. Beijing: Zhongyang bianyi chubanshe, 2011.

Pan Wei. *Nongmin yu shichang: Zhongguo jiceng zhengquan yu xiangzhen qiye* [Peasants and the market: China's grassroots political power and rural enterprises]. Beijing: Shangwu yinshuguan, 2003.

Pan Wei, ed. *Zhongguo moshi: jiedu renmin gongheguo de 60 nian* [The China model: Understanding 60 years of the People's Republic]. Beijing: Peking University Press, 2009.

Perdue, Peter C. *China Marches West: The Qing Conquest of Central Eurasia.* Cambridge,MA: Harvard University Press, 2004.

Perry, Elizabeth. "Explaining the Rise of China: A Challenge to Western Social Science Theories?" panel discussion. Harvard University, April 5, 2010, http://www.harvard-yenching.org/sites/harvard-yenching.org/files/featurefiles/Rise%20of%20China%20Transcript_final.pdf.

Pieke, Frank N. *The Good Communist: Elite Training and State Building in Today's China.* Cambridge, UK: Cambridge University Press, 2009.

Pieke, Frank N. "The Communist Party and Social Management in China." *China Information* 26:2 (2012): 149–165.

Pieke, Frank N., and Elena Barabantseva, eds. "Old and New Diversities in Contemporary China." Special issue of *Modern China* 38:1 (2012): 3–133.

Qin Hui. "Zhongguo jingji fazhan de di renquan youshi" [The advantage of poor human rights in China's economic development]. (November 2, 2007). http://www.aisixiang.com/data/detail.php?id=16401.

Qin Yaqing. "Guoji guanxi lilun Zhongguo pai shengcheng de keneng he biran" [The Chinese school of international relations theory: Possibility and necessity]. *Shijie jingji yu,* no. 3 (2006): 7–13.

Ramo, Joshua Cooper. *"The Beijing Consensus."* London: Foreign Policy Centre, May 2004.

Reid, Anthony, and Yangwen Zheng, eds. *Negotiating Asymmetry: China's Place in Asia.* Honolulu: University of Hawaii Press, 2010.

Romney, Mitt. *No Apology: Believe in America: The Case for American Greatness.* New York: St. Martin's Griffin, 2011.

Rorty, Richard. *Achieving Our Country: Leftist Thought in Twentieth-Century America.* Cambridge, MA: Harvard University Press, 1998.

Rozman, Gilbert. *Chinese Strategic Thought toward Asia.* New York: Palgrave, 2010.

Said, Edward. *Orientalism.* New York: Vintage, 1978.

Saunders, Phillip C. "Will China's Dream Turn into America's Nightmare?" *China Brief* 10:7 (April 1, 2010), http://www.jamestown.org/single/?no_cache=1&tx_ttnews%5Btt_news%5D=36217.

Sautman, Barry. "Peking Man and the Politics of Paleoanthropological Nationalism in China." *Journal of Asian Studies* 60:1 (2001): 95–124.

Schwartz, Benjamin I. *In Search of Wealth and Power: Yen Fu and the West.* Cambridge, MA: Harvard University Press, 1964.

Shanghai World Expo Organizing Committee. *Chengshi fazhan zhong de Zhonghua zhihui* [Chinese wisdom in urban planning]. Shanghai: Wenhui chubanshe, 2010.

Shi Yinhong. *Quanqiuxing de tiaozhan yu Zhongguo: Duoshi zhi qiu yu Zhongguo de zhanlüe xuyao* [China and global challenges: China's strategic needs in an era of many troubles]. Changsha: Hunan renmin chubanshe, 2010.

State Council. "China's Peaceful Development Road." Beijing: Xinhua, December 22, 2005.

State Council. "China's Peaceful Development." Beijing: Xinhua, September 6, 2011.

Studwell, Joe. *The China Dream: The Quest for the Last Great Untapped Market on Earth.* New York: Grove Press, 2003.

Su Wei, Yang Fan, and Liu Shiwen. *Chongqing moshi* [The Chonqging model]. Beijing: Zhongguo jingji chubanshe, 2011.

Su Xiaokang. "River Elegy." *Chinese Sociology and Anthropology* 24:2 (Winter 1991–92): 7–18.

Sun Yat-sen. *San Min Chu I: The Three Principles of the People*, trans. Frank W. Price. Shanghai: The Commercial Press, 1928.

Sun Yatsen [Sun Zhongshan]. *Sanmin zhuyi.* Beijing: Zhongguo Chang'an chubanshe, 2011.

Teng, Emma Jinhua. *Taiwan's Imagined Geography: Chinese Colonial Travel Writing and Pictures, 1683–1895.* Cambridge, MA: Harvard University Press, 2004.

Thompson, Laurence G. "Biographical Sketch of K'ang Yu-wei" in *Ta T'ung Shu: The One-World Philosophy of K'ang Yu-wei*, by Kang Youwei, 11–25. London: George Allen & Unwin, 1958.

Thornton, John L. "Foreword." In *China in 2020: A New Kind of Superpower*, by Hu Angang, vi–vii. Washington, DC: Brookings Institution Press, 2011.

Vogel, Ezra. *Japan as Number One: Lessons for America.* Cambridge, MA: Harvard University Press, 1979.

Waldron, Arthur. "The Rise of China: Military and Political Implications." *Review of International Studies* 31:4 (2005): 715–733.

Wang, Yuan-kang. "The Chinese World Order and War in Asian History." Presented at the American Political Science Association annual conference, Toronto (September 2009).

Wang, Yuan-Kang. *Harmony and War: Confucian Culture and Chinese Power Politics.* New York: Columbia University Press, 2011.

Weller, Robert P. *Alternative Civilities: Democracy and Culture in China and Taiwan.* Boulder, CO: Westview Press, 1999.

Wishik, Anton. "The Bo Xilai Crisis: A Curse or a Blessing? An Interview with Cheng Li." Seattle: National Bureau of Asian Research, April 18, 2012.

Woodside, Alexander. "The Asia-Pacific Idea as a Mobilization Myth." In *What Is in a Rim? Critical Perspectives on the Pacific Region Idea*, ed. Arif Dirlik, 37–52. 2d ed. Lanham, MD: Rowman & Littlefield Publishers, 1998.

World Bank. *China 2030: Building a Modern, Harmonious and Creative High-Income Society*. Washington, DC: World Bank.

Wu Jinglian, Yu Keping, and Robert Fogel, eds. *Zhongguo weilai 30 nian* [China: 30 years in the future]. Beijing: Zhongyang bianyi chubanshe, 2011.

Wu Ming. *Zhongguo xin lingxiu: Xi Jinping zhuan*, zengding xinban [China's new leader: Xi Jinping, rev. ed.]. Hong Kong: Wenhua yishu chubanshe, 2010.

Xi Jinping, ed. *Kexue yu aiguo: Yan Fu sixiang xintan* [Science and patriotism: New explorations of Yan Fu's thought]. Beijing: Qinghua daxue chubanshe, 2001.

Xiang Lanxin. *2025: Zhongguo meng* [2025: The China dream]. Changsha: Hunan renmin chubanshe, 2010.

Xu Jilin. "Pushi wenming, haishi Zhongguo jiazhi? Jin shinian zhongguo lishi zhuyi sichao zhi pipan" [Universal civilization, or Chinese values? A critique of the Chinese historicism trend over the past decade]. *Kaifang shidai*, no. 5 (2010), http://www.usc.cuhk.edu.hk/PaperCollection/Details.aspx?id=7909.

Xu Jilin. "Shanghai Culture Lost," trans. Geremie R. Barmé. *China Heritage Quarterly*, no. 22 (June 2010).

Xu Jilin. "Zhongguo xuyao liweidan? jin shinian lai Zhongguo guojiazhuyi sichao zhi pipan" [Does China need a Leviathan? Critique of the Statist Trend in China]. *Gongshiwang* (January 23, 2011).

Xu Jinglei, dir. "Du Lala shengzhi ji" [Du Lala's Promotion Diary; or Go Lala Go!] (2010).

Xu Jinglei. *Gongkai! Lao Xu de Nanfei yingwen shu* [Showtime! Lao Xu's South African English book]. Shanghai: Shanghai jinxiu wenzhang chubanshe, 2008.

Yan Xuetong. "The Rise of China and Its Power Status." *Chinese Journal of International Politics* 1:1 (2006): 5–33.

Yan Xuetong. "Xun zi's Thoughts on Interstate Politics and Their Implications." *Chinese Journal of International Politics* 2 (2008): 135–165.

Yan Xuetong. *Ancient Chinese Thought, Modern Chinese Power*, ed. Daniel A. Bell and Sun Zhe. Princeton, NJ: Princeton University Press, 2011.

Yan Xuetong, and Xu Jin, eds. *Wangba tianxia sixiang ji qiyou* [Thoughts on world leadership and implications]. Beijing: Shijie zhishi chubanshe, 2009.

Yang Jisheng. *Tombstone: The Great Chinese Famine, 1958–1962*, trans. and eds., Edward Friedman, Stacy Mosher, and Jian Guo. New York: Farrar, Straus and Giroux, 2012.

Yang Qianru. "An Examination of the Research Theory of Pre-Qin Interstate Political Philosophy." In *Ancient Chinese Thought, Modern Chinese Power*, ed. Daniel A. Bell and Sun Zhe, 147–160. Princeton, NJ: Princeton University Press, 2011.

Yang Sizhuo. "Weilai xuejia jiang 'Zhongguo gushi': Du Zhongguo da qushi" [Futurist tells 'the China story': Reading *China's Megatrends*]. *Mingzuo xinshang* no. 4 (2010): 110.

Yang Yao. "The End of the Beijing Consensus: Can China's Model of Authoritarian Growth Survive?" *Foreign Affairs* (February 2010).

Yu Jie. *Zhongguo yingdi: Wen Jiabao* [China's best actor: Wen Jiabao]. Hong Kong: Xin shiji chubanshe, 2010.

Yu, Zhansui. "Questioning the Chinese Model of Development: A Critical Reading of *Shengshi: Zhongguo 2013.*" TheChinaBeat.org (July 28, 2010).

Zha, Jianying. *Tide Players: The Movers and Shakers of a Rising China.* New York: New Press, 2011.

Zhang Minchang. "Liu Xiaobo hu nuojiang, pushi jiezhi de shengli!" [Liu Xiaobo wins Nobel Prize: A victory for universal values!]. Boxun blog (October 12, 2010).

Zhang Shuguang. "Tianxia lilun he shijie zhidu" [Tianxia theory and world order]. *Zhongguo Shuping,* no. 5 (2006).

Zhang Wei-wei. *Ideology and Economic Reform under Deng Xiaoping.* London: Kegan Paul, 1996.

Zhang Wei-wei. *Transforming China: Economic Reform and its Political Implications.* New York: St. Martin's Press, 2000.

Zhang Wei-wei. "Yige qijo de pouxi: Zhongguo moshi jiqi yiyi" [The Analysis of a Miracle: The China Model and Its Significance]. *Qiushi,* no. 6 (2011), http://www.qstheory.cn/hqwg/2011/201106/201103/t20110325_74156.htm.

Zhang Wei-wei. *Zhongguo zhenhan: Yige 'wenming xing guojia' de jueqi* [China Shock: The rise of a "civilization-state"]. Shanghai: Renmin chubanshe, 2011.

Zhang Wenmu. *Lun Zhongguo haiquan,* 2d ed. [China's sea power, 2d ed.]. Beijing: Haiyang chubanshe, 2010.

Zhang Yiwu. "'Anti-gravity': A Surge of Chinese Imagination and the Significance of 'Peasant da Vincis.'" In *Nongmin dafenqi* [Peasant da Vincis], by Cai Guoqiang, 28–36. Guilin: Guangxi shifan daxue chubanshe, 2010.

Zhang, Feng. "Chinese Exceptionalism in the Intellectual World of China's Foreign Policy." In *China Across the Divide: The Domestic and Global in Politics and Society,* ed. Rosemary Foot. New York: Oxford University Press, 2013.

Zhao Tingyang. *Tianxia tixi: Shijie zhidu zhexue daolun* [The under-heaven system: The philosophy for the world institution]. Nanjing: Jiangsu jiaoyu chubanshe, 2005.

Zhao Tingyang. *Tianxia tixi: Shijie zhidu zhexue daolun* [The under-heaven system: The philosophy for the world institution, rev. ed.]. Beijing: Zhongguo renmin chubanshe, 2011.

Zhao Tingyang. "Guanyu hexie shijie de sekao" [Thoughts on the harmonious world]. *Shijie jingji yu zhengzhi,* no. 9 (2006): 1.

Zhao Tingyang. "All under Heaven." *China Security* 4:2 (2008): 15.

Zhao Tingyang. *Huai shijie yanjiu* [Investigations of the bad world]. Beijing: Zhongguo renmin daxue chubanshe, 2009.

Zhao, Tingyang. "Rethinking Empire from a Chinese Concept 'All-under-Heaven' (Tian-xia)." *Social Identities* 12:1 (2006): 29–41.

"Zhongguo guan yinxiang" [Impressions of the China pavilion]. Shanghai: Zhongguo chuban jutuan, 2010.

Zhonghua Renmin Gongheguo guomin jingji he shehui fazhan di shier ge wunian guihua gangyao [Outline 12th Five-Year Programme for National Economic Social Development of the People's Republic of China]. Beijing: Renmin chubanshe, March 2011.

Who's Who

Ai Weiwei (1957–), artist and social activist; imprisoned in 2011 for 81 days

Bo Xilai (1949–), party secretary of Chongqing (2007–2012), minister of commerce of the People's Republic of China (2004–2007); promoter of the Chongqing model that included social welfare programs, singing communist songs, and cracking down on organized crime; ejected from the Communist Party in 2012 because of abuse of power

Cai Guoqiang (1957–), world-famous artist who explores Chinese identity; his Peasant da Vincis exhibit (2010) critiqued the China model

Chan Koonchung [Chen Guanzhong] (1952–), novelist, magazine editor, filmmaker; born in Shanghai, raised in Hong Kong, now lives in Beijing; wrote *The Fat Years* [*Shengshi*] (2009)

Cui Zhiyuan (1963), political science professor at Tsinghua University's School of Public Policy and Management; leading member of the New Left; chronicler of the Chongqing model

Deng Xiaoping (1904–1997), paramount leader of China (1978–1997); started the reform and opening policy in 1979; ordered the June 4th massacre in 1989

Du Lala (born in the 1980s), fictional character in *Du Lala's Promotion Diary* (2007), which became a film (2010); a "good girl" who learns how to be modern by working in an American transnational corporation; represents people born in the 1980s

Han Han (1982–), novelist, blogger, professional race car driver; famous for the biting social commentary on his blogs; represents people born in the 1980s

He Dongsheng (born in the 1950s), fictional character in Chan Koonchung's *The Fat Years* (2009); creates a plan to save China from economic disaster that includes a massacre; supports authoritarian capitalism

Hu Angang (1953–), top economist and forecaster; professor in the School of Public Policy and Management at Tsinghua University (Beijing), director of the China Studies Center

Hu Jintao (1942–), general secretary of the Chinese Communist Party (2002–2012); president of the People's Republic of China (2003–2013)

Lin, Justin Yifu (1952–), professor of economics at Peking University; vice president and senior economist, World Bank (2008–2012); born in Taiwan, defected to the PRC in 1979; adviser to the Chinese government

Kang Xiaoguang (1963–), professor of regional economics and politics and dean of the Non-Profit Organization Research Center at Renmin University, Beijing; advocates Chinese exceptionalism and the Confucianization of China

Kang Youwei (1858–1927), scholar and government official in the Qing dynasty; intellectual inspiration for the Hundred Days Reform movement (1898); wrote *The Book of Great Harmony*

Jiang Rong (1946–), pseudonym for Lü Jiamin; author of best-selling novel *Wolf Totem*; political science professor at the China Institute of Industrial Relations, Beijing; imprisoned for two years for his role in the Tiananmen Square protests of 1989; his novel has environmentalist and fundamentalist messages

Li Keqiang (1955–), deputy general secretary of the Chinese Communist Party (2012–); premier of the People's Republic of China (2013–)

Liu Mingfu (1951–), senior colonel in the People's Liberation Army, professor at China's National Defense University and former director of the university's Army Building Research Institute; wrote *The China Dream* (2010) to argue that the PRC needs to build its military power

Liu Xiaobo (1955–), literary critic, writer, pro-democracy activist; Nobel Peace Prize (2010); at present in jail

Lou Jing (1989–), singer on *Go Oriental Angel*, China's *American Idol*–like program (2009); daughter of Han Chinese mother and African-American father; suffered racial abuse from Chinese netizens

Lung Ying-tai [Long Yingtai] (1952–), writer, social commentator, and democracy activist in greater China; minister of culture for Taiwan (2012–)

Mao Zedong (1893–1976), communist revolutionary and first leader of the People's Republic of China; his egalitarian ideals still inspire China's New Left intellectuals and projects like the Chongqing model

Pan Wei (1960–), director of China and World Affairs at Peking University; main theorist of the China model

Wen Jiabao (1942–), deputy general secretary of the Chinese Communist Party (2002–2012); premier of the People's Republic of China (2008–2013)

Xi Jinping (1953–), general secretary of the Chinese Communist Party (2012–); president of the People's Republic of China (2013–)

Xu Jilin (1957–), historian at East China Normal University, Shanghai; well-known historian of Chinese thought; promotes democratic civilization

Xu Jinglei (1974–), award-winning actor, director, editor, blogger based in Beijing; graduate of the Beijing Film Academy (1997); directed and starred in *Du Lala's Promotion Diary* (2010); represents people born in the 1980s

Zhang Wei-wei (1955–), professor of international relations at the Geneva School of Diplomacy, Switzerland; translator for Deng Xiaoping in the 1980s; promoter of the China model.

Zhao Tingyang (1961–), philosophy professor at the Chinese Academy of Social Sciences; wrote *The Under-Heaven System* (2005) to describe a Chinese-influenced world order; influential among strategists and policymakers

Index

CPSIA information can be obtained at www.ICGtesting.com
Printed in the USA
BVOW02s1621190315

392394BV00001BA/4/P